Paradigms in Economic Development

Paradigms in Economic Development

Classic Perspectives, Critiques, and Reflections

RAJANI KANTH

Editor

M.E. Sharpe

Armonk, New York
London, England

Library of Congress Cataloging-in-Publication Data

Paradigms in economic development : classic perspectives, critiques,
and reflections / edited by Rajani K. Kanth.
p. cm.
Includes bibliographical references and index.
ISBN 1-56324-329-6 (cloth).   ISBN 1-56324-330-X (pbk.)
1. Economic development.
I. Rajani Kannepalli Kanth.
HD75.P36   1993
338.9--dc20
93-31934
CIP

Printed in the United States of America

The paper used in this publication meets the minimum requirements of
American National Standard for Information Sciences—
Permanence of Paper for Printed Library Materials,
ANSI Z39.48–1984.

∞

BM (c) 10 9 8 7 6 5 4 3 2 1
BM (p) 10 9 8 7 6 5 4 3 2 1

For Antara, Indrina, Malini, Cory—
and Kesavan Kesari (1914–1992)

Contents

PART III: AFTERTHOUGHTS ON DEVELOPMENT

Acknowledgments

The chapters in this book are taken from the following sources. Permissions to reprint are gratefully acknowledged.

1. Reprinted from H. Myint, "An Interpretation of Economic Backwardness," *Oxford Economic Papers* Vol. 6, no. 6 (June 1954): 132–63. Reprinted by permission of Oxford University Press.

2. Reprinted from R. Nurkse, "Some International Aspects of the Problem of Economic Development," *American Economic Review* vol. XLII, no. 2 (May 1952): 571–83. Reprinted by permission from *The American Economic Review*.

3. Reprinted from W. A. Lewis, "Economic Development with Unlimited Supplies of Labour," *The Manchester School* vol. XXII, no. 2. (May 1954): 139–91. Reprinted with permission from Basil Blackwell, Publishers.

4. Reprinted from W. W. Rostow, *The Stages of Economic Growth: A Non-Communist Manifesto* (Cambridge, England: Cambridge University Press, 1960), pp. 4–12. Copyright 1960 Cambridge University Press. Reprinted with the permission of Cambridge University Press and the author.

5. Reprinted from A. Gerschenkron, *Economic Backwardness in Historical Perspective* (Cambridge, MA: Harvard University Press, 1962), pp. 31–51. Copyright 1957 *L'industria*, Milan, no. 2 (1957).

6. Reprinted from P. Baran, *The Political Economy of Growth* (New York: Monthly Review Press, 1957), pp. 134–62. Copyright © 1957 by Monthly Review Inc. Reprinted by permission of Monthly Review Foundation.

7. Reprinted from A. G. Frank, "The Development of Underdevelopment," *The Monthly Review* vol. 18, no. 4 (September 1966): 17–31. Copyright © 1966 by Monthly Review Inc. Reprinted by permission of Monthly Review Foundation.

8. Reprinted from S. Amin, *Unequal Development* (New York: Monthly Review Press, 1976), pp. 198–203. Copyright © 1976 by Monthly Review Press. Reprinted by permission of Monthly Review Foundation.

9. Reprinted from R. Prebisch, "The Latin American Periphery in the Global System of Capitalism," *CEPAL Review* no. 13 (E/CEPAL/G.1145), Santiago de Chile (April 1981): 143–50. United Nations publications, Sales No. E.81.II.G.2. Reprinted by permission of the Publications Board, United Nations.

10. Reprinted from J. Banaji, "For a Theory of Colonial Modes of Production," *Economic and Political Weekly* no. 52 (December 23, 1972): 2498–2502. vol. 7 no 52.

11. Reprinted from A. Hirschman, *Essays in Trespassing: Economics to Politics and Beyond* (Cambridge, England: Cambridge University Press, 1981), pp. 1–24. Copyright 1981 Cambridge University Press. Reprinted with the permission of Cambridge University Press and the author.

12. Reprinted from A. K. Sen, "Development: Which Way Now?" *The Economic Journal* 93 (December 1983): 745–62. Reprinted with the permission of Basil Blackwell, Publishers, and the author.

13. Reprinted from D. Lal, "Misconceptions of Development Economics," *Finance and Development* 22 (June 1985): 10–13.

14. Reprinted from V. Shiva, *Staying Alive* (London: Zed Books, 1989; originally published in New Delhi: Kali for Women, 1988), pp. 1–13. Copyright 1988 Kali for Women. Reprinted with the permission of Zed Books (world excluding South Asia) and Kali for Women (South Asia).

Paradigms in Economic Development

RAJANI KANTH

Introduction: The Oeuvre of Development Studies—An Overview

Preamble

It was the year 1917 that defined the decisive watershed in the history of the twentieth century, marking a fission and eventually a series of fissures that were to have a devastating impact on the self-confidence of European capitalist civilization, as much as on its outreach in captive colonies and neocolonies on far-flung continents. Much like the French Revolution of 1789,[1] which divided Europe fundamentally and irreversibly, from almost all of its prehistory, the Bolshevik Revolution altered the map of world capitalism, throwing up an important, if only an initial, barricade against its predatory expansionism and providing an early spark of hope of national liberation for the host of non-European peoples who were chafing under the yoke of European imperialism. The emergent socialist republic of the Soviet Union, though weak and impoverished in itself, was nonetheless to provide for the next seventy years political, diplomatic, and military support for both national liberation struggles and struggles for socialist transformation, within the context of what was eventually to be termed the "Third World" or, more apologetically, the "developing countries."[2]

However, fortuitous circumstances aided the Soviet resolve: The near-collapse of the capitalist order in the Great Depression of the late 1920s and early 1930s (at a time when even Stalinist misery was producing impressive economic strides in the USSR) and the consequent imperialist war of the late capitalist comers—Japan, Italy, and Germany—against the traditional supremacy of Anglo-American capitalism weakened the center of world capitalism decisively, given the near destruction of "civilized" Europe in the holocaust of imperialist struggles. While the "West" (with the critical exception of the United States, protected as it was by two rather sizable, and conveniently placed, oceans) lay critically—almost mortally—wounded, the USSR was to emerge as a new industrial giant, pushed to economic extremes by the terror unleashed by the forces of the Third Reich. It was the confluence of these two processes that ensured that at least formal decolonization would, henceforth, be firmly on the agenda of European powers. The final push toward this objective, of course, came from liberation struggles "internal" to the colonies, whether nationalist or (nominally) "socialist," across Asia and Africa; and, with the breaking free of the torpid Chinese giant from European, American, and Japanese colonialism, the process was to become irreversibly encoded into history. The Third World had been invented, through the machinations of cold war politics, the heroic struggles of oppressed non-European peoples, and the steadfast support of the USSR, of the newly created fringe republics of Eastern Europe, and of newly emergent Maoist China.

Regardless of how Third World nations themselves viewed the matter (an issue treated only as a regrettable infelicity), the *macro* logic of the world economy, locked now in a life-and-death struggle between a resurgent (but restructured) Western capitalism (with the forced admission of defeated Japan into its ranks) and a militarily powerful Eastern-bloc socialism, dictated that the Third World would now be destined to be the pawn in a deadly East–West struggle for the hearts, minds, factories, and paddyfields of the ex-colonies.[3] The future of both capitalism and socialism appeared to rest on the uncertain backs of the restless, anarchic, and effulgent masses in Asia and Africa, still staggering unsteadily after the long, deep, dark, and dismal slumber of colonial rule. Their "development"—in directions suitable to either capitalist or socialist agendas— was too important a matter to be left to the nations themselves or to the class struggles therein. While the USSR quietly went about building and bolstering anti-imperialist forces in these regions, Western governments and agencies—far richer than the Soviets and almost infinitely more sophisticated in their array of techniques—went about toppling governments and imposing procapitalist (or, more simply, pro-Western) dictatorships wherever possible, through means fair, foul, and unspeakable.[4] But such clandestine and covert activities required more positive backstopping. Accordingly, Western economic policy—a potent adjunct of what might be termed North Atlantic Treaty Organization foreign policy— was now directed, with the assistance of a dozen newly created "international" agencies, to assure the conditions of capitalist reproduction in the Third World. The USSR had not merely provided the political and military provocation for decolonization; it had also, by dint of the example of its own internal transformation, provided the nucleus of the idea of a "planned" or "guided" development (in both theory and practice) that would be seized upon eagerly by development-mongers who anxiously sought to plan (hastily) for capitalism in the periphery.[5]

The availability of vast amounts of funds, dispersed through various banks, foundations, and institutes, created the basis, as intended, for a healthy and vigorous new academic "discipline" called, neutrally, "development studies," the crux of whose efforts—internalizing the policy slant to perfection—was the creation and stabilization of capitalist social institutions[6] in the near-exotic conditions of a non-European cultural milieu. All of mainstream development theory, whether conservatively laissez-faire or social democratically interventionist, grappled with this central problematic in the early years of the formation of the "field" of development studies (during the first and second "Development Decades," as the United Nations was to christen them). Indeed, the grappling continues to this day, despite the recent sorry collapse of the so-called Soviet threat (although it is obviously still premature to pass final judgment on a situation essentially in flux) that had originally spurred the not-quite-dispassionate and apparently seamless "inquiry." The collection of works in Part I reflects—sometimes self-consciously, sometimes not—this abiding, dominant preoccupation. It could not be otherwise, for social theory—inevitably—is only a masquerade for policy.

Mainstream Initiatives

Given the policy context just outlined, one begins to appreciate the enormous significance of the article by W. Arthur Lewis (chapter 3), which defined the implicit problematic explicitly, even if at a practical level it left the matter somewhat indeterminate. Employing a formal model of "dualism" loosely approximating the Marxian departmental schemata in *Capital* (and reminiscent in some respects of Rosa Luxemburg's analysis of the importance of precapitalist societies for capitalism) and the similar analyses employed in practice by early Stalinist planners, which profoundly influenced Keynesian ideologists, Lewis went on to sketch the fundamental importance of capital formation to the scheme of things in the context of "growth" (not a novel idea, given the heritage of classical economics, but quite exotic given the usual dominance of the unreal dream world of neoclassical economics). Lewis's article, though quite artless in outward appearance and cast in the tautological reasoning and the argument by assumption that are endemic to mainstream economic science, nonetheless was geared to an important affirmation of the true goals and objectives of the development crusade. Indeed, in this regard the paper makes only two rather simple, but politically critical, points: (a) that the initiation of capitalist economic growth requires the existence of a capitalist/entrepreneurial class; and (b) that subsequent capitalist evolution requires that income distribution be skewed in favor of this same "saving" class.

In effect, Lewis defined the "problem" of the Third World to a nicety: to "invent" an industrial bourgeoisie and to ensure its continued hegemony over state power. An obvious catch existed, however: how is one to "produce" a capitalist class where, under presumption, it does not exist? The traditional route of social revolution was blocked off by cold-war strategy: A revolution was too dangerous to risk because its outcome was uncertain—in a revolutionary situation peasants and workers might seize power just as easily as the bourgeoisie, even when the latter came equipped with foreign assistance. For instance,

A. Gerschenkron (chapter 5) advanced the thesis that, even in the case of Europe, the trajectory of "late" industrialization had always been "explosive." Lewis offered two possibilities: a capitalist class could be imported from abroad (the classic neocolonial solution, in what was to be called, not always satirically, "industrialization by invitation"[7]); or some form of state capitalism might be pursued, along the lines of India or Egypt, creating domestic capital on "public account."[8] His sketch did, however, prove quite prophetic, for the trajectory of peripheral capitalism has, historically, taken both of these different forms, from neocolonial Hong Kong to state-capitalist India. Nonetheless, given the fragility of autonomous capitalist development, it is probably fair to say that Lewis was far more successful in identifying the key problematic than in offering any ultimately satisfactory resolution.

W. W. Rostow's work (chapter 4) followed on the heels of Lewis's, with a slightly more avowedly antisocialist stance.[9] Lewis's hesitancy and caution about the success of a capitalist development of the periphery was now corrected with an historicism (Gerschenkron offers a partial corrective to this misuse of history in chapter 5) that was necessarily quite specious. As remarked, Lewis had put more emphasis on the "problem" of capitalist infusion than on the means to its achievement. Rostow, though adding little to this latter analysis and being remarkable only for his bleakness in this regard (a pessimism echoed by H. Myint in chapter 1), nonetheless secured something rather important for "free-world" ideology: the idea of the inevitability of such a transformation by reference to a mechanistic, bowdlerized "history" of economic change, forced into altogether too tidy, preset, "stages" of economic growth that assured—as if history were a grand drama enacted for a specific purpose—the eventual approximation, for all, of the standard (and style) of living of the United States. The "take-off" being only a question of time, Somalia would surely turn into Sweden—someday. Curiously, Rostow tried to turn the specific history of the English bourgeois Industrial Revolution (much like many an errant Marxist) into a general scheme of world history, echoing Marx's well-known—if rather dubious—phrase, penned in 1867, to the effect that, "The country that is more developed industrially only shows, to the less developed, the image of its own future."[10]

At another remove, as early as 1952, while the colonies and ex-colonies were only barely finding their feet in the new world order created by the crisis of imperialism and the rise of Soviet power, Ragnar Nurkse (chapter 2) defined a fairly comprehensive ecopolitical agenda for "developing" countries, with primary responsibility for growth to be placed in the hands of the Third World governments themselves. In so doing, Nurkse introduced into the idiom of development studies the enduring characteristic of Western development-mongers, a dualism of sorts that did not escape the attention of either conservatives or radicals: *of preaching Smith (laissez-faire) at home and Keynes (intervention) abroad.* Given the world situation, the West could not afford to wait for tardy, privately inspired, laissez-faire capital accumulation. Instead, the state was adjured to carry out the essential tasks of what Marx had termed "primitive accumulation," in hothouse fashion. The key to success was to be the ability of state power to extract revenues from noncapitalist sectors so as to channel them into capitalist use, or "public finance," as the euphemism went. Astonishingly, and in chilling revelation of its real agenda, no stricture was placed upon the form of government: As Jeanne Kirkpatrick was to enunciate the doctrine later, quite plainly the issue was not despotism per se but whether or not the despots were pro-Western. (Myint [chapter 1] made the same point as Nurkse: that the "free play of economic forces" could not be expected to break the vicious cycle of poverty or the low-level equilibrium trap in these regions but that some form of organized direction and "countervailing power" was needed.) Nurkse urged "balanced growth," an essentially undefinable notion—and vagueness has its uses—drawn both from Marxian departmental schemes and from Keynesian adaptations of the same. (In this idea, as much as in the specificity of the need for state direction, Nurkse was following a path laid by Rosenstein-Rodan in 1943.) Much was made of breaking the "vicious cycle" of poverty—yet this was to be done by *reducing consumption further!* Given Third World political structures, there could have been no doubt as to which of the social classes would be called to bear the burden of this belt-tightening, enforced by state power. At any rate, Nurkse—by suggesting that the burden of the funds should be raised through internal, domestic policies of legal seizure and confiscation by a strong, mobilized state—offered a major policy alternative to Lewis's idea of massive capital transfers, the latter more along the lines of a Marhsall Plan, involving a considerable international transfer of resources. The West was to find it quite congenial to advocate aggressive state direction for the "backward peoples" (the choice, if telling, phrase of Myint) while full of the pious platitudes of individual liberties and personal freedoms for denizens closer to home.

The Radical Response

The reaction to the various policies of imperialism came from various sources—indeed, diverse sources—gathering strength in the 1950s and 1960s as the world experienced an efflorescence of revolutionary activity in not merely the Third World but the First and Second worlds as well. It was the age of Fidel and Che and Mao and of the heroic peasants of Vietnam who were to teach the premier imperialist nation a lesson it would never forget. Neo-Marxist, Third-Worldist, and New Left perspectives bloomed, indiscriminately, worldwide: from Havana to Paris and from Prague to Peking. Not all of these perspectives were necessarily socialist or working class, or even peasant based, however. Indeed, a good bit of this nominal Third-Worldism, as with the Nehrus, Nassers, and Nkrumahs, was simply a good old-fashioned economic nationalism, with incipient ruling classes in newly emergent nations chafing at the tight economic straitjacket they faced in world markets under the firm control of imperialist world centers.[11]

Although the so-called non-aligned group of nations were always a potpourri of strange bedfellows, a great many among them—India and Egypt, for instance—concealed their eminently bourgeois aims under a pseudo "socialist" rhetoric. This had the triple advantage of getting Soviet support, disarming the Left opposition domestically, and blackmailing the West for economic aid. A good example of this kind of dissatisfaction with the place of the Third World in the economic world order of capitalism is the work of Raúl Prebisch (first published in 1950 and summarized effectively in the 1981 article included as chapter 9 of this volume), an Argentinian who became director of the United Nations Economic Commission for Latin America (ECLA) in Chile, as represented in what came to be called the "ECLA manifest" in 1950.

Latin America, of course, was somewhat different from Asia and Africa, in the sense that direct colonial rule had been successfully overthrown, for the most part, a good century earlier, and also in the important sense that (native traditions notwithstanding) it represented a continuation of the original, settler European culture. However, the continent was quite clearly a neocolony, primarily of the United States and secondarily of Great Britain, Spain, and other European metropolitan centers. Prebisch's work must be seen only as a protest against the subordinate status of Latin America within Western capitalism. In essence his analysis, though critical of neoclassicism, was nonetheless cast within its frame of discourse. The fundamental problem of "peripheral capitalism" was in the adverse terms of trade, between the periphery and the metropoles, arising from various "structural" factors. Indeed, "structuralism" was the term applied to this perspective, although a loosely defined "institutionalism" might have been a better term. One structural factor was the excessive reliance of peripheral capitalism on primary commodity exports, leading to a drain of resources such that "underdevelopment" was continually re-created in the periphery. The alternative was to be termed "programmed industrialization," enabling domestic accumulation, not under laissez-faire capitalism or socialism but rather within an uncertain mix of what might be termed, for want of a better phrase, *Keynesian social democracy.*

More serious and profound than this rather tame national bourgeois agenda was the work of Paul Baran (chapter 6), stemming, however, from the radical provenance of Marxism and quite antipodal to the current vogue of the Western academic Marxian tradition that views imperially exported capitalism as good medicine for the colonial world.[12] Essentially, Baran was repeating the Leninist thesis of the retrograde and reactionary nature of capital in its imperialist phase: Boldly and categorically, with the example of India in mind, Baran forwarded the thesis (obviously unpopular with Eurocentric Marxists) that it was the captive markets of the Third World that fueled England's otherwise unaccountable take-off into sudden industrial supremacy, while the simultaneous colonial "capture" of the "economic surplus" of colonies was to generate their chronic economic regression. The proposition had splendid dialectical relish to it: Historically, contact between the First and Third worlds accentuated development in the former and retardation in the latter. This idea was destined to remain an abomination to both imperialist scholars and orthodox Western Marxists.

The challenge of Baran's thesis was soon to be supported by the work of easily the most recognizable, if notorious, name in development studies: André Gunder Frank (chapter 7). Original scholarship, moral vision, and revolutionary fervor mark his work with a special, indelible character. With Latin American country studies as initial examples, Frank established the case for two major theses: that the periphery only develops when freed of metropolitan strangleholds; and that only a systematic *delinking*[13] with world capitalism could ensure the prospects for an autonomous escape from underdevelopment, defined as the condition of being either directly or indirectly colonized. Reinforcing Baran's idea, Frank permanently enshrined the distinction between *undevelopment*, a more "natural" condition, and *underdevelopment*, a distorted construction of colonialism, *a distinction that is arguably fundamental to any serious study of the Third World*. Indeed, it is with Frank (and Amin, who indeed preceded Frank in published work) that EuroMarxism suffers a first cut (hence the odium imposed on Frank by a generation of EuroMarxists), later on to be further lacerated by a host of Third World scholars[14] led by Samir Amin, a prolific theorist of world capitalism whose work (though authored in French in the early fifties, was to find reception in English only decades later) is represented in chapter 8. Amin was to craft Frankian ideas—although developed independently—into an historical, nonethnocentric,[15] Marxian mold, developing important conceptual tools to understand the complex, disarticulated modalities of peripheral capitalism,[16] as opposed to the logic of First World *autocentrism*. A more potent challenge to the pretensions of mainstream theory and policy than the Frank-Amin school can hardly be visualized. And, for a while, it looked as if mainstream theorizing, if not mainstream policies, overt and covert, would simply fall apart of its own sustained weightlessness. In point of historical fact, of course, it both did and did not—as we shall see.[17] At any rate, the papers in Part II capture the important countercurrents to the mainstream initiatives that, for a period, took hold and dominated the literature.

Afterthoughts and Reconsiderations

The crisis of the 1970s for world capitalism was deep and severe. The growing military equity between East and West, coupled with uncontrollable Third World challenges to Western capitalism and European cultural domination, had profoundly shaken the confidence and might of the West. Never had countervailing forces against the West been either so strong or so successful: Even the predacious World Bank, under the stewardship of Vietnam war architect Robert McNamara, was to admit, weakly and in conciliatory fashion, to a short-lived "basic needs" strategy, an idea first touted vigorously by the more Third-Worldist International Labour Organisation in 1976. Economically staggering under stagflation and the recessionary gloom of the 1970s (auguries of the breakdown of postwar Fordism,[18] politically hounded by the increasingly organized and unified protests of poorer nations in the United Nations, and militarily checked by a strong Eastern bloc, even the ideological establishment—"development" economists among them—started to show chinks in its armor. Established journals of corporate imperialism started to pay attention to "dependency" arguments, and the more apolitical members of the tribe of development studies began to suspect that they were indeed standing on shaky, if not actually shallow, ground; that, perhaps, the field of economics, as conventionally constituted, simply did not have all of the answers to the seemingly intractable development dilemma. Traces of this otherwise atypical melancholia are to be found in the influential essay by A. Hirschman (chapter 11), in which he laments the passing of an age, in a somber, retrospective mood: "I cannot help feeling that the old liveliness is no longer there, that new ideas are ever harder to come by and that the field is not adequately reproducing itself."

But history, as always (a fact not always appreciated by determinists, of both Left and Right), is full of surprises. The crisis of imperialism was resolved not by the amelioration of a transition to a true social democracy, as might have been expected at the time, but by a fierce and quite unexpected turn to the *right*. The Thatcher-Reagan era marked a profound restructuring of capitalist institutions and ideology, with the inauguration of a new, rapaciously predatory, stance toward both the Soviet Union and its Third World allies. With a post-Maoist China[19] implicitly giving support (or at least neutralized, for the most part), the instruments of an international, right-wing capitalist crusade were very quickly forged. Direct U.S. military interventions, the Grand Intimidation of the Strategic Defense Initiative (a *coup de grace* of sorts), and increased covert and overt political and economic strikes by a coordinated Western alliance, against both socialism and Third World nationalism, were to alter the balance (of terror) yet again in favor of Western interests. This wholesale revival of right-wing market ideology was to rub off, creditably, on economics as well. The retrospective soon turned into a promising prospective; Deepak Lal's article (chapter 13), full of World Bank platitudes and the simple, if antediluvian, free-trade rhetoric of "getting prices right," catches the mood of new-found success quite succinctly.

More cautious, as befits a brilliant, mature scholar, but no less supportive of the essential thrust of mainstream development strategies, is the retrospective by Amartya Sen in chapter 12. Sen robustly defends the entire enterprise (within which, of course, he was a significant entrepreneur). That much was only self-defense, however; more importantly and interestingly, Sen calls, quietly, for an abandonment of older perspectives and a shift toward recognition of the sociopolitical "rights" and priorities (expressed in terms of the neologisms of "entitlements" and "capabilities") of peoples as better indices of development, away from traditional economic criteria that usually focus on per capita availability of goods and services. For the radical, all this was far from original (except in the nether world of mainstream economics), being only a paraphrase of ideas that radicals and Marxists had fought hard to be heard on and about, unsuccessfully, for decades, both in and out of academe. Despite the hoary nature of these pronouncements, however, mainstream development theorists embraced these ideas warmly, correctly seeing in them hope for a new lease on life for an otherwise discredited, humbled profession.

A much more convincing retrospective comes from the pen of Vandana Shiva (chapter 14), whose torrid but refreshing Third World *ecological feminism* tells, easily and convincingly—indeed, passionately!—of all that had been (wantonly) missing in the Western (and socialist) crusade, the horrors of which are still visible in the many scars on both the physical and cultural landscape of the world as a whole, in all its first, second, and third segments.[20] Hers is an eloquent plea for doing away with factory fetishism, ecological degradation, and racial and sexual oppression, and for putting people—not policies!—at last at the center of things. From World Bank ideology to Third World ecofeminism, the papers in Part III span the gamut of the varying extant moods and reflect the obvious uncertainties of a new order, one that is still in the making.

Postface

Looking at it now, in the 1990s, it is clear that the original cold war is now over, having been won decisively in a military sense by the West and in a much more important political sense by the East. The peoples of the Eastern bloc have won important new freedoms, even if at a cost they have yet to realize; the peoples of the West, of course, have won nothing. The fractured European family is now united again, a fact of overriding significance. The original barricade against Western expansion, the USSR, now lies prostrate (although not totally enfeebled), and its many dependencies in the Third World stagger about, shaken and uncertain, naked to all their enemies. The *age of imperialism* is upon us now a second time; it is one world again, alas, a world renewedly under the European capitalist heel (as the recent Middle Eastern conflagration illustrates profoundly and prophetically)—back to pre-1917, one might speculate, except on a higher technological plane. And so the wheel of the twentieth century has turned full circle. Indeed, the self-confidence of the West has been restored to the point of major international funding agencies, Ford and Rockefeller, for example, having quietly packed up their "development" kit bags to go back to supporting their local philharmonics; the fate of the Third World, being now securely within Western purview, is of no further significance. My own little Postscript, written in 1991, speculates on the nature of the resistance to come (if not already leading an embryonic existence) to this *"new world order,"* endorsing the objections already present in the Shiva article, toward an affirmation of the fundamental principle, sagely ignored in all of development studies by most traditions, Marxist or mainstream: the right of peoples, clans, tribes, villages, and so forth to *self-determination*—to say *No* to the plans of others involving them. In some respects, therefore, we have regressed back to beginnings in the development psyche and circumstance; while, in others, we have traversed millennia, trespassing into visions of the future.

Notes

1. See E. J. Hobsbawm, *The Age of Revolution 1789–1848* (New York: Mentor, 1962), for an important discussion of the (aptly termed) world-historical significance of the French Revolution.

2. Today, with the "discovery" of the so-called Newly Industrializing Countries, mainstream theory identifies a *fourth* world within the third: and, if one adds the special status occupied by the OPEC countries, then we have a fifth, as well, and so on.

3. A credible account of the policy thrust toward what was to be termed "modernization" is available in Ankie Hoogvelt, *The Third World in Global Development* (London: Macmillan, 1982).

4. From the deposition of Arbenz in Guatemala, to Mossadegh in Iran, Lumumba in the Congo, and Nkrumah in Ghana; from Allende in Chile to Manley in Jamaica; from the occupation and invasion of Panama, Grenada, Nicaragua, etc., the Western record of suppressing and sabotaging popular regimes in the Third World (while propping up reactionary dictatorships) is a sorry one, indeed, and occupies a choice place in the annals of shame.

5. Much of the inspiration for the much-acclaimed Harrod ("An Essay in Dynamic Theory," *Economic Journal*, vol. 49, March 1939, pp. 14–33) and Domar ("Expansion and Employment," *American Economic Review*, vol. 37, March 1947, pp 34–55) models of growth were the informed consequence of the Soviet planning experiment.

6. See Rajani Kanth, "The Conflictual Aspects of Structural Change: Development Strategy and Structural Crisis in the Third World," in *Explorations in Political Economy*, ed. R. Kanth and E. K. Hunt (Savage, MD: Rowman and Littlefield, 1990), pp. 203–17.

7. For a critical discussion of this strategy with respect to the region of the Caribbean—Arthur Lewis's original focus—see the chapter on "Dependency Theory in Action," in M. Blomstrom and B. Hettne, *Development Theory in Transition* (London: Zed Books, 1984).

8. For this thesis of deliberately nurtured state capitalism, see Amiya Bagchi, *Political Economy of Development and Underdevelopment* (Cambridge, England: Cambridge University Press, 1982).

9. For an exposé of the ideological stance contained in Rostow's work, see P. Baran and E. J. Hobsbawm, "A Non-Communist Manifesto," in P. Baran, *The Longer View* (New York: Monthly Review Press, 1969), pp. 52–67.

10. K. Marx, *Capital*, Vol. 1, (NY: International Publishers, 1967, p. 19); See Rajani Kanth, "Marxism and Dependency: The Real Divide," in R. Kanth, *Capitalism and Social Theory: The Science of Black Holes* (Armonk, NY: M. E. Sharpe, Inc., 1992, pp. 199–210), for an examination of the nature of Eurocentric extrapolations from history.

11. Quite opportunistically, EuroMarxists of the genre of Bill Warren (*Imperialism: Pioneer of Capitalism* [London: Verso, 1980]) and Robert Brenner ("The Origins of Capitalist Development," *New Left Review* no. 104 [1977]: 25–92) conflate radical dependency theory with bourgeois dependency theory, dismissing both of them as expressions of a dispensable "nationalism."

12. As, say, in Warren, *Imperialism: Pioneer of Capitalism* (London: Verso, 1980).

13. For a full account of the sociopolitical meaning of delinking, see Samir Amin, *Delinking* (London: Zed Books, 1990).

14. An example of this is J. Banaji's valiant attempt (chapter 10) to theorize a "colonial" mode of production free of EuroMarxist stereotypes.

15. For Amin's recent work on this issue, see his *Eurocentrism* (London, Zed Books, 1989).

16. A current and detailed analysis of the disarticulation of African economies is to be found in Amin's *Maldevelopment: Anatomy of a Global Failure* (London, Zed Books, 1990).

17. For a purely academic perspective on the *theory* underlying development studies, quite unmediated by any political rationale, see Diana Hunt, *Economic Theories of Development* (Savage, MD: Barnes and Noble Books, 1989).

18. For one account of the breakdown of the so-called Fordist regime, see Alain Lipietz, *Mirages and Miracles: The Crisis of Global Fordism* (London: Verso, 1987).

19. For more on the politics of post-Maoism in China, see William Hinton, *The Great Reversal* (New York: Monthly Review Press, 1990).

20. For an account of the ecological and social ravages of the much touted "Green Revolution" in India, by way of example, see V. Shiva's *The Violence of the Green Revolution* (London: Zed Books, 1991).

Part I

Early Mainstream Perspectives

1

H. MYINT

An Interpretation of Economic Backwardness

In current discussions the terms "underdeveloped" and "backward" are generally used as though they were completely interchangeable by applying them to aggregate geographical concepts such as "countries," "areas," and "regions," or by equating them with certain broad indices such as low incomes or capital investment per head. It is more illuminating, in my view, to give these terms different connotations by using the former to mean underdeveloped *resources*, and the latter to refer to the backward *people* of a given area. In this paper I shall argue that this distinction is fundamental to the understanding of the nature of economic backwardness.

I

The difference in approach in terms of "underdeveloped resources" and in terms of "backward people"[1] can best be illustrated by examining the current fashion of including not only the natural resources but also the so-called "human resources" under the generic heading of "underdeveloped resources," which seems to imply that the two terms we have distinguished really overlap. But is it merely a matter of taste or tact whether we choose to speak of "backward people" or of "underdeveloped human resources"? On a close examination it will be seen that each term has its own hinterland of associated ideas and the two cannot be superimposed on each other without creating a number of serious logical difficulties.

EDITOR'S NOTE: *In one of the earliest of the classic works in the field, Myint anticipated many later themes such as poverty reduction and basic needs, albeit with a distinctly Eurocentric (and pessimistic) tone about the practical possibility of elevating the "backward" [sic] peoples, given their inevitable location within a regressive international division of labor that fosters institutional inequalities. Not a masterpiece of analytics, by any means, but respectable in the mainstream tradition all the same.*

In common-sense terms, a "backward people" may be defined as a group of people who are in some fashion or other unsuccessful in the economic struggle to earn a livelihood. Thus we are starting from a Classical or Marshallian distinction between man, on the one hand, and his environment on the other: only then can we think of a group of people as being successful or otherwise in adapting themselves to their environment. Further, the idea of "backwardness" inevitably implies a comparison of different degrees of success in this economic struggle: some groups of people are less successful or "backward" compared with other more successful or "advanced" groups. Thus the nature of backwardness would lose much of its significance if applied to a homogeneous group of people without international economic relations. It is when a self-sufficient primitive or medieval economy has been opened up to outside economic forces and its people come into contact with other economically more"advanced" people that the idea of backwardness suggests itself.

This way of approach at once raises a number of issues. Firstly, we shall have to make a more systematic analysis of the continuous process of mutual adaptation between wants, activities, and environment which we have described as "economic struggle." Secondly, in order to make a valid comparison of the varying degrees of success in the economic struggle of different groups of people we require the assumption that these different groups are in fact pursuing the same or comparable sets of ends. This is a big assumption which will have to be examined closely. Finally, we shall have to consider whether it is sufficient to measure the degree of "backwardness" or "advancement" of different groups of people merely in terms of the relative distribution of final incomes among them; or whether the pattern of distribution of economic activity among the different groups and the different roles they play in economic life might not in the long run offer a more significant clue to the future potential development of each group.

These will be discussed at a later stage (section IV). For the purpose of a preliminary contrast, however, it is sufficient to note that when we adopt the approach in terms of "backward people" we are by definition making their failure in the economic struggle the centre of the problem and that this involves: (a) a fundamental contrast between them (the "backward people") and the natural resources and the economic environment of their country, and (b) a deliberate concentration of attention on their share of incomes or economic activity either within their own country or in relation to the world at large as distinct from the total volume of output or economic activity.

When we turn to the approach in terms of "underdeveloped resources," however, we are led to quite a different set of ideas. To treat "human resources" on exactly the same footing as natural resources as part of the common pool of "underdeveloped resources" is to abandon the older man-against-environment approach in favour of the modern "allocative efficiency" approach. We are then concerned, not with the success or failure of a given group of people in their struggle against their economic environment (including other groups of people), but with the allocation of given "resources" among alternative uses as determined by the price system or by the central planner or by a mixture of both. The aim of this allocative process is to maximize total output, and "underdevelopment" becomes a species of deviation from the productive optimum defined in some sense or other.

We can now see that although, physically speaking, the same people are involved when we speak of "backward people" and of "underdeveloped human resources," the standpoint adopted in each case is different. From the first standpoint, these people are regarded as actors (even if unsuccessful ones) in the economic struggle. From the second, they are regarded as impersonal units of "underdeveloped" resources not distinguishable from units of other types of underdeveloped resources except by the degree of underdevelopment defined in some functional sense. Thus we are not specially concerned with "human resources" more than with other types of resources except in so far as it could be shown that "developing" the human resources would in fact increase the total output by a greater extent than by developing other "material" resources.

The difference between the "backwardness" and the "underdevelopment" approach becomes very clear when we exclude human resources from the definition of "underdeveloped resources" and confine it entirely to natural resources. This is by no means an unusual or deliberately contrived "strong case" to boost our distinction. As a matter of fact, much of the thinking on the subject is still influenced by the idea of "underdeveloped countries" as those which (whatever their "human resources") possess a greater amount of potential natural resources waiting to be developed compared with the "developed countries" whose natural resources have already been fully brought into use. We may also note how the use of such expressions as "underdeveloped countries," "underdeveloped areas," "underdeveloped regions," etc., tends to foster this belief in the existence of potential natural resources.

Here, once we have excluded the human beings from the "underdeveloped resources," a number of propositions emerge. Since they will recur again in the course of our argument, they may be summarily stated at this stage. (1) "Underdevelopment" of natural resources and "backwardness" of people are two distinct phenomena and they need not even always coexist: thus the inhabitants of the "overpopulated" countries which admittedly have very little natural resources left for further unaided development are also generally "backward." (2) When "underdeveloped" natural resources and "backward" people coexist, they mutually aggravate each other in a "vicious circle"; but this mutual interaction is an essentially dynamic and historical process taking place over a period of time and may be too complicated and qualitative to be easily fitted into the formal quantitative framework of optimum allocation of resources (including capital resources) suggested by the pure "underdevelopment" approach. (3) Although the "underdevelopment" of natural resources may cause the "backwardness" of the people, it does not necessarily follow that any efficient development of natural resources resulting in an increase in total output will always and *pari passu* reduce the backwardness of people. On the contrary, the problem of economic backwardness in many countries has been made more acute, not because the natural resources have remained "underdeveloped," but because they have been as fully and rapidly developed as market conditions permitted while the inhabitants have been left out, being either unable or unwilling or both to participate fully in the process.

II

Let us now turn to the logical difficulties which arise from attempts to superimpose the "backwardness" and the "underdevelopment" approach on each other. These can be best illustrated by examining some of the typical arguments in favour of increasing the flow of investment from the "advanced" to the"underdeveloped" countries.

Advocates of plans for the international economic development of the underdeveloped countries generally start by saying that the case for alleviating the poverty and discontent, ill health and ignorance of the peoples of these countries can be made whether we approach the subject from a humanitarian standpoint or purely in self-defence to ease the storm-centres of international relations. At this stage therefore the problem seems to be set out in terms of human misery and discontent, in terms of "backwardness" rather than in terms of "underdevelopment" of resources. Indeed, the existence of "underdeveloped" natural resources at least, far from creating a "problem" in the relevant sense, may be regarded as part of the means of solving it. When, however, we pass from this initial statement of the problem to the later parts of the economic development plans which contain a more technical treatment of the proposals and "target figures" for investment, we generally encounter a shift from the "backwardness" to the "underdevelopment" approach. The existence of "underdeveloped" natural resources is no longer regarded as the means of solving the problem; it has become the problem itself. The argument then proceeds as though the phenomenon of the "backwardness" of the people can be satisfactorily accounted for purely in terms of the "underdevelopment" of the resources and deviations from the optimum allocation of world's capital resources (cf., for example, United Nations Report, *Measures for the Economic Development of the Underdeveloped Countries*, ch. viii).

It is now time to consider the meaning of "underdeveloped resources" more closely. In the language of optimum theory, it seems to describe two types of deviation: (i) less than optimum amounts of these "underdeveloped" resources have been used in producing final output, and (ii) less than optimum amounts of capital have been invested to augment the quantity and improve the quality of these "underdeveloped" resources. Where the first occurs by itself it would be possible to increase the total output of the underdeveloped countries without outside investment merely by reorganizing their own existing resources by such measures as legal and administrative reforms, the mobilizing of domestic savings, and so on. In current discussion, although this possibility is admitted, it is considered that as a rule the two types of deviation occur simultaneously, the first caused by the second. That is to say, the scope for a more productive reorganization or "development" of the resources of the underdeveloped countries is limited without first removing the basic cause of "underdevelopment," viz. an insufficient flow of investment from the "advanced" countries.

The typical arguments in favour of increasing investment in the underdeveloped countries may now be examined. They may be classified according to the degree of optimism concerning the richness of the "underdeveloped resources."

i. The most optimistic type of argument assumes that as a rule underdeveloped countries possess *natural* resources capable of being developed by private investors on a purely commercial basis and this process will automatically help to raise the standard of living of the people of these countries. "Underdevelopment" is therefore caused by "artificial" obstacles and restrictions to the free international movement of private capital. Whatever our views about the richness of potential natural resources, this type of argument serves to illustrate a sharp clash between the "underdevelopment" and the "backwardness" approach. For, on a closer examination, it turns out that the only type of investment which private investors are willing to undertake in the underdeveloped countries is the exploitation of raw materials, e.g. petroleum, and it is precisely in this field that the governments of the underdeveloped countries are frequently unwilling to admit private foreign capital because they fear that this "nineteenth-century type of investment" will merely develop the natural resources and not the people and will result in "foreign economic domination" aggravating the economic "backwardness" of their peoples. This is a genuine deadlock to which no satisfactory answer can be given in terms of the simple "underdevelopment" approach. And to dismiss the whole thing merely as irrational economic nationalism seems suspiciously like throwing the baby away with the bath water (see section VI below).

ii. The next type of argument may be regarded as an attempt to retrieve the "underdevelopment" approach by introducing the Pigovian concept of the "social" productivity as distinguished from the "private" productivity of investment. Here it is argued that although the underdeveloped countries may not possess (or are unwilling to make available) resources which can be developed by private enterprise, they can nevertheless very profitably absorb large sums of international investment in the form of public enterprises using a broader criterion of "social" productivity. These enterprises would include public utilities, transport, hydro-electric and irrigation schemes, etc., which offer economies of large scale and scope for complementary investment and where only a public agency can collect the diffused social returns by means of taxation. A good example of a direct application of this argument may be found in the United Nations Report on

National and International Measures for Full Employment. Here the authors, after recommending that the International Bank for Reconstruction and Development should be used as the main channel of inter-governmental lending to reduce political risks on both sides, lay down the following conditions.

> The criteria of worthwhileness for the loans should be their effect on national income, taxable capacity and export capacity. The Bank should *not* in general lend, unless it is convinced that in consequence of the loan, the borrowing country's current balance of payments will improve sufficiently to permit interest and amortisation payments to be made.[2]
> Development loans should be made at interest rates uniform for all borrowing countries. (Op. cit., pp. 93–94.)

These two conditions may be regarded as the logical limits to which the investment policy towards the underdeveloped countries can be liberalized on the basis of the Pigovian concept of "social" productivity of investment. It may be noted that fairly substantial amounts of capital can still be absorbed by some of the underdeveloped countries within these limits. But comparing this view with the general run of discussions on the subject, it soon becomes apparent that many advocates of international development plans would consider the Pigovian conditions as too restrictive to be regarded as a serious basis of investment policy towards the underdeveloped countries. There are two possible ways out of this impasse. The first, which we shall recommend in the later part of this paper, is to make a clean break with the whole "underdevelopment" approach and to adopt a more direct approach to the problem of economic backwardness of the people. The second and more popular alternative is to try to broaden the "underdevelopment" approach still further; and this brings us to the third type of the under-investment argument.

iii. The argument at this stage consists in attempts to stretch the concept of "social productivity" or "desirability" by invoking (a) the principle of "needs," and (b) the dynamic principle of trying to stimulate further rounds of loan investment by "productive" grants to "improve social capital," particularly in the fields of public health, education, and communications. A good example of this may be found in a later United Nations Report on *Measures for the Economic Development of the Underdeveloped Countries.*

Here the authors argue:

(a) that 'the amount that can be profitably invested at a 4 per cent. rate of interest depends on the amount which is being spent at the same time on improving social capital; and especially on public health, on education and on roads and communications. There is much to be done in this way in the underdeveloped countries before they will be in a position to absorb large amounts of loan capital' (para. 269);

(b) that the underdeveloped countries 'cannot borrow' for these purposes, presumably because 'they could not meet the full burden of loan finance' (paras. 270 and 277);

(c) that, therefore, grants-in-aid should be made to the underdeveloped countries, but purely for 'productive' purposes (paras. 271 and 276).

The authors do not, however, hesitate to invoke the principle of needs. Thus:

> The principle that the better off should help to pay for the education, the medical services and other public services received by the poorer classes of the community is now well established within every Member nation of the United Nations. The idea that this principle should also be applied as between rich and poor countries is relatively new. It has however been put into practice on several occasions. (Para. 272.)

How far are these attempts to stretch the idea of "social" productivity successful?

To begin with, there is an important shift in the basic definition of the "underdeveloped countries" which is not as clearly stated as it might be. Up to now the main burden of the argument has been on the proposition that "underdeveloped countries" possess a greater amount of "underdeveloped" resources than the developed countries and that therefore the "social" productivity of investment is higher in the former than in the latter. From now on the emphasis has shifted to the fact that the underdeveloped countries have lower *per capita* incomes and therefore suffer from greater needs than the developed countries.

The introduction of the principle of needs does not create any difficulties provided we are prepared to keep it clearly apart from the principle of productivity. Then loans should continue to be made strictly on the productivity principle while grants should be made *separately* on the need principle.

This, however, results in somewhat unpalatable conclusions. (a) When we are allocating loans, our main concern is to maximize the total world output and not to equalize international incomes. Thus the social productivity curves of investment must be constructed objectively, and independently of our value judgements concerning needs. This means that capital should not be diverted in the form of low interest loans or grants to the poorer countries simply because they are poor. A more *economic* way of reducing inequalities in the international distribution of income is to allocate the world capital resources in uses where its social productivity is highest even if it happens to be in the richest countries, and to redistribute the resultant output after first ensuring that it is maximized. (b) Conversely, when we are allocating grants, our concern is with a more equitable international distribution of incomes and not with their effects on total output. Thus grants should be made in the form of final consumers' goods and services, directed not only towards the poorer countries but also towards the poorer sections within each country. The principle of need in its strict form is an argument for diverting final incomes from the richer to the poorer countries for consumption purposes and not an argument for diverting capital grants for "productive" purposes.

These conclusions are not without relevance to the practical issues of economic policy in the underdeveloped countries. Thus critics of the unsuccessful developmental ventures of the British Overseas Food Corporation and the Colonial Development Corporation may reasonably maintain that the root cause of the failure lies not as much in the wrong choice of men and inefficient methods of administering the ventures but in the vagueness of the mandate itself which tries to compromise between the principle of obtaining economic returns and the principle of needs. They may say that rather than waste huge sums of money by investing in projects which cannot be justified on the strict productivity principle, it were better to distribute them as free gifts of consumers' goods and services among the poor of Africa. Again, individuals and governments in underdeveloped countries sometimes find themselves with large sums of money which they cannot profitably or safely invest locally; and then, following the strict productivity principle and the need to protect their capital, they have found it wiser to invest it in the most developed countries such as the U.S.A. or the U.K.

The last example, however, brings out the unsatisfactoriness of trying to apply the static rules of the productive optimum to the problem of the underdeveloped countries. This, however, is rather damaging to the conventional definitions of the "underdeveloped" countries both in terms of "underdeveloped" resources and in terms of low *per capita* incomes. For now it begins to transpire: (a) that if we take the productivity curves of international investment on the basis of existing economic conditions in the "developed" and the "underdeveloped" countries, more often than not capital is likely to be more productive in the former than the latter and the Pigovian distinction between "social" and "private" product will not appreciably change the broad picture; (b) that therefore if we were to allocate capital according to the existing productivity curves, even taking a generous view of "social" productivity, this would still result in relatively greater quantities of capital being invested in the "developed" than in the "underdeveloped" countries, accentuating the unequal rate of economic development between the two types of country; and (c) that a policy of a more equal redistribution of international incomes based on the pure principle of needs, although it may relieve the burden of cumulative unequal rates of economic development, does not touch the heart of the problem; for fundamentally the problem of the "underdeveloped" countries is not merely that of low or unequal distribution of final incomes but also that of unequal participation in the processes of economic activity.

Faced with these considerations, those who wish to retain the "underdevelopment" approach are obliged to "dynamize" it and to refer to social productivity in the *longer run* as distinct from the *present* social productivity of investment.

We are now in a position to examine the argument of the authors of the United Nations Report on the *Measures for the Economic Development of the*

Underdeveloped Countries. It will be seen that the crux of their argument lies in the question how far "improving social capital" in public health, education, and communications, whether financed by grants or loans, can successfully stimulate further rounds of loan capital. Thus the authors' appeal to the principle of need in para. 272 (also implicit earlier on, e.g. para. 248) turns out to be a side-issue. It is a confusing side-issue at that because the requirements for creating incentives for further investment and those for promoting economic equality do not always conveniently coincide in the same policy as the authors have implied. On the contrary, there are many instances where the incentives for further investment can be created only by pursuing relatively disequalizing policies, such as control of domestic wages, tax exemptions to new (foreign) enterprises, etc. (Cf., for instance, "Industrialisation of Puerto Rico," *Caribbean Economic Review*, Dec. 1949, by Prof. A. Lewis, one of the authors of the Report.)

Turning to their main argument, the extent to which further rounds of loan investment can be effectively stimulated by a policy of "improving social capital" by grants must depend on a wide variety of circumstances which vary from country to country and about which no definite generalizations can be made. We are no longer in the static world where "under-investment" in a particular line can be deduced in principle by an inspection of the *given* social marginal productivity curves and where there is a definite functional relationship between the quantity of capital invested and the quantity of "returns" in the form of final output. Thus given favourable circumstances, a small amount of "investment" in social capital might start a chain-reaction and yield "returns" in the form of secondary rounds of investment out of all proportion to the initial investment. On the other hand, if circumstances are not favourable, even a larger amount of initial investment might not successfully start these secondary rounds of activities, and there is no real guarantee that increasing the amount of the initial investment still further would induce the desired results. In reply to such objections, the authors can only appeal to the general presumption that if average incomes per head or expenditure per head in the type of social sciences they have chosen is low, then longer-run social productivity of investment in "social capital" is likely to be high. This general presumption is not as strong as it appears, and there are two general arguments which may be advanced against it.

The first is clearest in the case of education and technical training although it can be applied also to other types of "social capital." It is the fairly common experience of the underdeveloped countries to find themselves, not merely with an overall shortage of educated people, but also with a relative shortage of those regarded as "socially productive," such as engineers and doctors, combined with a relative abundance of those regarded as less socially productive, such as lawyers and clerks. The reason for this is, of course, that with the existing social and economic organization of these countries there is a relatively greater market demand for the latter type of person than the former. This would seem to suggest that the problem of creating and organizing demand for trained personnel in the underdeveloped countries may even be more important than the problem of creating the supply by investment in "social capital." Given the demand, the supply of trained personnel of most types (including those trained abroad) would seem to respond more automatically and to a greater extent than is usually allowed for. On the other hand, there is less indication that the demand can be effectively stimulated merely by creating the supply without simultaneously introducing far-reaching changes into the economic structure. Thus most underdeveloped countries can provide numerous instances of graduates from technical and agricultural colleges who cannot be absorbed, because the existing economic structure cannot be changed quickly enough to absorb them, although in terms of broad averages the amount of money spent per head of education and technical training is quite modest. The common fate of these people is to suffer a form of intellectual "disguised unemployment" by taking up appointments as clerks and ordinary school teachers (cf. J. S. Furnivall, *Colonial Policy and Practice*, pp. 380–2). Thus there is a genuine tendency for a great deal of investment in "social capital" to be wasted, although the full extent of this wastage is concealed because expenditure on education and technical training is classed under the head of social services and not subject to the strict profit-and-loss accounting of other types of state enterprises.

This leads us to the second argument, which is rather disconcerting to the economic theorist. The application of fairly sophisticated economic theory involving concepts of social productivity and induced investment tends to create the impression that we have now opened up new possibilities of investment in the underdeveloped countries which were unappreciated and unexplored by the governments and administrators of these countries. This, however, overlooks two circumstances. Firstly, a substantial part of capital inflow into the underdeveloped countries was in the form of government borrowing even in the heyday of private investment. Secondly, the governments of the newly-opened-up countries have always been impelled by a powerful "self-interest" to try to obtain adequate revenues to meet the expanding costs of administration. Thus, untutored as they may be in economic theory, they have been obliged by practical necessity to borrow and deploy their loans and grants in ways not so different from the recommendations of the present-day economic experts. The moral of this argument is not merely that there is less scope for the deployment of "productive" loans and grants (as distinct from those social service expenditures which are frankly based on the principle of need) than appears at first sight. There is a further consideration which cuts across the whole of the "underdevelopment" approach. For, as we shall see, ironically enough, where the governments of the underdeveloped countries have been successful in stimulating private (foreign) investment, the result has frequently been too great and rapid an expansion in a few lines of primary production for export which further aggravated the problem of the adjustment of the indigenous peoples of these countries to outside economic forces. Thus again, we are led back from the consideration of the total quantity of investment and the total volume of output and economic activity to a consideration of the type of investment and the distribution of economic activities and economic roles between the backward peoples and the others.*

This is a convenient point at which to pause and summarize our argument so far. (i) The problem of the so-called "underdeveloped countries" consists, not merely in the "underdevelopment" of their resources in the usual senses, but also in the economic "backwardness" of their peoples. (ii) Where it exists, the "underdevelopment" of *natural* resources and the backwardness of people mutually aggravate each other in a "vicious circle." (iii) While (ii) is very important, it needs to be handled with care, for it is liable to distract our attention from the real problem of economic backwardness. Thus, impressed by the connexion between the "backwardness" of the people and the "underdevelopment" of the resources, many have sought to superimpose these two concepts on each other and to explain the former entirely in terms of the latter. In doing so, however, they are continually obliged to stretch and shift the basis of their argument: from the "underdeveloped" *natural* resources to the "underdeveloped" *human* resources; from the "private" to the "social" productivity of investment; from the principle of "productivity" to the principle of "need"; and finally, from the static idea of the optimum allocation of investible resources to the dynamic idea of stimulating further rounds of investment by "productive" grants. It is fair to say that, in spite of all these contortions, the real issues of backwardness seem to have eluded the grasp of the "underdevelopment" approach. (iv) Thus in order to push our analysis farther to the heart of the problem, it would seem desirable to make a clean break with the "underdevelopment" approach and to recognize the problem of "backwardness" as a major problem in its own right which may occur even where there is no important "underdevelopment" of resources in any of the acceptable senses. To emphasize this we shall speak from now on of "backward" and not "underdeveloped" countries.

III

At this stage it will be seen that there are at least two other "obvious" explanations of "backwardness" which must be considered as seriously as "underdevelopment" in relation to some of the backward countries. But like "underdevelopment" itself, we shall have to leave them aside in our search for a more general approach to the problem.

The first, of course, is the "overpopulation" approach which not so long ago

---

*In some cases, however, there may be an important divergence between the social productivity of investment to the community and the "private" productivity to the government interpreted narrowly in terms of quick revenue receipts. Sometimes governments may actually discourage new domestic industries to protect their vested interests in customs and excise duties.

used to occupy a central position in discussions now dominated by the idea of "underdevelopment." Here again we may agree that backward peoples generally tend to have high birth-rates and that therefore "overpopulation" and "backwardness" tend to aggravate each other in another of those "vicious circles" which are a feature of the whole subject. But this still leaves important gaps in the explanation. While overpopulation may be a major cause of backwardness in some countries, it does not explain why other countries not suffering from manifest population pressure should also be similarly backward. Moreover, some backward countries, e.g. most of those in south-east Asia, initially started from sparse populations in relation to their natural resources. It is only after they have been "opened up" to international trade that they have tended to become overpopulated, partly because their death-rates have been reduced and partly because their resources have been developed in a few special lines of primary production for export which are subject to diminishing returns. Here, overpopulation cannot be regarded as the cause of backwardness; rather it is a manifestation of the maladjustment of backward peoples to outside economic forces at the physical level. Nor need this maladjustment always take the form of overpopulation. In some cases of extreme backwardness the size of the backward populations has been known to diminish to the point of extinction. Finally, the degree of overpopulation depends, not only on the relation between the physical quantity of natural resources and the size of population, but also on the level of technical and economic development of the people. Thus advanced industrial countries can usually maintain a denser population at a higher standard of living than the backward agricultural and pastoral countries. Further, in the past the advanced countries have absorbed very large increases in population without lowering their standard of living; indeed, many would maintain that these increases were a necessary part of their even greater rates of expansion in output and economic activity.[3] Thus to try to account for economic backwardness purely in terms of population pressure is to leave unanswered the question why the economically backward peoples have been unable to increase their productivity to match the increase in their population while the economically advanced people have managed to increase their standard of living on top of large increases in population.

The second possible line of approach is in terms of the deliberate and legalized political, economic, and racial discriminations imposed on the "backward" peoples by the "advanced" peoples. Here again, although this appears to be a major factor in certain countries, notoriously in Africa, it does not explain why the indigenous peoples of other countries who are not subject to such obvious discriminations to the same extent should also be similarly backward. Here, of course, the definition of the nature and extent of discriminations raises very formidable difficulties which we must frankly by-pass if we are to get farther on with our analysis. We shall thus content ourselves with drawing a somewhat crude working distinction between the deliberate and therefore directly remediable causes of backwardness in the form of open and legalized *discriminations* and the more fortuitous and intractable *disequalizing factors* which may operate even where there is a perfect equality of formal legal rights between different groups of people in their economic relations with each other (cf., however, section V below).

We are now able to sketch the general outlines of our problem. When the backward countries were "opened up" to economic relations with the outside world, their peoples had to face the problem of adapting themselves to a new environment shaped by outside economic forces. In this, whatever their degree of cultural advance in other spheres, they seem to have been conspicuously unsuccessful or "backward" compared with the other groups of economically "advanced" people—whatever their degree of cultural advance in other spheres. Our problem is to explain this gap, to explain why the backward people cannot stand on a "competitive footing" with the advanced people in this "economic struggle." The problem is further complicated by the fact that the gap between the advanced and backward peoples instead of being narrowed has been frequently widened by the passage of time. Thus an inquiry into the causes of economic backwardness essentially consists in searching for those disequalizing factors which instead of being neutralized are cumulatively exaggerated by "the free play of economic forces."

In order to isolate these disequalizing factors, we can adopt a "model" of a backward country which has the following broad negative specifications. (i) Initially the country started with a fairly sparse population in relation to its potential natural resources; so it cannot be said to have been suffering from "overpopulation" to begin with. (ii) Its natural resources are then "developed," usually in the direction of a few specialized lines of primary production for export, as fully as the world market conditions permit. This process of "development" is generally carried out by foreign private enterprise under conditions of *laissez-faire*, but frequently the process may be aided by a government policy of stimulating expansion in investment, export, and general economic activity motivated by a desire to expand taxable capacity. So the country's natural resources cannot be said to be obviously "underdeveloped." (iii) Whatever its political status, its native inhabitants at least enjoy a perfect equality of formal legal rights in their economic relations with other people, including the right to own any type of property and to enter into any type of occupation; so they cannot be said to suffer from obvious discriminations in economic matters.

To those who are firmly wedded to the conventional explanations of economic backwardness this may seem like assuming away the entire problem. But when we turn and survey the different types of backward countries, it will be seen that there is a large group, for example those in south-east Asia, British West Africa, Latin America, which approximates more to our model than to any models of obvious "underdevelopment," "overpopulation," or "discrimination" or a combination of all of them, if the first and the second can in fact be combined. Further, even in the other groups of backward countries where these conventional explanations are obviously very important, our model is still useful in turning attention to the residual causes of backwardness which may turn out to be by no means negligible.

IV

Before we consider our "model" further let us examine the concept of economic backwardness more closely. We may begin by distinguishing between the "backward country" as an aggregate territorial and economic unit and the "backward people" who frequently form merely a group within it confined to certain sectors of the economy. Now the disequalizing factors which we are seeking must be considered as operating, not only between the backward and the advanced countries as aggregate units, but also between the backward and advanced groups of peoples within the same backward country itself. Obviously a complete analysis of economic backwardness must take into account both sets of disequalizing factors which are closely interrelated with each other. Even so, we shall come to realize that the familiar "countries A and B" approach of the conventional theory of international trade is seriously inadequate for our purpose and that to study the actual impact of outside economic forces on the backward people we shall have to go behind these macro-economic units to those disequalizing factors which operate within the backward country itself.

But much still remains to be done even in terms of the conventional approach, using these versatile letters A and B to denote the "advanced" and the "backward" countries respectively. It is only recently that the general run of economists have turned their attention to the long-run problem of unequal rates of economic growth and productivity among the different countries participating in international trade. But even so, it is fair to say that this has somewhat shaken the belief in the adequacy of the static theory of comparative costs to deal with the essentially dynamic process of growth of the international economy. Thus it is now increasingly admitted that the existing ratios of comparative costs are by no means immutable and rigidly related to the original natural resources of the countries but may be influenced to a great extent by such factors as education, experience, technical skills, and so on, which arise out of the process of international trade itself and may exert a cumulatively disequalizing influence against the countries which have a later start. Following on from this, it would seem that the gains from international trade cannot be adequately measured merely in the form of the conventional "terms of trade" and the distribution of final incomes among the participating countries; we must also take into account the distribution of economic activities, in the form of induced investment and secondary rounds of employment, growth of technical knowledge and external economies, and all those dynamic stimuli which each participating country receives as a consequence of a given increase in the volume of its trade (cf. H. W. Singer, "The Distribution of Gains between Investing and Borrowing Countries," *American*

Economic Review, Papers and Proceedings, May 1950). Although different views may be held about the practical policies most likely to induce these secondary rounds of investment and economic activity, there is little doubt that the concept of "induced" investment affords great theoretical insight into the nature of economic backwardness. In a sense, one might say that the difference between the "advanced" and the "backward" country lies in the fact that the former, subject to the powerful "accelerator" effect, can generate its own trade-cycle while the latter merely receives the fluctuations transmitted to it from outside, although of course the size of the impact need not be smaller for that reason.

Having said this, however, it is necessary to add that an approach to backwardness which stops short at this level will be seriously inadequate and that many of the discussions on the subject have been vitiated precisely because they are couched in terms of such geographical aggregates as "countries," "areas," "territories," etc. A natural consequence of this is a preoccupation with such macro-economic quantities as the aggregate and *per capita* national income, total volume of exports, total and average amount of investment, etc. Whence follow those economic development plans which aim to increase either the total or the *per capita* national income by a certain percentage by means of target figures for investment calculated on the basis of average capital requirements per head of population.

This type of macro-economic model of economic development may be suitable for the advanced countries,[4] but there are a number of reasons why it cannot be satisfactorily extended to the backward countries. To begin with, the advanced country, by definition, is in the middle of a self-generating process of economic growth characterized by a steady rate of technical innovation and increase in productivity. Thus it seems reasonable to rule out diminishing returns and assume that a given rate of net investment will, on the whole, result in a corresponding rate of increase in total output or productive capacity. Further, certain basic ratios, such as the propensity to consume, are not obviously unstable and may be used as constants for the process analysis. When we turn to the backward country, however, these assumptions are no longer plausible. The problem here is not to trace the working of the process of economic growth on the basis of certain constant proportions but to try to start that process itself. We cannot stop short at thinking in terms of overall rates of net investment and increase in total output because the two rates are no longer connected in a determinate manner by a stable average ratio of capital to output.[5] Indeed, even if we could assume constant average productivity of capital, this will not be sufficient for the purpose of many economic development plans because they rely to varying degrees on the assumption of "external economies" and increasing returns to scale. Further, none of the basic ratios required as constants for the process analysis can be assumed to be stable for the relevant long period. Under the impact of outside economic forces, most of these ratios, such as propensity to consume and import, population growth, etc., have been changed or are in the process of changing.

Here again it is the accepted task of economic development policy, not merely to accept these ratios as given, but to try to change them in directions considered to be favourable for development. This is not to say that all economic development plans based on macro-economic analysis will always fail. It is merely to say that it is not sufficient to stop short at this level and assume as a matter of course that, provided the required supply of capital[6] is forthcoming, the process of economic growth will work itself out automatically as it does in the advanced countries. Thus the very nature of our problem, which is to start this process of economic growth, obliges us to go behind the macro-economic units and investigate the actual structure and "growing-points" of the backward economy. For the same reason, we cannot treat the changes in the basic ratios and propensities as "exogenous" changes in data but must inquire into their nature and causes.

So far we have been concerned only with the mechanical difficulties of applying the macro-economic models to the backward countries. Even more serious difficulties are encountered when we inquire into the meaningfulness of macro-economic quantities such as the aggregate, national income or the *per capita* income to the peoples of the backward countries. These arise in addition to the complication already noted—that "backward peoples" normally form only a sector of the economy of their "countries"—so that the fortunes of the "country" and the "people" cannot be closely identified.

Even in the advanced countries, such concepts as the increase in national income or aggregate output capacity create serious problems of interpretation once we drop the static assumption of given and constant wants and enter the real world of a continual stream of new wants and commodities and improvements in the quality of existing goods. We can, however, put aside these "index-number" problems in favour of a "common-sense" interpretation, since we can assume that the "measuring rod of money" and physical productivity are meaningful to the individuals concerned and broadly approximate to the social goals they are pursuing as groups in a fairly simple and straightforward manner. When we come to the backward countries, however, this assumption has to be carefully re-examined. The peoples of backward countries have had shorter periods of contact with the "money economy" so that the habits of mind and the symbolism associated with monetary accounting may not be deep rooted in their minds.[7] Further, as groups, they are subject to complex pulls of nationalism and racial status, so that there may not be a simple means–end relationship between the increase in national output and the achievement of their social goals. Thus, in many backward countries, people seem to desire up-to-date factories and other trappings of modern industrialism, not so much for the strictly material returns they are expected to yield as for the fact that they are in themselves symbols of national prestige and economic development. Following Veblen, one might describe this as a case of "conspicuous production."

There is then a greater need in the study of backward countries than in that of the advanced countries to go behind the "veil" of conventional social accounting into the real processes of adaptation between wants, activities, and environment which we have described earlier on as the "economic struggle." When we do this we shall see that the "problem" of the backward countries as it is commonly discussed really has two distinct aspects: on the subjective side it might be described as the economics of discontent and maladjustment; on the objective side it might be described as the economics of stagnation, low *per capita* productivity and incomes. In principle the latter should be a counterpart to the former and provide us with quantitative indices of it. In practice there is a real danger of the macro-models of economic development "running on their own steam" without any reference to the fundamental human problems of backwardness on the subjective side.

To illustrate this, let us begin by considering the backward country as a stationary state. In terms of the objective approach this is a standard case of economic backwardness and "overpopulation" popularly attributed to the classical economists.[8] In terms of the subjective approach the situation may not appear so gloomy. Many of the backward countries before they were "opened up" were primitive or medieval stationary states governed by habits and customs. Their people might live near the "minimum subsistence level" but that, according to their own lights, did not appear too wretched or inadequate. Thus in spite of low productivity and lack of economic progress, there was no problem of economic discontent and frustration: wants and activities were on the whole adapted to each other and the people were in equilibrium with their environment. This is not to say that everything was idyllic: there may have been frequent tribal wars and insecurity of life and property. But on the whole it is fair to say that there was no "problem" of backward countries in the modern sense and that the situation perhaps resembled J. S. Mill's picture of the stationary state more than that of his predecessors (cf. Mill, *Principles*, bk. iv, ch. vi).

Now consider the second stage particularly in the second half of nineteenth century and the beginning of twentieth century when these stationary backward societies were opened up to the outside economic forces. Here we can see why the term "backward" which we have been obliged to use for lack of a better alternative is so loose and liable to different interpretations. For at this stage, and to a certain extent even today, the economic backwardness of a society was simply measured by the lack of response of its members to monetary incentives. This in effect meant measuring the backwardness of a people, not by their inefficiency and inaptness in satisfying their given wants or in pursuing their own social goals, but by their tardiness in adopting new Western standards of wants and activities. Measures for "economic development" then consisted mainly in attempts to persuade or force the backward people into the new ways of life represented by the money economy—for example, by stimulating their demand for imports and by taxing them so that they were obliged to turn to cash crops or work in the newly opened mines and plantations. Whether it was meaningful or not to the people, the accepted yardstick of economic development of a "country" was its export and taxable capacity.

"Backwardness" in the sense of economic discontent and maladjustment does not fully emerge until the third stage of the drama when the natural resources of the backward countries have been "developed" to a large extent, usually by foreign private enterprise, and when the backward peoples have been partly converted to the new ways of life. Here the irony of the situation lies in the fact that the acuteness of the problem of backwardness at this stage is frequently proportional to the success and rapidity of "economic development" at the second stage. To begin with, it becomes apparent that the backward peoples can be only too successfully converted to new ways of life on the side of wants and aspirations while this cannot be matched by a corresponding increase in their earning capacity. We then have a progressive maladjustment between wants and activities, the former outstripping the latter at each round of "education" and contact with the outside world. (This may spread from the individual to the national level when at the fourth stage the independent national governments of the backward countries find their resources insufficient to carry out ambitious schemes of economic development and social welfare.) Further, the backward peoples now find that they cannot successfully adapt themselves to the new economic environment shaped by outside forces and that they lag behind in the "economic struggle" with other economically advanced groups of people who have initiated the "opening-up" process. Thus they find themselves with a relatively smaller share of the economic activities and the national incomes of their countries although these may be rapidly increasing in the aggregate (at least up to the limits set by the diminishing returns in the new lines of the primary production for export). Here then we have the problem of economic backwardness in its full efflorescence charged with the explosive feeling of discontent and grievance against "lop-sided economic development," "foreign economic domination," "imperialistic exploitation," and so on.

We can now see why it is so unsatisfactory to approach the problem of the backward countries as the source of international tension purely at the macro-economic level of the conventional development plans. Aggregates such as the total national income and volume of exports are very unsatisfactory as indices of economic welfare of a "plural society" made up of different groups of people such as that which exists in many backward countries. Here the well-known maxim of static welfare economics, that the economic welfare of a country is increased if some people can move to a better position while leaving the others exactly as they were before, must sound somewhat galling to the backward peoples who frequently happen to be those left "exactly as they were before."

Nor is *per capita* income very satisfactory as an index of "poverty." The sort of maladjustment between wants and earning capacity which we have been describing may occur even if *per capita* incomes are rising. Indeed a greater amount of discontent may be created where incomes rise enough to introduce new commodities into the consumers' budget and then fluctuate and decline (a common experience in export economies) than where incomes per head remain stationary or decline slowly. Further, we should note that the degree of discontent depends, not as much on the absolute level of *per capita* incomes as in their *relative* ranking. Thus motives of "conspicuous consumption" and the external diseconomies of consumption of higher income groups associated with Veblen and more recently with Professor J. S. Duesenberry should be taken into account (cf. Ragnar Nurkse, *Some Aspects of Capital Accumulation in Underdeveloped Countries*, Cairo, 1952, Third Lecture).

It is important to point this out since low income per head has now crystallized into the definition of backward countries. Some have even tried to put it on a "scientific" basis by arguing that since the existing low incomes of the backward peoples are insufficient to provide them with the minimum nutritional requirements, their physical efficiency and productivity is lowered, thus creating a "vicious circle." While this may be an important long-run factor, it is a dangerous over-simplification of the complex motivations and aspirations of the backward peoples both at the individual and national levels to assume that Communism can be "contained" by calories. Even in the backward countries, perhaps particularly there, men do not live by bread alone. Thus as a *Times* correspondent has recently written about the wage claims in the African Copper Belt:

> Another factor which drives the African to make demands is his increasing needs. He is beginning to buy smarter clothes; to eat foods he never did before; to drink wine and English beer instead of native liquor. It is, indeed, an almost impossible task to-day to compile a reasonable family budget because of this traditional stage in African 'consumer' requirements. This, too, however much people may disapprove of the elaborately dressed up African 'spiv' with his cowboy hat, sunglasses, and new bicycle, is a healthy trend; it is obviously essential if the African is to be weaned from a subsistence to a cash economy that he should develop the needs that create incentive. (*The Times*, 19 January 1953.)

If the backward peoples as individuals desire those commodities one associates with the "American way of life," at the national level they seem to desire the latest models of social security schemes associated with the "British Welfare State." It would thus be a crowning-point of irony if some backward countries were to turn towards Communism through an excessive fondness for the American and British ways of life.

V

In the light of what has been said above, the study of the "disequalizing factors" at work against the backward peoples within the economies of their countries emerges as an essential link between the two aspects of the problem of backwardness: the economics of discontent and maladjustment on the one side and the economics of stagnation or relatively slow rates of growth in total or *per capita* national income and productivity on the other.

When we consider these "disequalizing factors" we shall see that the exclusion of the "obvious" explanations in terms of "underdevelopment," "overpopulation," and "discrimination" still leaves us with a great variety of residual causes of backwardness. To analyse them in detail is beyond the scope of this paper. For our purpose of obtaining a general interpretation of the nature of backwardness it is sufficient to point out certain broad patterns of backwardness in which the initial differences in experience, opportunities, capital supply, etc., between the economically backward and advanced groups of people seem to have been "fossilized" or accentuated by the "free play of economic forces." We shall illustrate these patterns with reference to the backward peoples in their typical roles as unskilled workers, peasant producers, and borrowers of capital which between them cover most types of economic contacts between the backward and the advanced peoples.

In order to do this we shall introduce three characteristic features of the "opening-up" process into our "model" of the backward economy.

i. The first concerns the nature of "specialization" for the export market. Now it is commonly realized that "specialization" does not merely mean moving along the given "production-possibility" curve of the textbook; and that in practice it involves an irreversible process whereby much of the resources and the productive equipment, e.g. transport and communications, of the backward economy have been moulded and made specific to satisfy the special requirements of the export market. (Hence the well-known argument for diversification.) But the habit of thinking in terms of "countries" or "areas" leads to the inadequate appreciation of one further fundamental fact: in spite of the striking specialization of the inanimate productive equipment and of the individuals from the economically advanced groups of people who manage and control them, there is really very little specialization, beyond a natural adaptability to the tropical climate, among the backward peoples in their roles as unskilled labourers or peasant producers. Thus the typical unskilled labour supplied by the backward peoples is an undifferentiated mass of cheap manpower which might be used in any type of plantation or in any type of extractive industry within the tropics and sometimes even beyond it.[9] This can be seen from the range of the primary industries built on the immigrant Indian, Chinese, and African labour. Thus all the specialization required for the export market seems to have been done by the other co-operating factors, the whole production structure being built around the supply of cheap undifferentiated labour.

When we turn to the backward peoples in their role as peasant producers, again the picture is not appreciably changed. Some backward economies "specialize" on crops which they have traditionally produced, and thus "specialization" simply means expansion along the traditional lines with no perceptible change in the methods of production (e.g. rice in south-east Asian countries). Even where a new cash crop is introduced, the essence of its success as a *peasant* crop depends on the fact that it does not represent a radical departure from the existing techniques of production[10] (e.g. yams and cocoa in West Africa). Thus as a historian has said about the palm-oil and ground-nuts trade of West Africa: "They made little demand on the energies or thought of the natives and they effected no revolution in the society of West Africa. That was why they were so readily grafted on to the old economy and why they grew as they did" (A. McPhee, *The Economic Revolution of West Africa*, pp. 39–40). Here again one is tempted to say that much of the "specialization" seems to have been done by nature and the complementary investment in transport and processing. On the side of productive activities, the fact that the crop is sold for the export market instead of for domestic consumption is an accidental detail. It is only on the side of wants that disturbing changes seem to have been introduced, including a decline of skills in the domestic handicraft industries now no longer able to compete against the imported commodities. To prevent misunderstanding, it should be added that frequently the peasant methods are found to have lower costs than the "modern" scientific methods, and that is the reason why peasant production has been able to withstand the competition of the plantation system in some countries. But at the best this merely means the survival of old skills rather than a steady improvement in the methods of production through "specialization" for the export market.

Thus, paradoxically enough, the process of "specialization" of a backward economy for the export market seems to be most rapid and successful when it leaves the backward peoples in their unspecialized roles as unskilled labour and peasant producers using traditional methods of production.

ii. The second characteristic feature of the "opening-up" process is the monopoly power of varying degrees which the foreign business concerns exercise in relation to the backward economy. Here again the actual process of the growth of trade between the advanced and the backward countries differs from the textbook picture of two countries coming into trading relations with each other under conditions of perfect competition. Indeed, if we were to insist on applying the rules of perfect competition to foreign enterprises, very few backward countries would have been "developed." The process of opening up a new territory for trade is an extremely risky and costly business, and it is only by offering some sort of monopolistic concessions that foreign business concerns can be induced to accept the risks and the heavy initial costs, which include not only those of setting up transport and communications and other auxiliary services but may also include the ordinary administrative costs of extending law and order to places where it does not exist. Hence the age-old method of economic development by chartered companies. In the case of mining this is reinforced by the technical advantages of large-scale enterprise.

Even where there is no formal concession of monopoly power, as in a peasant economy, conditions are generally very favourable for its growth. To begin with, only fairly big firms with large enough reserves to meet the heavy initial costs and risks may venture into the new territory. Further, although there may be no restriction to free entry, potential competitors may be put off by the "economies of experience" which give a great differential advantage to the pioneers. Thus there are usually a small number of fairly big export-import firms engaged in a "cut-throat" competition with each other in their effort to increase their turnover and spread their heavy overhead costs. This need not be limited to "horizontal" competition among the export-import firms; it may also result in a "vertical" competition between the export-import firms and the steamship companies which control the trade routes. After some time this trade war generally results in "pools" and "combinations" both of the horizontal and vertical types,[11] for "the small trader must grow to greatness, either in himself, or in combination with others. The alternative is his failure and ultimate disappearance. In fact, economic conditions of England are exhibited on an intenser scale in West Africa, where businesses grow, decay and combine with mushroom rapidity." (McPhee, op. cit., p. 103; cf. W. K. Hancock, *Survey of British Commonwealth Affairs*, vol. ii, part 2, ch. iii, sec. iii; also J. S. Furnivall, *Colonial Policy and Practice*, pp. 95–97 and pp. 197–8.)

Thus in a typical process of "development," the backward peoples have to contend with three types of monopolistic forces: in their role as unskilled labour they have to face the big foreign mining and plantation concerns who are monopolistic buyers of their labour; in their role as peasant producers they have to face a small group of exporting and processing firms who are monopolistic buyers of their crop; and in their role as consumers of imported commodities they have to face the same group of firms who are the monopolistic sellers or distributors of these commodities.

iii. The third characteristic feature of the "opening-up" process is the growth of the middlemen between the big European concerns and the economically backward indigenous populations. They are the necessary adjuncts to any process of rapid economic development and fill in the gaps between the highly specialized Western economic structure and the relatively unspecialized roles of the backward peoples. Although they may operate in the labour market, they are more important in their activities as collectors of produce from the peasant farmers, as distributors of imported articles to the indigenous consumers, and, most important of all, as money-lenders. In most backward countries they seem to owe their special position to their longer contact with Western economic life; frequently they may start as immigrant labour and work their way up as small traders and money-lenders. The racial distribution of the middlemen groups among the backward countries is familiar: thus we have the Indians and Chinese in south-east Asia, Indians in East Africa, Syrians and "Coast Africans" in West Africa, etc. Thus the economic hierarchy of a typical backward country is generally a pyramid with Europeans on top, then the middlemen, and lastly the indigenous people at the bottom.

Each of the characteristic features outlined above tends to reduce the relative share of the national incomes of the backward countries accruing to the indigenous peoples. But, as we have said before, the nature of economic backwardness cannot be fully appreciated until we go beyond the distribution of incomes to the distribution of economic activities: for "it is to changes in the forms of efforts and activities that we must turn when in search for the keynotes of the history of mankind" (Marshall, *Principles*, p. 85.)

When we consider the backward peoples in their role as unskilled labour, it is important to ask, not merely why their wages have remained low but why they have been frozen into their role of cheap undifferentiated labour with little vertical mobility into more skilled grades. Here, apart from the monopsony power of the employers, various complex factors are at work to stereotype their role; out of these we may select three as being fairly typical (cf. Wilbert E. Moore, *Industrialization and Labor*, ch. v, for a more systematic analysis).

The first is the very high rate of turnover of indigenous labour, partly because the backward peoples are unused to the discipline of the mines and plantations, and partly because they have one foot in their traditional tribal and village economies which make them look upon wage labour not as a continuous permanent employment but as a temporary or periodical expedient to earn a certain sum of money. Given this rapid rate of labour turnover, there is no opportunity to acquire the experience and skill for promotion to skilled grades. If this were the only cause, one might assume that this is a transitional problem which would gradually disappear with the breakdown of the traditional social institutions and the spread of money economy. But unfortunately there are other obstacles.

This brings us back to the difficulties which we by-passed when defining the nature and extent of "discrimination" against backward peoples. Here, with reference to the lack of vertical mobility of indigenous labour, we must frankly admit that our distinction between "discrimination" and "disequalizing factor" wears very thin in many backward countries. Even where there is no official colour bar, unofficial industrial colour bar is fairly widespread (for example, say, the Rhodesian copper-mines). Even where "discrimination" has not hardened into a "bar" of any sort, the natural and frequently unconscious tendency of the white employers to mark off "native" or "coloured" occupational categories irrespective of individual differences in ability and skill can be very damaging to the backward peoples; for the educational effect of apprenticeship and promotion to skilled grades in ordinary economic life is more far-reaching than huge sums of money spent on educational institutions.

The third factor which has contributed to the fossilization of the "cheap labour" convention is the additional supplies of labour which mines and plantation can draw, either from the breakdown of tribal societies (e.g. the Ashanti Wars in West Africa) or from the human reservoirs of India and China. Importation of immigrant labour has been blessed by liberal economic policy as contributing to the international mobility of labour; and it may be freely admitted that "economic development" and the rapid growth of output of tropical raw materials could not have been achieved without it. But as a solution to the problem of human backwardness it has been somewhat unhappy. It has not appreciably relieved the population pressure in the donating countries; and in the receiving countries, apart from the complex social problems it has created, it has robbed the indigenous people of the chance to acquire vertical mobility in the labour market through the automatic operation of the laws of supply and demand and the principle of substitution.

Let us now turn to the backward peoples in their role as peasant producers in relation to the middlemen and the big export-import firms. Here we have the familiar disequalizing factors, such as the peasants' ignorance of market conditions, which are extremely unstable, their lack of economic strength to hold out against middlemen and speculators, and their need to borrow money at high rates of interest, which have reduced the relative share of incomes accruing to the backward peoples. It may also be freely admitted that this has been helped by their well-known "extravagance" and lack of thrift which are after all the logical consequences of too successful a policy of creating economic incentives for the production of cash crops. The formal framework which offers perfect equality of economic rights offers no protection, and the result of the "free play of economic forces" under conditions of fluctuating export prices is the well-known story of rural indebtedness, land alienation, and agrarian unrest (cf. Furnivall, *Colonial Policy and Practice*, passim). Here again we should go beyond the distribution of incomes to the distribution of economic activities. We shall then see that the real damage done by the middlemen lies not in their "exploitation," considerable as it may be in many cases, but in the fact that they have put themselves between the backward peoples and the outside world and have robbed the latter of the educating and stimulating effect of a direct contact (cf. Hancock, op. cit., pp. 225–7). As a consequence, even after many decades of rapid "economic development" following the "opening-up" process, the peoples of many backward countries still remain almost as ignorant and unused to the ways of modern economic life as they were before. On the side of economic activities they remain as backward as ever; it is only on the side of wants that they have been modernized, and this reduces their propensity to save and increases their sense of discontent and inequality (cf. Ragnar Nurkse, *Some Aspects of Capital Accumulation in Underdeveloped Countries*, 1952, Third Lecture).

Finally, we may comment briefly on the backward peoples in their role as borrowers. Here, when we inquire closely why they are obliged to borrow at very high rates of interest from the money-lenders, we frequently find that high risks and the difficulties of finding suitable outlets for liquid funds may be more important than an overall shortage of saving. It is true that the rigid sterling exchange standard of some backward countries (which works like the gold standard) may have a deflationary bias, particularly during periods of rapid extension of the money sector. But, in spite of this, it is difficult to establish that there is an overall shortage of saving for the backward economy as a whole. In the "advanced" or Western sectors at least, big business concerns can raise loans on the international market on equal terms with the borrowers from the advanced countries and the banks generally tend to have a very high liquidity ratio.

This leads us to the problem which is apt to be obscured by the "underinvestment" approach which stresses the overall shortage of capital supply. It is the problem of organizing the *distribution* of credit as distinct from the problem of increasing the total supply of saving. The "retail distribution" of credit among peasant producers is beyond the capacity of the ordinary commercial bank and, in spite of the rise of the co-operative movement, still remains one of the unsolved problems of the backward countries which may have greater long-run significance than the more spectacular projects for economic development. Further, there is a great need to extend credit facilities not only to the peasant producers but also to the growing class of small traders and business men among the backward peoples who would like to enter into the traditional preserves of the middlemen. Here many would-be business men from the backward groups frequently complain of the "discrimination" against them by the commercial banks when the truth of the matter is that they are simply caught up in a vicious circle of lack of business experience resulting in a lack of credit-worthiness. The banks, far from discriminating, are playing strictly according to the "rules of the game," but these rules tend to put the heaviest handicap on the weakest players.

That the real "bottleneck" may frequently lie in the difficulties of organizing the distribution of credit and finding suitable outlets for existing savings, rather than in the overall shortage of saving, may also be seen from the fact that domestic saving even where it exists in sizeable amounts is normally used for money-lending on the basis of land and jewellery mortgage since this yields a very much higher rate of return to the savers than any other available form of "productive" investment.

VI

The idea of economic backwardness put forward in this paper may be better appreciated in terms of the deviations, not from the static concept of the allocative optimum, but from the dynamic presumption concerning the beneficial effects of free trade held by the older generation of liberal economists. For it will be remembered that the classical case for free competition was based, not as much on the purely static considerations of allocative efficiency as on dynamic considerations of economic expansion. Thus it was believed that the growth of individualism and economic freedom would encourage initiative and enterprise, thrift, industriousness, and other qualities favourable to the dynamic expansion of the economy both horizontally, through the international division of labour and the extension of the market, and vertically, through capital accumulation and technical innovations. (Cf. L. Robbins, *The Theory of Economic Policy*, p. 16; also H. Myint, *Theories of Welfare Economics*, ch. iv.)

This line of thought is worth pursuing. The Classical economists did not claim that the free play of economic forces would necessarily lead to a more equitable distribution of wealth; as a matter of fact, they believed that inequalities of incomes (on the basis of equal opportunities) were necessary to provide the incentives for economic expansion: thus a redistribution of incomes from the rich to the poor might discourage saving, and poor relief (whether on a national or an international scale) might aggravate the population problem. As a corollary to this, they denied that the free play of economic forces would set up disequalizing factors which would ultimately inhibit the expansion in the total volume of output and economic activity.

As is well known, this Classical vision of harmonious economic growth through free enterprise has been shattered by two major factors: the growth of monopoly and imperfect competition, and the growth of unemployment. These did not, however, immediately lead to a reconsideration of the long-run theory of economic development on the Classical lines, for many economists have been too preoccupied with the purely static effects of imperfect competition, as in much of modern welfare economics, or with purely short-run problems, as in much of modern Keynesian economics. It is only fairly recently that the tide has turned, and the economics of backwardness, apart from its practical interest, may now come to occupy an important position in its own right as an essential element in the new theory of long-run economic development.

One of the most interesting developments in the long-run theory of economic development is Professor Schumpeter's well-known argument that the growth of monopoly, which from a static view would result in a maldistribution of resources, might actually favour technical innovations and economic development (J. Schumpeter, *Capitalism, Socialism and Democracy*, chs. vii and viii). We have already seen a parallel case of this argument when we were led to the conclusion that monopoly was an essential element in the "opening-up" process of the backward countries to international trade. The question then arises: can the Schumpeter argument be extended to the backward countries or is there a fundamental difference in the operation of monopoly in the backward countries as compared with the advanced countries?

Recently Professor J. K. Galbraith has put forward a theory which seems to provide a part of the answer. He maintains that the growth of monopoly in the advanced countries, particularly in the U.S.A., has been accompanied by a growth of "countervailing power" on the opposite side of the market, e.g. trade unions, retail chain stores, co-operative societies, farmers' unions, etc. The growth of monopoly increases the gains from building up the countervailing power and induces its growth and this provides a new self-regulatory mechanism to the economy in a world of monopoly (J. K. Galbraith, *American Capitalism*, "The Concept of Countervailing Power"). In Professor Galbraith's terminology, then, economic backwardness may be described as a phenomenon which arises because the process of "economic development" has been too rapid and the initial conditions too unfavourable to give rise to an effective "countervailing power" to check the "foreign economic domination" of the backward peoples. One remarkable thing about Professor Galbraith's argument is that although he is concerned with the economically most advanced country in the world, the U.S.A., the sectors of the economy which he regards as being particularly in need of the countervailing power—agriculture, consumers' goods market, and the labour market—are exactly paralleled in the backward countries with their export-import monopolies and large scale mining and plantation businesses (cf. Galbraith, op. cit., chs. x and xi).

Now if we were merely concerned with the problem of backwardness in its subjective aspect as the economics of discontent it would be sufficient to show how the working of the disequalizing factors set up by the free play of economic forces in the absence of countervailing power has resulted in the present situation. But we must go on to the other side of the problem and investigate the relation between the disequalizing factors and economic stagnation or the slow rate of growth in total output and economic activity (apart from the unfavourable effects of political and social unrests, both on present production and future investment).

Here, as we have noted above, we must be on guard against the convenient supposition that the requirements of economic equality and economic development always work in the same direction. Bearing this in mind, when we consider the typical process of "economic development" of most backward countries there seem to be prima facie reasons for thinking that the disequalizing factors have affected not merely the distribution but also the rate of growth in the total volume of output and economic activity.

The fundamental assumption of liberal economics is that the free play of economic forces would lead to the maximum development of *individual* talents and abilities; whereas in practice the free play of economic forces in backward countries has resulted, not in a division of labour according to individual abilities, but in a division of labour according to stratified groups. The accurate selection of the different types and qualities of natural resources by the automatic market mechanism contrasts dramatically with its lack of selectivity concerning human resources which has resulted in the "fossilization" of the backward peoples in their conventional roles of undifferentiated cheap labour and unspecialized peasant producers. Thus, unless we are prepared to subscribe to the doctrine of inherent racial inferiority of the backward peoples, there seems to be a strong presumption that the potential development of the backward countries has been inhibited by this waste of human resources, leading to a stultification of the possible "growing-points" of the economy. Nor can the loss of educational opportunities be adequately remedied by "investment in human capital" as is frequently assumed. Mere increase of expenditure on technical training and education, although it may offer a partial relief, is really too weak and unselective to be an active countervailing force to the deep-seated disequalizing factors. Too great an emphasis on the "under-investment in human capital" therefore tends to confuse the issues and distract attention from the more potent disequalizing factors.

Further, the disequalizing factors work not only on the supply side but also on the demand side, and unequal distribution of incomes and of activities combine with each other to inhibit economic development. One of the most important reasons why the backward countries have been prevented from enjoying the stimulating effect of manufacturing industry is not the wickedness of foreign capitalists and their exclusive concern with raw material supplies but merely the limitation of the domestic market for manufactured articles (cf. Ragnar Nurkse, *Some Aspects of Capital Accumulation in Underdeveloped Countries*, First Lecture).

When we were discussing the concept of "social productivity" towards the end of section II above, we remarked on the tendency of economic practice to forestall economic theory. So also here, with the concept of "countervailing power." Long before the economists were aware of the problem, practical administrators and economic historians of the backward countries were impressed by the fact that the peoples of these countries seem to need some sort of countervailing power to enable them to stand up against the "free play of economic forces." Some have sought the countervailing power in the preservation of the traditional social institutions and, in extreme cases, have even toyed with the idea of a retreat into the self-sufficiency of the traditional stationary state. Others, more forward-looking, have tried to foster countervailing power in the form of co-operative societies and, more recently, by means of trade unions and marketing boards for the peasant produce. Above all this, the disequalizing forces themselves have generated a fierce nationalism among the backward peoples which is the most powerful source of countervailing power in the present times. So we are already in a position to learn a few lessons about the nature and limitations of the countervailing power in the backward countries.

The first lesson is that some sources of countervailing power, like the co-operative societies, themselves need a fairly high degree of business-like behaviour and "economic advance" and can only be fostered very slowly in the backward countries. The second lesson is that it is easier to redistribute existing incomes than to redistribute and stimulate economic activity by the use of countervailing power. The governments of some backward countries are now able to obtain a larger share of the income from the exploitation of the natural resources, either by striking better bargains with foreign mining concerns or by means of marketing boards in the case of peasant produce; but they are still faced with the problem of reinvesting the money in a directly productive way as distinct from increasing expenditure on general social services. It is difficult enough to find outlets for productive investment in backward countries; it is far more difficult to find those outlets which will increase the direct participation of the backward peoples in the processes of economic activity. It is important to stress this point because the governments of the backward countries, in their desire to have rapid and spectacular economic development, may be tempted to embark on those large-scale projects which, even if they were successful as business concerns, might not appreciably increase the participation of their peoples in the new economic activities.[12] Apart from its failure as a business concern, the fundamental weakness of the famous "Ground Nut Scheme" of the British Overseas Food Corporation was that in an attempt to have rapid results on a large scale the Corporation was obliged to minimize the African participation in it.

The final lesson to be learnt is the danger of an excessive use of the countervailing power combined with an extreme economic nationalism. As a countermeasure to the disequalizing forces at the international level, discriminatory and protective measures to change the existing terms of comparative costs and foster the national economies of the backward countries have their place. In certain circumstances, they may even have a favourable effect on the volume of international trade in the long run. But, on the other hand, the dangers of an excessive nationalist policy should not be underrated. The loss to the backward countries in this case is not merely consumers' loss through having to pay a higher price or through having to put up with poorer qualities of commodities substituted for imports; a far heavier loss may lie in the sphere of economic activities when cut off from the stimulating contact with the outside world. This is also true of trade unions. In some backward countries trade unions have the very important function of breaking the industrial colour bar; but in others they may become a crippling burden on the economy and inhibit economic progress (cf. *Report on Cuba,* by the Economic and Technical Mission of the International Bank for Reconstruction and Development, pp. 138–59).

These considerations should not, however, blind us to the genuineness of the disequalizing factors working against the backward peoples and their real need for countervailing power. From the point of view of these peoples this is where the real rub lies. It is, however, precisely on this point that economists, both of liberal and of central-planning persuasion, have shown the least sympathy and understanding. The liberal economist is apt to believe that the disequalizing factors do not exist and that all attempts to use the countervailing power are the result of "irrational economic nationalism." The central planner is apt to seek a solution of the essentially distributive and structural problems of economic backwardness in terms of bigger and better aggregate economic development plans. Thus the study of the disequalizing factors at work against the backward peoples has never really been allowed to emerge from the intellectual underworld of extreme economic nationalism.

Notes

1. In order to avoid misunderstanding I had better say at once that in speaking of "a backward people," in contrast to "an advanced people," I am referring only to economic

life and do not in the least imply general cultural "backwardness." The qualifying word "economic" is dropped merely for the sake of brevity.

2. We are not concerned here with the question how far this rule can be reconciled with the authors' practical proposals for stabilizing longer-term lending by fixing target figures. Cf. also A. E. Kahn, "Investment Criterion for Development Programmes," *Quarterly Journal of Economics*, Feb. 1951.

3. Cf. J. R. Hicks, *Value and Capital*, p. 302 n.

4. Cf., however, T. Wilson, "Cyclical and Autonomous Inducements to Invest," *Oxford Economic Papers*, March 1953.

5. "The law of large numbers" is unconvincing when applied to the industrial sector of backward economics, where instead of *n* number of firms in full working order the State is trying to start a few odd new industrial units.

6. Including "productive" grants to stimulate investment. Cf. section II above.

7. Cf. S. H. Frankel, *Some Conceptual Aspects of International Economic Development of Underdeveloped Countries* (Princeton, May 1952), now reprinted in *The Economic Impact on Underdeveloped Societies* (Blackwell, Oxford, 1953). My debt to my colleague Professor Frankel cannot, however, be adequately expressed in terms of specific points, for I have had the benefit of discussing with him the fundamental issues of the subject for several years. I cannot, of course, claim his authority for the particular conclusions I have arrived at in this paper.

8. Cf., however, Ricardo's *Principles*, Sraffa ed., p. 99 and p. 100 n.

9. Cf. S. H. Frankel, *Capital Investment in Africa*, pp. 142–6.

10. If this condition is not fulfilled, the peasant system soon gives way to the plantation system or the peasant is so supervised and controlled that he is reduced to the status of wage-earner except in name (cf. J. H. Boeke, *The Evolution of Netherland Indies Economy*, p. 11).

11. This "vertical integration" may also spread downwards towards a greater supervision and control of peasant producers resulting in a "mixed" system between peasant and plantation systems (cf. Boeke, op. cit., ch. i).

12. In some countries excessive central planning may give rise to a new class of "middlemen" in the guise of government agents or officials.

2

Ragnar Nurkse

Some International Aspects of the Problem of Economic Development

"A country is poor because it is poor." This seems a trite proposition, but it does express the circular relationships that afflict both the demand and the supply side of the problem of capital formation in economically backward areas. This paper will discuss some international aspects of the difficulties on both sides. It will take up only a few points and cannot even attempt to give anything like a balanced picture.

I

The inducement to invest is limited by the size of the market. That is essentially what Allyn Young[1] brought out in his reinterpretation of Adam Smith's famous thesis. What determines the size of the market? Not simply money demand, nor mere numbers of people, nor physical area. Transport facilities, which Adam Smith singled out for special emphasis, are important; reductions in transport costs (artificial as well as natural) do enlarge the market in the economic as well as the geographical sense. But reductions in any cost of production tend to have that effect. So the size of the market is determined by the general level of productivity. Capacity to buy means capacity to produce. In its turn, the level of productivity depends—not entirely by any means, but largely—on the use of capital in production. But the use of capital is inhibited, to start with, by the small size of the market.

EDITOR'S NOTE: *Nurkse added new vocabulary to the jargon of development economics with his ideas on "balanced growth" (a Marxian notion, drawn from Marx's famous departmental schemes in* Capital, *but traveling incognito and introduced to the literature by Rosenstein-Rodan), the suggested antidote to the so-called vicious circle of poverty and underdevelopment that doomed the Third World to its well-known deprivations. The practical policy advice was to use domestic public finance to generate the necessary savings for the big industrial leap forward.*

Where is the way out of this circle? How can the market be enlarged? Although in backward areas Say's Law may be valid in the sense that there is generally no deflationary gap, it never is valid in the sense that the output of any single industry, newly set up with capital equipment, can create its own demand. Human wants being various, the people engaged in the new industry will not wish to spend all their income on their own products.[2] Suppose it is a shoe industry. If in the rest of the economy nothing happens to increase productivity and hence buying power, the market for the new shoe output is likely to prove deficient. People in the rest of the economy will not give up other things in order to buy, say, a pair of shoes every year, if they do not have enough food, clothing, and shelter. They cannot let go the little they have of these elementary necessities. If they were willing to give up some of their present consumption in exchange for an annual pair of new shoes, these things would be available for the shoe workers to make up the balance in their own consumption needs. As it is, the new industry is likely to be a failure.

The difficulty is not due fundamentally to discontinuities in the technical forms of capital equipment, though these may accentuate it. It is due above all to the inevitable inelasticity of demands at low real income levels. It is in this way that lack of buying power cramps the inducement to invest in any individual industry.

The difficulty is not present, however, in the case of a more or less synchronized application of capital to a wide range of different industries. Here the result is an over-all enlargement of the market and hence an escape from the deadlock. People working with more and better tools in a number of complementary projects become each other's customers. Most industries catering for mass consumption are complementary in the sense that they provide a market for, and thus support, each other. This basic complementarity stems, of course, from the diversity of human wants. The case for "balanced growth" rests ultimately on the need for a "balanced diet."

The notion of balance is inherent in Say's Law. Take Mill's formulation of it: "Every increase of production, if distributed without miscalculation among all kinds of produce in the proportion which private interest would dictate, creates, or rather constitutes, its own demand."[3] Here, in a nutshell, is the case for balanced growth. An increase in the production of shoes alone does not create its own demand. An increase in production over a wide range of consumables, so balanced as to correspond with the pattern of consumers' preferences, does create its own demand.

How do we get balanced growth? Ordinary price incentives may bring it about by small degrees, though here the technical discontinuities can be a serious hindrance; besides, slow growth is just not good enough where population pressure exists. In the evolution of Western industrial capitalism, rapid growth was achieved, in Schumpeter's view, through the action of creative entrepreneurs producing spurts of industrial progress. Even though innovations originated each time in a particular industry, the monetary effects and other circumstances were such as to promote each time a wave of new applications of capital over a whole range of industries. It is easy to see how a frontal attack of this sort can succeed while yet any sizable investment in any particular industry may be discouraged by the limits of the existing market.

Other types of society may feel a need for some degree of central direction to produce the desired effect—at any rate initially. But whether balanced growth is enforced by government planning or achieved spontaneously by private enterprise is, in a sense, a question of method. Whichever method is adopted, the nature of the solution aimed at may be the same, though the "miscalculation" Mill warned against seems hard to avoid in either case.

II

On the international plane, these general considerations apply first of all to the problem of international investment. Why is it that private business investment abroad has tended in the past—in the last few years as well as in the nineteenth century—to shy away from industries working for the domestic market in under-developed areas and to concentrate instead on primary production for export to the advanced industrial centers? The facts do not support the view that the so-called "colonial" type of investment—in mines and plantations producing for export to the industrial creditor countries—was typical of nineteenth century foreign investment as a whole. They do suggest, however, that it was, and still is, fairly typical of private business investment in backward areas. American direct investments abroad definitely conform to this pattern. In underdeveloped countries, they work mostly in extractive industries—oil fields, mines, and plantations—producing for export markets; only in advanced areas (Canada and Western Europe) do they, significantly, show any great interest in manufacturing for local consumption.[4]

The reluctance of private business capital to go to work for domestic markets in underdeveloped countries, in contrast with its eagerness in the past to work there for export to the industrial nations, reflects no sinister conspiracy or deliberate policy. There is the obvious economic explanation: on the one hand, the poverty of the local consumers in the backward countries; on the other, the large and, in the nineteenth century, vigorously expanding markets for primary products in the world's industrial centers. In these circumstances it was natural for foreign business investment to form mere outposts of the industrial creditor countries, to whose needs these outposts catered.

Incidentally, the weakness of the market incentive for private investment in the domestic economy of a low-income area can affect domestic as well as foreign capital. It may help in some degree to account for the common observation that such domestic saving as does take place in underdeveloped countries tends to be used unproductively: hoarded, exported, or put into real estate.

Private investment generally is governed by the pull of market demand, and private international investment is no exception to this. A particular instance of the relation between investment incentives and market demand appears in our old friend the acceleration principle. The relation holds, albeit in a different way, in space as well as in the time dimension. The conventional theory of factor proportions and capital movements is that in countries where there is little capital in relation to land and labor, the marginal productivity and hence the yield of capital will be high, and that, if it were not for extraneous impediments, capital would move to these countries from the areas where it is relatively abundant. This view is subject to the qualification that the high potential yield of capital in capital-poor areas may be capable of realization only through investment undertaken simultaneously in a number of complementary industries (or in public overhead facilities that serve to raise productivity in a number of different lines). A balanced increase in production generates external economies by enlarging the size of the market for each firm or industry. There is on this account as well as for other possible reasons, a discrepancy between the private and the social marginal productivity of capital. Even if we abstract from political and other risk factors, there is no guarantee that the motives that animate individual businessmen will automatically induce a flow of funds from the rich to the poor countries. The marginal productivity of capital in the latter compared with the former may be high indeed, but not necessarily in private business terms.

While the doctrine of balanced growth leaves plenty of room for international investment, it does reveal limits to the role of direct business investment. An individual foreign investor may not have the power, even if he had the will, to break the deadlock caused by low productivity, lack of real buying power, and deficient investment incentives in the domestic economy of a backward area. Even in the heyday of private foreign investment, however, capital outlays carried on by public authorities by means of private foreign loans were an important form of international investment. Loans to governments accounted for 30 per cent of Britain's total overseas investments outstanding in 1914, with another 40 per cent in railway securities and 5 per cent in public utilities.[5] Clearly this does not leave any major proportion for the strictly colonial type of investments—in mines and plantations producing for the creditor countries.

Investment by public authorities financed from private—or public—foreign funds is a form of "autonomous" investment, since it does not depend closely, if at all, on the current state of market demand. By contrast, direct business investment must be classed as a form of "induced" investment since it generally has to be induced by tangible market demand, already existing or visibly coming into existence. Thus the general distinction between autonomous and induced investment is applicable in a certain sense to international investment as well.

International investment on private business account is attracted by markets, and for the poorer countries the big markets in the past were the markets for export to the great industrial centers. Investment was induced by the investing countries' own demand. Foreign investment in extractive industries working for export is not to be despised, since it usually carries with it various direct and indirect benefits to the country where it is made. Why is even this type of investment now flowing out in only a small trickle? Aside, again, from the obvious political impediments, perhaps the answer is that the export markets for primary commodities have not been enjoying anything like the same rate of secular expansion as that which came about in the nineteenth century from the extraordinary growth of population as well as productivity in the Western industrial countries, and also from Britain's willingness to sacrifice her own agriculture to the requirements of international specialization. In recent decades, synthetic substitutes have affected unfavorably the demand for a number of staple products. The present raw-material boom is widely regarded as being due to special circumstances which may not last. In any case, it may take more than a boom—it may take something like a secular expansion of demand—to induce private foreign investment in underdeveloped areas for the production of primary commodities for export.

Reliance on direct business investment for the capital needed for economic development is therefore liable to a double disappointment. Not only is there little or no incentive for private business capital to go to work for the expansion of the domestic economies of low-income countries; even for the expansion of raw-material supplies for export, private business funds may not want to move out in any steady or sizable flow. But this, I repeat, applies to induced investment. It does not, or need not, affect international investment of the autonomous sort.

III

The case which the underdeveloped countries advance in favor of their "balanced growth" and "diversification" is not always well received. Does it not mean turning away from the principle of comparative advantage? Why do these countries not push their exports of primary products according to the rules of international specialization, and import the goods they need for a balanced diet? The answer is: because the notion of balance applies on the global scale as well. For fairly obvious reasons, expansion of primary production for export is apt to encounter adverse price conditions on the world market, unless the industrial countries' demand is steadily expanding, as it was in the nineteenth century. To push exports in the face of an inelastic and more or less stationary demand would not be a promising line of development. If it is reasonable to assume a generally less than unitary price elasticity of demand for crude foodstuffs and materials, it seems reasonable also to contend that, under the conditions indicated before, economic growth in underdeveloped countries must largely take the form of an increase in production for the domestic market.

These are some of the considerations that explain the desire for balanced growth and provide some economic justification for it. They do not constitute a case for autarky. As productivity increases and the domestic market expands, while the composition of imports and exports is bound to change, the volume of external trade is more likely to rise than to fall. But even if it remains the same there is not necessarily any harm in balanced growth on the domestic front. Take a country like Venezuela: petroleum accounts for about 90 per cent of its exports but employs only about 2 per cent of its labor force; the majority of the people work in the interior for a precarious subsistence in agriculture. If through the application of capital and increased productivity the domestic economy were to grow so that people working formerly on the land alone would now supply each other with clothing, footwear, houses and house furnishings as well as food products, while all the time petroleum exports remained the same and imports likewise constant in total volume, nothing but gain would result to the inhabitants without any loss to the outside world. No doubt there would be a fall in the proportion of foreign trade to national income. But could it not be that this proportion, in the many peripheral countries of this type, has been kept unduly high in the past simply by the poverty of the domestic economy? World income is a more basic criterion of world prosperity than the volume of international trade.

The characteristically important role which international trade played in the world economy of the nineteenth century was partly due to the fact that there was a periphery—and a vacuum beyond. The trade pattern of the nineteenth century was not merely a device for the optimum allocation of a given volume of resources; it was, as D. H. Robertson put it, "above all an engine of growth,"[6] but of growth originating in and radiating from the early industrial centers. Even in this country we have been so accustomed to regard the early nineteenth century pattern as normal that we seldom stop to notice that the economic development of the United States itself has been a spectacular departure from it.

With the spread of industrialization, we have, however, noticed that the major currents of international trade pass by the economically backward areas and flow rather among the advanced industrial countries. Balanced growth is a good foundation for international trade, as well as a way of filling the vacuum at the periphery.

IV

Let us turn now to the supply side of the problem of capital formation for economic development. Here the circular relationship runs from the low-income level to the small capacity to save, hence to a lack of capital, and so to low productivity. It seems to be a common view that the capacity for domestic saving in underdeveloped countries depends on an initial increase in productivity and real income, because the existing level is too low to permit any significant margin of saving, and that some form of outside help—say, foreign investment—is required to bring about this initial improvement and so break the vicious circle.

This theory begins to look a bit shaky as soon as we realize that it is not only the absolute but also the relative level of real income that determines the capacity to save. Although the absolute level of even the poorest countries has risen, it is doubtful whether saving has become any easier; on the contrary, it may have become more difficult for them, because there has occurred at the same time a decline in their relative income levels in comparison with those of the economically advanced countries. The hypothesis seems to me plausible and, at any rate, worth considering. The great and growing gaps between the income levels of different countries, combined with increasing awareness of these gaps, may tend to push up the general propensity to consume of the poorer nations, reduce their capacity to save, and incidentally strain their balance of payments.

As we have seen from J. S. Duesenberry's recent book, *Income, Saving and the Theory of Consumer Behavior*, the hypothesis that individuals' consumption functions are interrelated rather than independent helps to account for certain facts that have seemed puzzling. The interdependence of consumers' preferences can affect, in particular, the choice between consumption and saving. The reason, for instance, why 75 per cent of families in the United States save virtually nothing (see page 39) is not necessarily that they are too poor to save or do not want to save; the main reason is that they live in an environment that makes them want new consumption goods even more. The reason is largely what Duesenberry calls the "demonstration effect" (page 27) of the consumption standards kept up by the top 25 per cent of the people. When individuals come into contact with superior goods or spending patterns, they are apt to feel a certain tension and restlessness: their propensity to consume is increased.

These forces, it seems to me, affect human behavior to a certain extent in international relations as well. The consumption functions of different countries are in some degree interrelated in a similar way. On the international plane, also, knowledge of or contact with superior consumption patterns extends the imagination and creates new wants.

The leading instance of this effect is at present the widespread imitation of American consumption patterns. The American standard of living enjoys considerable prestige in the world. And it is always easier to adopt superior consumption habits than improved production methods. True, American production methods are also widely imitated; sometimes, indeed, too closely. But generally this requires investible funds. The temptation to copy American consumption patterns tends to limit the supply of investible funds.

The intensity of the attraction exercised by the consumption standards of the economically advanced countries depends on two factors. One is the size of the gaps in real income and consumption levels. The other is the extent of people's awareness of them. Even though the poorer countries have probably all increased their per capita income over the last hundred years, the gaps have tended to widen. The position we have now reached is that two-thirds of the world's income goes to less than a fifth of the world's population in the most advanced countries, while at the bottom of the scale two-thirds of the world's population receives less than a sixth of the world's income; and that the average per capita income of the former group is about seventeen times as high as that of the latter.[7] The estimates on which these calculations are based are in many cases extremely crude, but probably not grossly misleading. They do not, of course, take account of voluntary leisure, which is one way in which the advanced nations have taken out their gains.

The gaps are great, but equally important is the fact that contact and communication are closer than ever before, so that knowledge of these gaps has increased. Think of such recent inventions as the radio, aviation, and the American movies. Communication in the modern world—in the free world at any rate—is close, and so the attraction of advanced consumption standards can exert itself fairly widely, although unevenly, in the poorer parts of the world.

This attraction is a handicap for the late-comers in economic development. It affects not only voluntary personal saving but also makes it politically more difficult to use taxation as a means of compulsory saving and to resist demands for government spending on current account. Some of the backward countries have large masses of disguised unemployment on the land, which could be mobilized for real capital formation, but not without strict curbs on any immediate rise in consumption. Others may hope to introduce improvements in agricultural techniques so as to release labor from primitive subsistence farming and make it available for capital works, but again not without restraints to prevent the increment from being immediately consumed. The use of potential domestic sources of capital can be seriously hampered by the dissatisfaction and impatience which the demonstration effect tends to produce.

The traditional view of international economic relations generally implies that a high level of productivity and real income in one country cannot hurt other countries and that, on the contrary, prosperity tends to spread. Of course there are many ways in which a country's prosperity will help its neighbors. But the particular effect now discussed is unfavorable. It puts an extra pressure on countries with a relatively low income to spend a high proportion of it. (This is quite apart from and in addition to the fact that some nations suffer from a cultural aversion to saving, due to the presence of traditional forms of conspicuous consumption. However, the "demonstration effect" imposes no additional strain on saving capacity when it leads merely to a switch from native to imported forms of consumption.)

A very poor society might find it extremely hard to do any saving even if it knew nothing about higher living standards in the outside world. The vicious circle that tends to keep down the volume of saving in low-income countries is bad enough by itself. The point is that it is made even worse by the stresses that arise from relative as distinct from absolute poverty.

V

The poorer nations, in contact with the richer, feel continually impelled to keep their money incomes and outlays above what is warranted by their own capacity to produce. The result is an inflationary bias at home and a persistent tendency towards disequilibrium in the balance of payments. The doctrine of comparative advantage is, in my opinion, an effective answer to the simpler forms of the productivity theory of the dollar shortage. Yet here we seem to have reached, by the back door as it were, a theory of balance-of-payments disequilibrium based similarly upon differences in general levels of productivity. However, the comparative cost principle is fully respected. Disequilibrium results, not because productivity determines a country's export costs and competitive strength in the world market, not because the most productive country necessarily undersells all the others in all lines; disequilibrium results because a country's productivity determines its real income and consumption level and because differences in levels of living, when they are very large and widely known, exert an upward pressure on the consumption propensity of the poorer countries. In the classical view, a lack of balance in international trade can persist only because some countries try to "live beyond their means." We have now a simple explanation of why some countries do, in fact, persist in trying to live beyond their means.

The inflationary pressures and balance-of-payments difficulties are not, as such, the basic trouble. They could conceivably come from increased capital outlays and not from consumer spending. The trouble is that the demonstration effect leads directly to increased consumption, or attempts at increasing consumption, rather than investment. At least it makes an increase in saving peculiarly difficult as and when incomes and investment increase. It is for this reason that international income disparities may have to be treated not merely as a source of strain in the balance of payments but actually as an impediment to capital formation in the poorer countries.

VI

The almost universal countermove of the underdeveloped countries both to suppress the disequilibrium in their balance of payments and, what is more important, to offset the attraction of superior consumption patterns is the restriction of imports and especially of imports of a so-called "luxury" or "semiluxury" character. There is a widespread notion that a country, by cutting down imports of consumption goods through direct controls or prohibitive duties, can make more real capital available for its economic development in the form of imports of capital goods. Governments seem convinced that they are promoting the formation of capital whenever, in their commercial policy, they banish consumable imports in favor of imports of machinery and equipment.

This simple idea that more capital can be got merely by pinching and twisting the foreign trade sector of the economy seems to me to be an instance of the fallacy of misplaced concreteness. The foreign trade sector of the economy enters into the circular flow of income. Every piece of capital equipment imported represents an act of investment which, in the absence of external financing, presupposes and necessitates a corresponding act of saving at home. If this act of saving is not forthcoming, the capital equipment imported may be offset by reduced investment or by disinvestment in the domestic economy, if the expenditure of money previously spent on consumable imports now draws away domestic factors from capital construction or maintenance. Only if this money is left unspent is the requisite saving generated quasi-automatically; this is possible but quite improbable. It is more likely that any net investment that may result from the increased imports of capital goods will be financed by the forced saving of inflation, as long as inflation has not yet passed the point where it ceases to be effective as an instrument of forced saving. It is possible, therefore, although not certain, that "luxury import restrictions" will lead to some increase in the rate of capital formation in an underdeveloped country.

Besides the quantity of investment, however, there is also a question of quality. Import restrictions unaccompanied by corresponding domestic restrictions will set up a special inducement to invest in domestic industries producing the goods—or substitutes for the goods—that can no longer be imported. If the domestic market is considered at all sufficient to warrant the establishment of such industries, the inducement may prove effective. But since it applies to the luxury and semiluxury type of goods, whose imports are restricted, the result will be that the country's capital supplies, scarce as they are, and painfully brought into existence, will be sucked into relatively unessential uses.

The luxury import restrictions of the underdeveloped countries in the world today seem to represent, in the last analysis, a desperate effort to offset the handicap which the demonstration effect imposes on the poorer nations—an effort to isolate the local consumption pattern from that of the advanced countries and so to make possible more domestic saving and capital formation. This effort deserves our sympathy. But it attacks only the surface of the problem. It attacks only that part of the propensity to consume which directly involves expenditure on imported goods. The demonstration effect tends, however, to operate through an upward shift in the general consumption function and not in the import consumption function alone. Luxury import restrictionism does not stop this pervasive indirect influence of international discrepancies in consumption levels. A more basic attack would be compulsory saving through public finance, although this is precisely one of the things that is made politically more difficult in the poorer countries by the great discrepancies in living standards.

Far more radical forms of isolation than luxury import restrictions have played a part in the development of two important countries. It is well known that Japan, in the early course of her industrialization, imitated the Western World in everything except consumption patterns. She had kept herself in a state of isolation for centuries, and it was comparatively easy for her to maintain this isolation in regard to consumption patterns. There is no doubt that this was part of the secret of her success in domestic capital formation.

The other instance of radical isolation is Soviet Russia's iron curtain (which of course is not merely a result of the present tension but was well established before World War II). While it certainly has other reasons for its existence, I am inclined to attach significance also to its economic function; that is, to the possible "materialist interpretation" of the iron curtain. Anyway, it illustrates the possibility that isolation may help to solve the economic problem of capital formation, in a world of great discrepancies in national living standards, by severing contact and communication among nations. Without communication, the discrepancies, however great, may become of little or no consequence and the "demonstration effect" may lose at least some of its potency.

That this might be a possible and perhaps a necessary solution is a disquieting thought, and one naturally turns in search of an alternative.

VII

Could it be that the alternative lies in unilateral income transfers or, in plain English, gifts from rich to poor countries? The foreign aid programs of the United States have certainly departed from traditional practices, and it may be that we have seen the beginnings of a system of international income transfers, comparable to the transfers that take place within a country as an automatic result of taxation proportional to income or, still more, of progressive taxation. A system of international grants-in-aid does not stem from any economic mechanism of the market place; nor does the principle of progressive taxation. Both are based on political value judgments, and both arise from pressures having to do with the coexistence and increasingly close association of people at widely different levels of material welfare.

Suppose we have a model, then, where on the one hand international income disparities open up gaps in the balance of payments and on the other unilateral income transfers come in to fill these gaps. Is this a sufficient and satisfactory solution to the problem of capital formation in the poorer countries? Clearly it is not. If nature is left to take its course, the income transfers coming in will be used in these countries for the satisfaction of the higher propensity to consume that is brought about by the disparity in real-income levels. No permanent basis will be created within the country for higher living standards in the future. It is nearly always possible to some extent to substitute foreign aid for domestic saving so that consumption is increased and no net contribution is made to the rate of total capital formation. It can happen even if the foreign resources are tied to specific productive projects. The point is not, of course, that this is bad, but that it fails to contribute to the foundations of economic development. The attraction of advanced living standards can thus interfere, not only with the harnessing of domestic saving potentials, but also with the effective use of external resources for economic development. It makes it more than ever necessary for an underdeveloped country to keep a tight rein on the national propensity to consume.

This applies obviously to autonomous international investment and, perhaps less obviously, also to improvements in the terms of trade. An improvement in the terms of trade puts at the country's disposal additional outside resources that can be used to promote economic development. By itself, however, it means simply an increment in the country's current income, derived from foreign trade. Without the corresponding domestic saving, this increment cannot lead to any net increase in the rate of investment. Here again the real task is not to extract more capital goods from foreign trade but to extract more saving from the national income.

The upshot is that external resources, even if they become available in the most desirable forms, are not enough. They do not automatically provide a solution to the problem of capital accumulation in underdeveloped areas. No solution is possible without strenuous domestic efforts, particularly in the field of public finance.

Notes

1. "Increasing Returns and Economic Progress," *Economic Journal*, December, 1928.
2. See Paul N. Rosenstein-Rodan, "Problems of Industrialization of Eastern and South-Eastern Europe," *Economic Journal*, June-September, 1943, p. 205.
3. J. S. Mill, *Essays in Some Unsettled Question of Political Economy* (London School of Economics reprint, 1948), p. 73.
4. See H. J. Dernburg, "Prospects for Long-Term Foreign Investment," *Harvard Business Review*, July, 1950, p. 42.
5. H. Feis, *Europe, The World's Banker, 1870–1914* (Yale University Press, 1930), p. 27.
6. "The Future of International Trade," *Economic Journal*, March, 1938, p. 5.
7. *National and Per Capita Incomes in 70 Countries, 1949* (Statistical Office of the United Nations, 1950).

3

W. Arthur Lewis

Economic Development with Unlimited Supplies of Labour

1. This essay is written in the classical tradition, making the classical assumption, and asking the classical question. The classics, from Smith to Marx, all assumed, or argued, that an unlimited supply of labour was available at subsistence wages. They then enquired how production grows through time. They found the answer in capital accumulation, which they explained in terms of their analysis of the distribution of income. Classical systems thus determined simultaneously income distribution and income growth, with the relative prices of commodities as a minor bye-product.

Interest in prices and in income distribution survived into the neo-classical era, but labour ceased to be unlimited in supply, and the formal model of economic analysis was no longer expected to explain the expansion of the system through time. These changes of assumption and of interest served well enough in the European parts of the world, where labour was indeed limited in supply, and where for the next half century it looked as if economic expansion could indeed be assumed to be automatic. On the other hand over the greater part of Asia labour is unlimited in supply, and economic expansion certainly cannot be taken for granted. Asia's problems, however, attracted very few economists during the neo-classical era (even the Asian economists themselves absorbed the assumptions and preoccupations of European economics) and hardly any progress has been made for nearly a century with the kind of economics which would throw light upon the problems of countries with surplus populations.

EDITOR'S NOTE: *The grandfather of mainstream development theory and policy for a generation, this essay, with its famous "dualism" and "surplus labor" notions and its conscious recourse to ideas intrinsic to classical economics, was to dominate official discussions in the early, optimistic period of "modernization." In policy, the bent was toward "industrialization by invitation" and/or the formation of state capitalism.*

When Keynes's *General Theory* appeared, it was thought at first that this was the book which would illuminate the problems of countries with surplus labour, since it assumed an unlimited supply of labour at the current price, and also, in its final pages, made a few remarks on secular economic expansion. Further reflection, however, revealed that Keynes's book assumed not only that labour is unlimited in supply, but also, and more fundamentally, that land and capital are unlimited in supply—more fundamentally both in the short run sense that once the monetary tap is turned the real limit to expansion is not physical resources but the limited supply of labour, and also in the long run sense that secular expansion is embarrassed not by a shortage but by a superfluity of saving. Given the Keynesian remedies the neo-classical system comes into its own again. Hence, from the point of view of countries with surplus labour, Keynesianism is only a footnote to neo-classicism—albeit a long, important and fascinating footnote. The student of such economies has therefore to work right back to the classical economists before he finds an analytical framework into which he can relevantly fit his problems.

The purpose of this essay is thus to see what can be made of the classical framework in solving problems of distribution, accumulation, and growth, first in a closed and then in an open economy. It is not primarily an essay in the history of economic doctrine, and will not therefore spend time on individual writers, enquiring what they meant, or assessing its validity or truth. Our purpose is rather to bring their framework up-to-date, in the light of modern knowledge, and to see how far it then helps us to understand the contemporary problems of large areas of the earth.

I. The Closed Economy

2. We have to begin by elaborating the assumption of an unlimited supply of labour, and by establishing that it is a useful assumption. We are not arguing, let it be repeated, that this assumption should be made for all areas of the world. It is obviously not true of the United Kingdom, or of North West Europe. It is not true either of some of the countries usually now lumped together as under-developed; for example there is an acute shortage of male labour in some parts of Africa and of Latin America. On the other hand it is obviously the relevant assumption for the economies of Egypt, of India, or of Jamaica. Our present task is not to supersede neo-classical economics, but merely to elaborate a different framework for those countries which the neo-classical (and Keynesian) assumptions do not fit.

In the first place, an unlimited supply of labour may be said to exist in those countries where population is so large relatively to capital and natural resources, that there are large sectors of the economy where the marginal productivity of labour is negligible, zero, or even negative. Several writers have drawn attention to the existence of such "disguised" unemployment in the agricultural sector, demonstrating in each case that the family holding is so small that if some members of the family obtained other employment the remaining members could cultivate the holding just as well (of course they would have to work harder: the argument includes the proposition that they would be willing to work harder in these circumstances). The phenomenon is not, however, by any means confined to the countryside. Another large sector to which it applies is the whole range of casual jobs—the workers on the docks, the young men who rush forward asking to carry your bag as you appear, the jobbing gardener, and the like. These occupations usually have a multiple of the number they need, each of them earning very small sums from occasional employment; frequently their number could be halved without reducing output in this sector. Petty retail trading is also exactly of this type; it is enormously expanded in overpopulated economies; each trader makes only a few sales; markets are crowded with stalls, and if the number of stalls were greatly reduced the consumers would be no whit worse off—they might even be better off, since retail margins might fall. Twenty years ago one could not write these sentences without having to stop and explain why in these circumstances, the casual labourers do not bid their earnings down to zero, or why the farmers' product is not similarly all eaten up in rent, but these propositions present no terrors to contemporary economists.

A little more explanation has to be given of those cases where the workers are not self-employed, but are working for wages, since it is harder to believe that employers will pay wages exceeding marginal productivity. The most important of these sectors is domestic service, which is usually even more inflated in over-populated countries than is petty trading (in Barbados 16 per cent. of the population is in domestic service). The reason is that in over-populated countries the code of ethical behaviour so shapes itself that it becomes good form for each person to offer as much employment as he can. The line between employees and dependents is very thinly drawn. Social prestige requires people to have servants, and the grand seigneur may have to keep a whole army of retainers who are really little more than a burden upon his purse. This is found not only in domestic service, but in every sector of employment. Most businesses in under-developed countries employ a large number of "messengers," whose contribution is almost negligible; you see them sitting outside office doors, or hanging around in the courtyard. And even in the severest slump the agricultural or commercial employer is expected to keep his labour force somehow or other—it would be immoral to turn them out, for how would they eat, in countries where the only form of unemployment assistance is the charity of relatives? So it comes about that even in the sectors where people are working for wages, and above all the domestic sector, marginal productivity may be negligible or even zero.

Whether marginal productivity is zero or negligible is not, however, of fundamental importance to our analysis. The price of labour, in these economies, is a wage at the subsistence level (we define this later). The supply of labour is therefore "unlimited" so long as the supply of labour at this price exceeds the demand. In this situation, new industries can be created, or old industries expanded without limit at the existing wage; or, to put it more exactly, shortage of labour is no limit to the creation of new sources of employment. If we cease to ask whether the marginal productivity of labour is negligible and ask instead only the question from what sectors would additional labour be available if new industries were created offering employment at subsistence wages, the answer becomes even more comprehensive. For we have then not only the farmers, the casuals, the petty traders and the retainers (domestic and commercial), but we have also three other classes from which to choose.

First of all, there are the wives and daughters of the household. The employment of women outside the household depends upon a great number of factors, religious and conventional, and is certainly not exclusively a matter of employment opportunities. There are, however, a number of countries where the current limit is for practical purposes only employment opportunities. This is true, for example, even inside the United Kingdom. The proportion of women gainfully employed in the U.K. varies enormously from one region to another according to employment opportunities for women. For example, in 1939 whereas there were 52 women gainfully employed for every 100 men in Lancashire, there were only 15 women gainfully employed for every 100 men in South Wales. Similarly in the Gold Coast, although there is an acute shortage of male labour, any industry which offered good employment to women would be besieged with applications. The transfer of women's work from the household to commercial employment is one of the most notable features of economic development. It is not by any means all gain, but the gain is substantial because most of the things which women otherwise do in the household can in fact be done much better or more cheaply outside, thanks to the large scale economies of specialisation, and also to the use of capital (grinding grain, fetching water from the river, making cloth, making clothes, cooking the midday meal, teaching children, nursing the sick, etc.). One of the surest ways of increasing the national income is therefore to create new sources of employment for women outside the home.

The second source of labour for expanding industries is the increase in the population resulting from the excess of births over deaths. This source is important in any dynamic analysis of how capital accumulation can occur, and employment can increase, without any increase in real wages. It was therefore a cornerstone of Ricardo's system. Strictly speaking, population increase is not relevant either to the classical analysis, or to the analysis which follows in this article, unless it can be shown that the increase of population is caused by economic development and would not otherwise be so large. The proof of this proposition was supplied to the classical economists by the Malthusian law of population. There is already an enormous literature of the genus: "What Malthus *Really* Meant," into which we need not enter. Modern population theory has advanced a little by analysing separately the effects of economic development upon the birth rate, and its effects on the death rate. Of the former, we know little. There is no evidence that the birth rate ever rises with economic development. In Western Europe it has fallen during the last eighty years. We are not quite sure why; we suspect that it was for reasons associated with development, and we hope that the same thing may happen in the rest of the world as development spreads. Of the death rate we are more certain. It comes down with development from around 40 to around 12 per thousand; in the first stage because better communications and trade eliminate death from local famines; in the second stage because better public health facilities banish the great epidemic diseases of plague, smallpox, cholera, malaria, yellow fever (and eventually tuberculosis); and in the third stage because widespread facilities for treating the sick snatch from the jaws of death many who would otherwise perish in infancy or in their prime. Because the effect of development on the death rate is so swift and certain, while its effect on the birth rate is unsure and retarded, we can say for certain that immediate effect of economic development is to cause the population to grow; after some decades it begins to grow (we hope) less rapidly. Hence in any society where the death rate is around 40 per thousand, the effect of economic development will be to generate an increase in the supply of labour.

Marx offered a third source of labour to add to the reserve army, namely the unemployment generated by increasing efficiency. Ricardo had admitted that the creation of machinery could reduce employment. Marx seized upon the argument, and in effect generalised it, for into the pit of unemployment he threw not only those displaced by machinery, but also the self-employed and petty capitalists who could not compete with larger capitalists of increasing size, enjoying the benefits of the economies of scale. Nowadays we reject this argument on empirical grounds. It is clear that the effect of capital accumulation in the past has been to reduce the size of the reserve army, and not to increase it, so we have lost interest in arguments about what is "theoretically" possible.

When we take account of all the sources we have now listed—the farmers, the casuals, the petty traders, the retainers (domestic and commercial), women in the household, and population growth—it is clear enough that there can be in an over-populated economy an enormous expansion of new industries or new employment opportunities without any shortage of unskilled labour becoming apparent in the labour market. From the point of view of the effect of economic development on wages, the supply of labour is practically unlimited.

This applies only to unskilled labour. There may at any time be a shortage of skilled workers of any grade—ranging from masons, electricians or welders to engineers, biologists or administrators. Skilled labour may be the bottleneck in expansion, just like capital or land. Skilled labour, however, is only what Marshall might have called a "quasi-bottleneck," if he had not had so nice a sense of elegant language. For it is only a very temporary bottleneck, in the sense that if the capital is available for development, the capitalists or their government will soon provide the facilities for training more skilled people. The real bottlenecks to expansion are therefore capital and natural resources, and we can proceed on the assumption that so long as these are available the necessary skills will be provided as well, though perhaps with some time lag.

3. If unlimited labour is available, while capital is scarce, we know from the Law of Variable Proportions that the capital should not be spread thinly over all the labour. Only so much labour should be used with capital as will reduce the marginal productivity of labour to zero. In practice, however, labour is not available at a zero wage. Capital will therefore be applied only up to the point where the marginal productivity of labour equals the current wage. This is illustrated in Figure I. The horizontal axis measures the quantity of labour, and the vertical axis its marginal product. There is a fixed amount of capital. *OW* is the current wage. If the marginal product of labour were zero outside the capitalist sector, *OR* ought to be employed. But it will pay to employ only *OM* in the capitalist sector. *WNP* is the capitalists' surplus. *OWPM* goes in wages to workers in the capitalist sector, while workers outside this sector (*i.e.* beyond *M*) earn what they can in the subsistence sector of the economy.

The analysis requires further elaboration. In the first place, after what we have said earlier on about some employers in these economies keeping retainers, it may seem strange to be arguing now that labour will be employed up to the point where the wage equals the marginal productivity. Nevertheless, this is probably the right assumption to make when we are set upon analysing the expansion of the capitalist sector of the economy. For the type of capitalist who brings about economic expansion is not the same as the type of employer who treats his employees like retainers. He is more commercially minded, and more conscious of efficiency, cost and profitability. Hence, if our interest is in an expanding capitalist sector, the assumption of profit maximisation is probably a fair approximation to the truth.

Next, we note the use of the terms "capitalist" sector and "subsistence" sector. The capitalist sector is that part of the economy which uses reproducible capital, and pays capitalists for the use thereof. (This coincides with Smith's definition of the productive workers, who are those who work with capital and whose product can therefore be sold at a price above their wages). We can think, if we like, of capitalists hiring out their capital to peasants; in which case, there being by definition an unlimited number of peasants, only some will get capital, and these will have to pay for its use a price which leaves them only subsistence earnings. More usually, however, the use of capital is controlled by capitalists, who hire the services of labour. The classical analysis was therefore conducted on the assumption that capital was used for hiring people. It does not make any difference to the argument, and for convenience we will follow this usage. The subsistence sector is by difference all that part of the economy which is not using reproducible capital. Output per head is lower in this sector than in the capitalist sector, because it is not fructified by capital (this is why it was called "unproductive"; the distinction between productive and unproductive had nothing to do

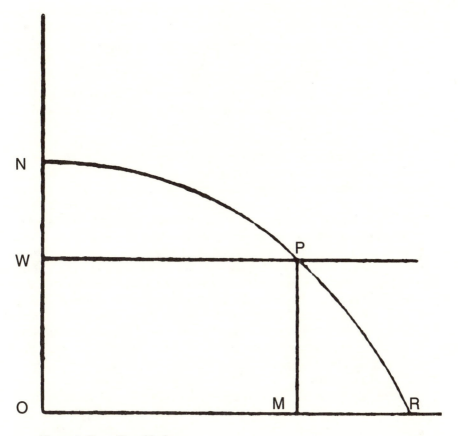

Figure I. **Quantity of Labour**

with whether the work yielded utility, as some neo-classicists have scornfully but erroneously asserted). As more capital becomes available more workers can be drawn into the capitalist from the subsistence sector, and their output per head rises as they move from the one sector to the other.

Thirdly we take account of the fact that the capitalist sector, like the subsistence sector, can also be subdivided. What we have is not one island of expanding capitalist employment, surrounded by a vast sea of subsistence workers, but rather a number of such tiny islands. This is very typical of countries in their early stages of development. We find a few industries highly capitalised, such as mining or electric power, side by side with the most primitive techniques; a few high class shops, surrounded by masses of old style traders; a few highly capitalised plantations, surrounded by a sea of peasants. But we find the same contrasts also outside their economic life. There are one or two modern towns, with the finest architecture, water supplies, communications and the like, into which people drift from other towns and villages which might almost belong to another planet. There is the same contrast even between people; between the few highly westernised, trousered, natives, educated in western universities, speaking western languages, and glorying in Beethoven, Mill, Marx or Einstein, and the great mass of their countrymen who live in quite other worlds. Capital and new ideas are not thinly diffused throughout the economy; they are highly concentrated at a number of points, from which they spread outwards.

Though the capitalised sector can be subdivided into islands, it remains a single sector because of the effect of competition in tending to equalise the earnings on capital. The competitive principle does not demand that the same amount of capital per person be employed on each "island," or that average profit per unit of capital be the same, but only that the marginal profit be the same. Thus, even if marginal profits were the same all round, islands which yield diminishing returns may be more profitable than others, the earliest capitalists having cornered the vantage points. But in any case marginal profits are not the same all round. In backward economies knowledge is one of the scarcest goods. Capitalists have experience of certain types of investment, say of trading or plantation agriculture, and not of other types, say of manufacturing, and they stick to what they know. So the economy is frequently lopsided in the sense that there is excessive investment in some parts and under-investment in others. Also, financial institutions are more highly developed for some purposes than for others—capital can be got cheaply for trade, but not for house building or for peasant agriculture, for instance. Even in a very highly developed economy the tendency for capital to flow evenly through the economy is very weak; in a backward economy it hardly exists. Inevitably what one gets are very heavily developed patches of the economy, surrounded by economic darkness.

Next we must say something about the wage level. The wage which the expanding capitalist sector has to pay is determined by what people can earn outside that sector. The classical economists used to think of the wage as being determined by what is required for subsistence consumption, and this may be the right solution in some cases. However, in economies where the majority of the people are peasant farmers, working on their own land, we have a more objective index, for the minimum at which labour can be had is now set by the average product of the farmer; men will not leave the family farm to seek employment if the wage is worth less than they would be able to consume if they remained at home. This objective standard, alas, disappears again if the farmers have to pay rent, for their net earnings will then depend upon the amount of rent they have to pay and in overpopulated countries the rent will probably be adjusted so as to leave them just enough for a conventional level of subsistence. It is not, however, of great importance to the argument whether earnings in the subsistence sector are determined objectively by the level of peasant productivity, or subjectively in terms of a conventional standard of living. Whatever the mechanism, the result is an unlimited supply of labour for which this is the minimum level of earnings.

The fact that the wage level in the capitalist sector depends upon earnings in the subsistence sector is sometimes of immense political importance, since its effect is that capitalists have a direct interest in holding down the productivity of the subsistence workers. Thus, the owners of plantations have no interest in seeing knowledge of new techniques or new seeds conveyed to the peasants, and if they are influential in the government, they will not be found using their influence to expand the facilities for agricultural extension. They will not support proposals for land settlement, and are often instead to be found engaged in turning the peasants off their lands. (Cf. Marx on "Primary Accumulation"). This is one of the worst features of imperialism, for instance. The imperialists invest capital and hire workers; it is to their advantage to keep wages low, and even in those cases where they do not actually go out of their way to impoverish the subsistence economy, they will at least very seldom be found doing anything to make it more productive. In actual fact the record of every imperial power in Africa in modern times is one of impoverishing the subsistence economy, either by taking away the people's land, or by demanding forced labour in the capitalist sector, or by imposing taxes to drive people to work for capitalist employers. Compared with what they have spent on providing facilities for European agriculture or mining, their expenditure on the improvement of African agriculture has been negligible. The failure of imperialism to raise living standards is not wholly to be attributed to self interest, but there are many places where it can be traced directly to the effects of having imperial capital invested in agriculture or in mining.

Earnings in the subsistence sector set a floor to wages in the capitalist sector, but in practice wages have to be higher than this, and there is usually a gap of 30 per cent. or more between capitalist wages and subsistence earnings. This gap may be explained in several ways. Part of the difference is illusory, because of the higher cost of living in the capitalist sector. This may be due to the capitalist sector being concentrated in congested towns, so that rents and transport costs are higher. All the same, there is also usually a substantial difference in real wages. This may be required because of the psychological cost of transferring from the easy going way of life of the subsistence sector to the more regimented and urbanised environment of the capitalist sector. Or it may be a recognition of the fact that even the unskilled worker is of more use to the capitalist sector after he has been there for some time than is the raw recruit from the country. Or it may itself represent a difference in conventional standards, workers in the capitalist sector acquiring tastes and a social prestige which have conventionally to be recognised by higher real wages. That this last may be the explanation is suggested by cases where the capitalist workers organise themselves into trade unions and strive to protect or increase their differential. But the differential exists even where there are no unions.

The effect of this gap is shown diagrammatically in Figure II, which is drawn on the same basis as Figure I. *OS* now represents subsistence earnings, and *OW* the capitalist wage (real not money). To borrow an analogy from the sea, the frontier of competition between capitalist and subsistence labour now appears not as a beach but as a cliff.

This phenomenon of a gap between the earnings of competing suppliers is found even in the most advanced economies. Much of the difference between the earnings of different classes of the population (grades of skill, of education, of responsibility or of prestige) can be described only in these terms. Neither is the phenomenon confined to labour. We know of course that two firms in a competitive market need not have the same average profits if one has some superiority to the other; we reflect this difference in rents, and ask only that marginal rates of profit should be the same. We know also that marginal rates will not be the same if ignorance prevails—this point we have mentioned earlier. What is often puzzling in a competitive industry is to find a difference in marginal profits, or marginal costs, without ignorance, and yet without the more efficient firm driving its rivals out of business. It is as if the more efficient says: "I could compete with you, but I won't," which is also what subsistence labour says when it does not transfer to capitalist employment unless real wages are substantially higher. The more efficient firm, instead of competing wherever its real costs are marginally less than its rivals, establishes for itself superior standards of remuneration. It pays its workers more and lavishes welfare services, scholarships and pensions upon them. It demands a higher rate on its marginal investments; where its competitors would be satisfied with 10 per cent., it demands 20 per cent., to keep up its average record. It goes in for prestige expenditure, contributing to hospitals, universities, flood relief and such. Its highest executives spend their time sitting on public committees, and have to have deputies to do their work. When all this is taken into account it is not at all surprising to find a competitive equilibrium in which high cost firms survive easily side by side with firms of much greater efficiency.

4. So far we have merely been setting the stage. Now the play begins. For we can now begin to trace the process of economic expansion.

The key to the process is the use which is made of the capitalist surplus. In so far as this is reinvested in creating new capital, the capitalist sector expands, taking more people into capitalist employment out of the subsistence sector. The surplus is then larger still, capital formation is still greater, and so the process continues until the labour surplus disappears.

OS is as before average subsistence earnings, and *OW* the capitalist wage [Fig III]. WN_1Q_1 represents the surplus in the initial stage. Since some of this is reinvested, the amount of fixed capital increases. Hence the schedule of the marginal productivity of labour is now raised throughout, to the level of N_2Q_2. Both the surplus and capitalist employment are now larger. Further reinvestment raises the

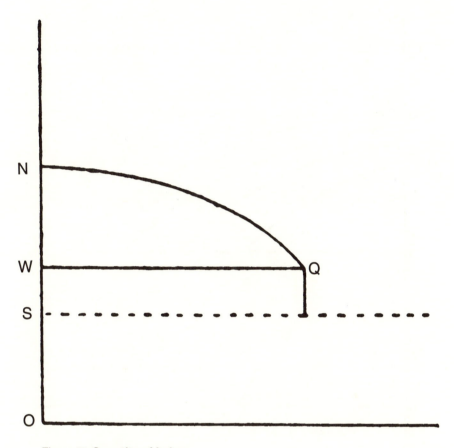

Figure II. **Quantity of Labour**

schedule of the marginal productivity of labour to N_3Q_3. And the process continues so long as there is surplus labour.

Various comments are needed in elaboration. First, as to the relationship
between capital, technical progress, and productivity. In theory it should be possible to distinguish between the growth of capital and the growth of technical
knowledge, but in practice it is neither possible nor necessary for this analysis.
As a matter of statistical analysis, differentiating the effects of capital and of
knowledge in any industry is straightforward if the product is homogeneous
through time, if the physical inputs are also unchanged (in kind) and if the
relative prices of the inputs have remained constant. But when we try to do it for
any industry in practice we usually find that the product has changed, the inputs
have changed and relative prices have changed, so that we get any number of

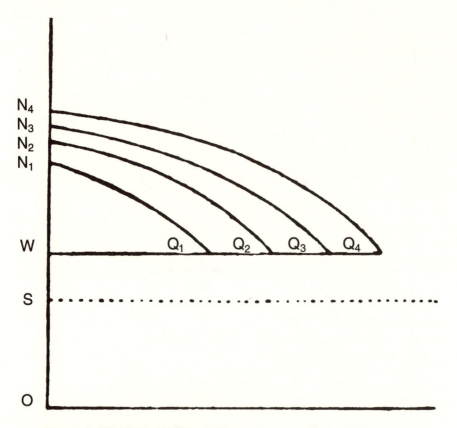

Figure III. **Quantity of Labour**

indices of technical progress from the same data, according to the assumptions and the type of index number which we use. In any case, for the purpose of this analysis it is unnecessary to distinguish between capital formation and the growth of knowledge within the capitalist sector. Growth of technical knowledge outside the capitalist sector would be fundamentally important, since it would raise the level of wages, and so reduce the capitalist surplus. But inside the capitalist sector knowledge and capital work in the same direction, to raise the surplus and to increase employment. They also work together. The application of new technical knowledge usually requires new investment, and whether the new knowledge is capital-saving (and thus equivalent to an increase in capital) or labour-saving (and thus equivalent to an increase in the marginal productivity of labour) makes no difference to our diagram. Capital and technical knowledge also work together in the sense that in economies where techniques are stagnant

savings are not so readily applied to increasing productive capital; in such economies it is more usual to use savings for building pyramids, churches, and other
such durable consumer goods. Accordingly, in this analysis the growth of productive capital and the growth of technical knowledge are treated as a single
phenomenon (just as we earlier decided that we could treat the growth of the
supply of skilled labour and the growth of capital as a single phenomenon in long
run analysis).

Next we must consider more closely the capitalist surplus. Malthus wanted to
know what the capitalists would do with this ever-growing surplus; surely this
would be an embarrassing glut of commodities? Ricardo replied that there would
be no glut; what the capitalists did not consume themselves, they would use for
paying the wages of workers to create more fixed capital (this is a free interpretation, since the classical economists associated the expansion of employment with
an increase of circulating rather than of fixed capital). This new fixed capital
would then in the next stage make possible the employment of more people in
the capitalist sector. Malthus persisted; why should the capitalists produce more
capital to produce a larger surplus which could only be used for producing still
more capital and so *ad infinitum*? To this Marx supplied one answer: capitalists
have a passion for accumulating capital. Ricardo supplied another: if they don't
want to accumulate, they will consume instead of saving; provided there is no
propensity to hoard, there will be no glut. Employment in the next stage will not
be as big as it would have been if they had created more fixed capital and so
brought more workers into the capitalist sector, but so long as there is no hoarding it makes no difference to the current level of employment whether capitalists
decide to consume or to save. Malthus then raised another question; suppose that
the capitalists do save and invest without hoarding, surely the fact that capital is
growing more rapidly than consumption must so lower the rate of profit on
capital that there comes a point when they decide that it is not worth while to
invest? This, Ricardo replied, is impossible; since the supply of labour is unlimited, you can always find employment for any amount of capital. This is absolutely correct, for his model; in the neo-classical model capital grows faster than
labour, and so one has to ask whether the rate of profit will not fall, but in the
classical model the unlimited supply of labour means that the capital/labour ratio,
and therefore the rate of surplus, can be held constant for any quantity of capital
(*i.e.*, unlimited "widening" is possible). The only fly in the ointment is that there
may develop a shortage of natural resources, so that though the capitalists get any
amount of labour at a constant wage, they have to pay ever rising rents to
landlords. This was what worried Ricardo; it was important to him to distinguish
that part of the surplus which goes to landlords from that part which goes to
capitalists, since he believed that economic development inevitably increases the
relative scarcity of land. We are not so certain of this as he was. Certainly
development increases the rent of urban sites fantastically, but its effect on rural
rents depends on the rate of technical progress in agriculture, which Malthus and

Ricardo both gravely under-estimated. If we assume technical progress in agriculture, no hoarding, and unlimited labour at a constant wage, the rate of profit on capital cannot fall. On the contrary it must increase, since all the benefit of technical progress in the capitalist sector accrues to the capitalists.

Marx's interest in the surplus was ethical as well as scientific. He regarded it as robbery of the workers. His descendants are less certain of this. The surplus, after all, is only partly consumed; the other part is used for capital formation. As for the part which is consumed, some of it is a genuine payment for service rendered—for managerial or entrepreneurial services, as well as for the services of public administrators, whether these are paid salaries out of taxes, or whether they live off their rents or *rentes* while performing unpaid public duties as magistrates, lord-lieutenants, or the like. Even in the U.S.S.R. all these functionaries are paid out of the surplus, and handsomely paid too. It is arguable that these services are over-paid; this is why we have progressive taxation, and it is also one of the more dubious arguments for nationalisation (more dubious because the functionaries of public corporations have to be paid the market rate if the economy is only partially nationalised). But it is not arguable that all this part of the surplus (*i.e.* the part consumed) morally belongs to the workers, in any sense. As for the part which is used for capital formation, the experience of the U.S.S.R. is that this is increased, and not reduced, by transforming the ownership of capital. Expropriation deprives the capitalists of control over this part of the surplus, and of the right to consume this part at some later date, but it does nothing whatever to transfer this part of the surplus to the workers. Marx's emotional approach was a natural reaction to the classical writers, who sometimes in unguarded moments wrote as if the capitalist surplus and its increase were all that counted in the national income (cf. Ricardo, who called it "the net revenue" of production). All this, however, is by the way; for our present interest is not in ethical questions, but in how the model works.

5. The central problem in the theory of economic development is to understand the process by which a community which was previously saving and investing 4 or 5 per cent. of its national income or less, converts itself into an economy where voluntary saving is running at about 12 to 15 per cent. of national income or more, This is the central problem because the central fact of economic development is rapid capital accumulation (including knowledge and skills with capital). We cannot explain any "industrial" revolution (as the economic historians pretend to do) until we can explain why saving increased relatively to national income.

It is possible that the explanation is simply that some psychological change occurs which causes people to be more thrifty. This, however is not a plausible explanation. We are interested not in the people in general, but only say in the 10 per cent. of them with the largest incomes, who in countries with surplus labour receive up to 40 per cent. of the national income (nearer 30 per cent. in more developed countries). The remaining 90 per cent. of the people never manage to save a significant fraction of their incomes. The important question is why does the top 10 per cent. save more? The reason may be because they decide to consume less, but this reason does not square with the facts. There is no evidence of a fall in personal consumption by the top 10 per cent. at a time when industrial revolutions are occurring. It is also possible that, though they do not save any more, the top 10 per cent. spend less of their income on durable consumer goods (tombs, country houses, temples) and more on productive capital. Certainly, if one compares different civilisations this is a striking difference in the disposition of income. Civilisations in which there is a rapid growth of technical knowledge or expansion of other opportunities present more profitable outlets for investment than do technologically stagnant civilisations, and tempt capital into productive channels rather than into the building of monuments. But if one takes a country only over the course of the hundred years during which it undergoes a revolution in the rate of capital formation, there is no noticeable change in this regard. Certainly, judging by the novels, the top 10 per cent. in England were not spending noticeably less on durable consumer goods in 1800 than they were in 1700.

Much the most plausible explanation is that people save more because they have more to save. This is not to say merely that the national income per head is larger, since there is no clear evidence that the proportion of the national income saved increases with national income per head—at any rate our fragmentary evidence for the United Kingdom and for the United States suggests that this is not so. The explanation is much more likely to be that saving increases relatively to the national income because the incomes of the savers increase relatively to the national income. The central fact of economic development is that the distribution of incomes is altered in favour of the saving class.

Practically all saving is done by people who receive profits or rents. Workers' savings are very small. The middle-classes save a little, but in practically every community the savings of the middle-classes out of their salaries are of little consequence for productive investment. Most members of the middle-class are engaged in the perpetual struggle to keep up with the Jones's; if they manage to save enough to buy the house in which they live, they are doing well. They may save to educate their children, or to subsist in their old age, but this saving is virtually offset by the savings being used up for the same purposes. Insurance is the middle-class's favourite form of saving in modern societies, yet in the U.K., where the habit is extremely well developed, the annual net increase in insurance funds from all classes, rich, middle, and poor is less than $1\frac{1}{2}$ per cent. of the national income. It is doubtful if the wage and salary classes ever anywhere save as much as 3 per cent. of the national income, net (possible exception: Japan). If we are interested in savings, we must concentrate attention upon profits and rents.

For our purpose it does not matter whether profits are distributed or undistributed; the major source of savings is profits, and if we find that savings are increasing as a proportion of the national income, we may take it for granted that this is because the share of profits in the national income is increasing. (As a refinement, for highly taxed communities, we should say profits net of taxes upon profits, whether personal income or corporate taxes). Our problem then becomes what are the circumstances in which the share of profits in the national income increases?

The modified classical model which we are using here has the virtue of answering the question. In the beginning, the national income consists almost entirely of subsistence income. Abstracting from population growth and assuming that the marginal product of labour is zero, this subsistence income remains constant throughout the expansion, since by definition labour can be yielded up to the expanding capitalist sector without reducing subsistence output. The process therefore increases the capitalist surplus and the income of capitalist employees, taken together, as a proportion of the national income. It is possible to imagine conditions in which the surplus nevertheless does not increase relatively to national income. This requires that capitalist employment should expand relatively much faster than the surplus, so that within the capitalist sector gross margins or profit plus rent are falling sharply relatively to wages. We know that this does not happen. Even if gross margins were constant, profits in our model would be increasing relatively to national income. But gross margins are not likely to be constant in our model, which assumes that practically the whole benefit of capital accumulation and of technical progress goes into the surplus; because real wages are constant, all that the workers get out of the expansion is that more of them are employed at a wage above the subsistence earnings. The model says, in effect, that if unlimited supplies of labour are available at a constant real wage, and if any part of profits is reinvested in productive capacity, profits will grow continuously relatively to the national income, and capital formation will also grow relatively to the national income.

The model also covers the case of a technical revolution. Some historians have suggested that the capital for the British Industrial Revolution came out of profits made possible by a spate of inventions occurring together. This is extremely hard to fit into the neo-classical model, since it involves the assumption that these inventions raised the marginal productivity of capital more than they raised the marginal productivity of labour, a proposition which it is hard to establish in any economy where labour is scarce. (If we do not make this assumption, other incomes rise just as fast as profits, and investment does not increase relatively to national income). On the other hand the suggestion fits beautifully into the modified classical model, since in this model practically the whole benefit of inventions goes into the surplus, and becomes available for further capital accumulation.

This model also helps us to face squarely the nature of the economic problem of backward countries If we ask "why do they save so little," the truthful answer is not "because they are so poor," as we might be tempted to conclude from the path-breaking and praiseworthy correlations of Mr. Colin Clark. The truthful answer is "because their capitalist sector is so small" (remembering that "capitalist" here does not mean private capitalist, but would apply equally to state capitalist). If they had a larger capitalist sector, profits would be a greater part of their national income, and saving and investment would also be relatively larger. (The state capitalist can accumulate capital even faster than the private capitalist, since he can use for the purpose not only the profits of the capitalist sector, but also what he can force or tax out of the subsistence sector).

Another point which we must note is that though the increase of the capitalist sector involves an increase in the inequality of incomes, as between capitalists and the rest, mere inequality of income is not enough to ensure a high level of saving. In point of fact the inequality of income is *greater* in over-populated under-developed countries than it is in advanced industrial nations, for the simple reason that agricultural rents are so high in the former. Eighteenth century British economists took it for granted that the landlord class is given to prodigal consumption rather than to productive investment, and this is certainly true of landlords in under-developed countries. Hence, given two countries of equal incomes, in which distribution is more unequal in one than in the other, savings may be greater where distribution is more equal if profits are higher relatively to rents. It is the inequality which goes with profits that favours capital formation, and not the inequality which goes with rents. Correspondingly, it is very hard to argue that these countries cannot afford to save more, when 40 per cent. or so of the national income is going to the top 10 per cent., and so much of rent incomes is squandered.

Behind this analysis also lies the sociological problem of the emergence of a capitalist class, that is to say of a group of men who think in terms of investing capital productively. The dominant classes in backward economies—landlords, traders, moneylenders, priests, soldiers, princes—do not normally think in these terms. What causes a society to grow a capitalist class is a very difficult question, to which probably, there is no general answer. Most countries seem to begin by importing their capitalists from abroad; and in these days many (*e.g.* U.S.S.R., India) are growing a class of state capitalists who, for political reasons of one sort or another, are determined to create capital rapidly on public account. As for indigenous private capitalists, their emergence is probably bound up with the emergence of new opportunities, especially something that widens the market, associated with some new technique which greatly increases the productivity of labour if labour and capital are used together. Once a capitalist sector has emerged, it is only a matter of time before it becomes sizeable. If very little technical progress is occurring, the surplus will grow only slowly. But if for one reason or another the opportunities for using capital productivity increase rapidly, the surplus will also grow rapidly, and the capitalist class with it.

6. In our model so far capital is created only out of profits earned. In the real world, however, capitalists also create capital as a result of a net increase in the supply of money—especially bank credit. We have now also to take account of this.

In the neo-classical model capital can be created only by withdrawing resources from producing consumer goods. In our model, however, there is surplus labour, and if (as we shall assume) its marginal productivity is zero, and if, also, capital can be created by labour without withdrawing scarce land and capital from other uses, then capital can be created without reducing the output of consumer goods. This second proviso is important, since if we need capital or land to make capital the results in our model are the same as the results in the neo-classical model, despite the fact that there is surplus labour. However, in practice the proviso is often fulfilled. Food cannot be grown without land, but roads, viaducts, irrigation channels and buildings can be created by human labour with hardly any capital to speak of—witness the Pyramids, or the marvellous railway tunnels built in the mid-nineteenth century almost with bare hands. Even in modern industrial countries constructional activity, which lends itself to hand labour, is as much as 50 or 60 per cent. of gross fixed investment, so it is not difficult to think of labour creating capital without using any but the simplest tools. The classical economists were not wrong in thinking of lack of circulating capital as being a more serious obstacle to expansion in their world than lack of fixed capital. In the analysis which follows in this section we assume that surplus labour cannot be used to make consumer goods without using up more land or capital, but can be used to make capital goods without using any scarce factors.

If a community is short of capital, and has idle resources which can be set to creating capital, it seems very desirable on the face of the matter that this should be done, even if it means creating extra money to finance the extra employment. There is no loss of other output while the new capital is being made, and when it comes into use it will raise output and employment in just the same way as would capital financed not by credit creation but out of profits. The difference between profit-financed and credit-financed capital is not in the ultimate effects on output, but in the immediate effects on prices and on the distribution of income.

Before we come to the effects on prices, however, we should pause a moment to notice what happens to the output of consumer goods in this model and the others while credit-financed capital is being created, but before it begins to be used. In the neo-classical model an increase in capital formation has to be accompanied by a corresponding fall in the output of consumer goods, since scarce resources can do one or the other. In the Keynesian model an increase in capital formation also increases the output of consumer goods, and if the multiplier exceeds 2, the output of consumer goods increases even more than capital formation. In our model capital formation goes up, but the output of consumer goods is not immediately affected. This is one of those crucial cases where it is important to be certain that one is using the right model when it comes to giving advice on economic policy.

In our model, if surplus labour is put to capital formation and paid out of new money, prices rise, because the stream of money purchases is swollen while the output of consumer goods is for the time being constant. What is happening is that the fixed amount of consumer goods is being redistributed, towards the workers newly employed, away from the rest of the community (this is where the lack of circulating capital comes into the picture). This process is not "forced saving" in the useful sense of that term. In the neo-classical model the output of consumer goods is reduced, forcing the community as a whole to save. In our model, however, consumer goods output is not at any time reduced; there is a forced redistribution of consumption, but not forced saving. And, of course, as soon as the capital goods begin to yield output, consumption begins to rise.

This inflationary process does not go on forever; it comes to an end when voluntary savings increase to a level where they are equal to the inflated level of investment. Since savings are a function of profits, this means that the inflation continues until profits increase so much relatively to the national income that capitalists can now finance the higher rate of investment out of their profits without any further recourse to monetary expansion. Essentially equilibrium is secured by raising the ratio of profits to the national income. The equilibrator need not however be profits; it might equally be government receipts, if there is a structure of taxes such that the ratio of government receipts to the national income rises automatically as the national income rises. This seems to be just about what happened in the U.S.S.R. In the crucial years when the economy was being transformed from a 5 per cent. to a (probably) 20 per cent. net saver, there was a tremendous inflation of prices (apparently prices rose about 700 per cent. in a decade), but the inflationary profits largely went to the government in the form of turnover tax, and by the end of the decade a new equilibrium was in sight.

It is not, however, always a simple matter to raise profits relatively to national income simply by turning on the monetary tap. The simplest and most extreme model of an inflation would be to assume that when the capitalists finance capital formation by creating credit, the money all comes back to them in the very next round in the form of an increase in their profits. In such a model profits, voluntary savings and capital formation can be raised to any desired level in a very short time, with only a small increase in prices. Something like this may well apply in the U.S.S.R. In real terms, however, this implies that there has been a fall in the share of the national income received by other people, including a fall in their real consumption, since they have had to release consumer goods for the previously unemployed who are now engaged in capital formation. It may be the farmers who are worse off, this showing itself in the prices of manufactures rising relatively to farm prices. Or it may be the workers in the capitalist sector who are worse off, because farm prices and the prices of manufactures rise faster than their wages. Or the blow may be falling upon salaried workers, pensioners, landlords or creditors. Now in the real world none of these classes will take this lying down. In the U.S.S.R., where the intention was that the capital formation should be at the expense of the farmers, it led in the end to organised violence on both sides. In our model it is hard to get away with it at the expense of the workers, since the wage in the capitalist sector must stand at a certain minimum level above subsistence earnings if labour is to be available. Generally, what happens as prices rise is that new contracts have to be made to take account of rising price levels. Some classes get caught, but only temporarily.

Now, if one pursued this argument logically, it would lead to the conclusion that equilibrium could never be reached—at any rate, so long as the banking system is content to supply all "legitimate" demands for money. If none of the other classes can be soaked, it seems impossible for profits to rise relatively the national income for more than a temporary space, and it therefore seems impossible to reach an equilibrium level of savings equal to the new level of investment. The inflation, once begun goes on forever. This, however, is not possible for another reason, namely the fact that the real national income is not fixed, but rising, as a result of the capital formation. Therefore all that is required is that capitalists' real incomes rise faster than other people's. Beyond the first year or two, when the additional consumer goods begin to appear, it is not necessary for any class to reduce its consumption. By the time the process of recontracting has begun, output has also begun to rise, and it is therefore possible to reach a *modus vivendi*.

We can give an exact description of this equilibrium in our modified classical model. In this model the average subsistence real income is given, and so also therefore is the real wage in the capitalist sector. It is not possible, by inflation or otherwise, to reach a new equilibrium in which the capitalist surplus has increased at the expense of either of these. If, therefore, the capitalists begin to finance capital formation out of credit, they lower the real incomes of the others only temporarily. Wages would then be chasing prices continuously but for the fact that, since output is growing all the time, profits are growing all the time. Hence the part of the investment which is financed out of credit is diminishing all the time, until equilibrium is reached. For example, suppose that an investment of £100 a year yields £20 a year profit, of which £10 a year is saved. Then, if capitalists invest an extra £100 a year, all of which in the first year is financed out of credit, by the eleventh year profits will be £200 a year greater, savings will be £100 a year greater and there will be no further monetary pressure on prices. All that will remain from the episode is that there will be £1,000 more useful productive capital at work than there would have if the credit creation had not taken place.

Thus we have two simple models marking the extreme cases. In the first, all the credit created comes back to the capitalists at once as profits (or to the state capitalist as taxes). Equilibrium is then reached easily, with the capitalists gaining at the expense of all others. In the other model the capitalists can only gain temporarily; equilibrium then takes much longer to reach, but it is reached eventually. In the first case we need only an expansion of money income; but in the second case it is the expansion of real income which eventually brings the capitalists the required proportion of the national income.

The fact that capital formation increases real output must also be borne in mind in the analysis of the effects of credit creation upon prices. The inflations which loom most in our minds are those which occur in war-time, when resources are being withdrawn from producing consumer goods. If the supply of money is increasing while the output of goods is falling, anything can happen to prices. Inflation for the purpose of capital formation, however, is a very different kettle of fish. For it results in increasing consumer goods output, and this results in falling prices if the quantity of money is held constant.

Perhaps it may be as well to illustrate a simple case. Suppose that £100 is invested every year, in the first instance by creating credit, and that each investment yields £30 a year in its second year and after. Suppose that it costs nothing to reap the yield; the price of £30 charged for the product being pure rent derived from its scarcity (investment in an irrigation works is a nearly perfect illustration). Then, if we use the Keynesian formula for a demand inflation, and assume the multiplier to be 2, money income will rise to an equilibrium level of +£200 a year. Output, however, will begin to increase by +£30 a year from the second year onward. By the eighth year output will have increased by +£210, while money income will have increased only by slightly less than +£200. Thereafter prices will be below the initial level, and will fall continuously. The alleged precision of this analysis is of course subject to all the usual objections against applying multiplier analysis to inflationary conditions, namely the instability of the propensity to consume, the effect of secondary investment, and the dangers of cost inflation. But though the precision is spurious, the result is nevertheless real. Inflation for purposes of capital formation is self-destructive. Prices begin to rise, but are sooner or later overtaken by rising output, and may, in the last state end up lower than they were at the beginning.

We may now sum up this section. Capital formation is financed not only out of profits but also out of an expansion of credit. This speeds up the growth of capital, and the growth of real income. It also results in some redistribution of the national income, either temporarily or permanently, according to the assumptions one makes—in the model we are using, the redistribution is only temporary. It also prevents prices from falling, as they otherwise would (if money is constant and output rising), and it may drive prices up substantially if (as in our model) the distribution of income cannot be altered permanently by monetary measures, since prices will then continue to rise until real output has risen enough to effect the required redistribution. Thereafter prices fall further, since inflation raises prices while capital is being created, but the increased output which then results brings them down again.

One point remains. We have seen that if new money is used to finance capital formation the rise of prices eventually peters out, as savings grow into equilibrium with investment; and reverses itself, as the output of consumer goods begins to pour out. The new equilibrium, however, may take a long time to reach, and if also the flow of new money is substantial the resulting rise of prices may strike fear into the hearts of the public. People do not panic if prices rise for two or three years; but after that they may begin to lose confidence in money, and it may become necessary to call a drastic halt. This is the most important practical limitation on the extent to which capital formation can be financed in this way. This is why the banking authorities have always tended to alternate short periods of easy credit with sharp periods of restriction. Bank credit moves three steps up and one step down instead of moving up continuously. This also brings us to the threshold of the trade cycle. If capital were financed exclusively out of profits, and if there were also no hoarding, capital formation would proceed steadily. It is mainly the existence of an elastic credit system which makes the trade cycle an integral part of the mechanism of economic development in an unplanned economy. It is not necessary, however, for us to enter into analysis of the cycle since in this respect the model we are using does not yield results different from those of other models.

7. We have said very little so far about the activities of government, since our basic model uses only capitalists, their employees, and subsistence producers. Governments affect the process of capital accumulation in many ways, however, and not least by the inflations into which they run. Many governments in backward countries are also currently anxious to use surplus man-power for capital formation, and as there is a great deal that can be done with labour and a few tools (roads, irrigation, river walls, schools and so on), it is useful to say something on the subject. We shall therefore in this section analyse the effect of inflation-financed government formation of capital, and thereby also give ourselves the chance to recapitulate the analysis of the previous section.

The results, it will be remembered, lie within two extremes. At one extreme all the money spent by the government comes back to it in taxes, and this is accepted by all classes. In this case, prices rise very little. At the other extreme, all classes refuse to accept a redistribution between themselves and the government. In this case prices tend to rise continuously, except that rising output (as a result of the capital formed) sooner or later catches up with prices and brings them down again. Rising output will also increase the government's "normal" share of the national income, and all monetary pressure will cease when the "normal" share has risen to the level of the inflated share which it was trying to get.

These results give us the questions we must ask. (1). What part of marginal income returns automatically to the government? (2). What effect does inflation have upon the various classes? And (3). What effect has government capital formation upon output?

(One other point must be remembered. In all this analysis so far we have assumed a closed economy. In an open economy inflation plays havoc with the balance of payments. We have therefore to assume that the government has strict control over foreign transactions. This assumption holds for some backward economies; others would get into an awful mess if they launched upon inflationary finance).

It is not possible that all the money spent by the government should come back to it in the first round, since this would presume that the government took 100 per cent. of marginal income. If the government takes any part of marginal income, some of the money will come back to it; but even the Keynesian multiplier will not bring it all back unless taxation is the only leakage (*i.e.* there is no saving). The larger the government's share of marginal incomes, the more it will get back, the quicker it will get it, and the smaller will be the effect on prices.

Since the second world war a number of governments of modern industrial states seem to be taking around 40 to 50 per cent. of marginal incomes in taxation, and this is one of the major reasons why their price levels have not risen more, despite heavy pressure on resources for capital formation, defence, etc. In backward countries, however, governments take only a very small part of marginal incomes. The best placed governments from this point of view are those in countries where output is concentrated in a few large units (mines, plantations) and therefore easily taxed, or where foreign trade is a large part of the national income, and is thus easily reached by import and export duties. One of the worst off is India, with a large part of its output produced by subsistence producers and small scale units, hard to reach, and with less than 10 per cent. of national income passing in foreign trade. In many cases, marginal taxation is less than average taxation, for when money incomes rise, the government continues to charge the same prices for railway travel or for stamps, and hesitates to raise land taxes on the peasants, with the result that money incomes rise faster than government receipts. No government should consider deficit financing without assuring itself that a large part of increases in money income will automatically come back to itself. By contrast, the U.S.S.R., with its very high rate of turnover tax, automatically mops up surplus funds injected into the system, before they are able to generate much demand inflation *via* the multiplier process.

The next question is the effect of inflation upon the distribution of income. The surplus money raises prices, some more than others. The government will probably try to prevent prices from rising, but will succeed better with some than with others. It is easy to apply price control to large scale enterprises, but very hard to prevent the farmers from raising food prices, or the petty traders from making big margins. From the point of view of capital formation, the best thing that can happen is for the surplus money to roll into the pockets of people who will reinvest it productively. The merchant classes would probably use it mainly for speculation in those commodities that are getting scarce. The middle-classes would mainly buy big American cars with it, or go on trips to Europe, wangling the foreign exchange somehow. The peasants ought to use it to improve their farms, but probably most would use it only to pay off debt, or to buy more land. There is really only one class that is pretty certain to reinvest its profits productively, and that is the class of industrialists. The effects of an inflation on secondary capital formation therefore depend first on how large the industrial class is, and secondly on whether the benefit goes largely to this class. In countries which have only a small industrial class, inflation leads mainly to speculation in commodities and in land, and to the hoarding of foreign exchange. But in any country which has a substantial industrialist class, with the passion this class has for ruling over bigger and better factories, even the most frightening inflations (*e.g.* Germany from 1919) leave behind a substantial increase in capital formation. (Have we hit here upon some deep psychological instinct which drives the industrialist to use his wealth more creatively than others? Probably not. It is just that his job is of the kind where passion for success results in capital formation. The peasant farmer wants to have more land, not more capital on his land [unless he is a modern capitalist farmer] so his passion is dissipated merely in changes in the price and distribution of land. The merchant wants to have a wider margin, or a quicker turnover, neither of which increases fixed capital. The banker wants more deposits. Only the industrialist's passion drives towards using profits to create a bigger empire of bricks and steel.) It follows that it is in industrial communities that inflations are most helpful to capital formation; whereas in countries where the industrial class is negligible there is nothing to show for the inflation when it is over, except the original investment which started it off. We should also note that many governments do not like the fact that inflation enables industrialists to earn the extra profits with which they create fixed capital, since this results in an increase of private fortunes. They therefore do all they can to prevent the inflation from increasing the profits of industrialists. More especially, they clamp down on industrial prices, which are also from the administrative point of view the easiest prices to control. Since it is the industrialist class which saves most, the result is to exacerbate the inflation. It would be much sounder to pursue policies which would result in the profits of industrialists rising more rapidly than other incomes, and then to tax these profits away, either immediately, or at death.

Inflation continues to be generated so long as the community is not willing to hold an amount equal to the increased investment expenditure. It is not therefore enough that savings should increase to this extent, for if these savings are used for additional investment the initial gap still remains. The gap is closed only if the savings are hoarded, or used to buy government bonds, so that the government can now finance its investments by borrowing, instead of by creating new money. Hence in practice, if the government wishes the inflation to be ended without reducing its investment, it must find means of bringing into its coffers as much in taxes or in loans as it is spending. If it is failing to do this, the inflation will continue; it is then better that it should continue because capitalists are spending their profits on further capital formation than because other classes are chasing a limited output of consumer goods; but if it is desired to end inflation as soon as possible, all classes should be encouraged to invest in government bonds rather than to spend in other ways.

Finally we come to the relation between capital and output. If the intention is to finance capital formation by creating credit, the best objects for such a policy are those which yield a large income quickly. To finance school building by creating credit is asking for trouble. On the other hand, there are a lot of agricultural programmes (water supplies, fertilisers, seed farms, extension) where quick and substantial results may be expected from modest expenditure. If there are idle resources available for capital formation it is foolish not to use them simply because of technical or political difficulties in raising taxes. But it would be equally foolish to use them on programmes which take a long time to give a small result, when there are others which could give a large result quickly.

We may sum up as follows. If labour is abundant and physical resources scarce, the primary effect on output is exactly the same whether the government creates capital out of taxation or out of credit creation: the output of consumer goods is unchanged, but is redistributed. Hence credit creation must be seen primarily as an alternative to taxation, which is worth the troubles it brings only if trying to raise taxes would bring even more troubles. Credit creation has however one further lead upon taxation in that if it also redistributes income towards the industrial class (if there is an industrial class), it will speed up capital formation out of profits. If it is impossible to increase taxation, and the alternative is between creating capital out of credit, and not creating it at all, the choice one has then to make is between stable prices or rising output. There is no simple formula for making this choice. In some communities any further inflation of prices would ruin their fragile social or political equilibrium; in others this equilibrium will be destroyed if there is not a sharp increase in output in the near future; and in still others the equilibrium will be ruined either way.

8. We may now resume our analysis. We have seen that if unlimited labour is available at a constant real wage, the capitalist surplus will rise continuously, and annual investment will be a rising proportion of the national income. Needless to say, this cannot go on forever.

The process must stop when capital accumulation has caught up with population, so that there is no longer surplus labour. But it may stop before that. It may stop of course for any number of reasons which are outside our system of analysis, ranging from earthquake or bubonic plague to social revolution. But it may also stop for the economic reason that, although there is a labour surplus, real wages may nevertheless rise so high as to reduce capitalists' profits to the level at which profits are all consumed and there is no net investment.

This may happen for one of four reasons. First, if capital accumulation is proceeding faster than population growth, and is therefore reducing absolutely the number of people in the subsistence sector, the average product per man in that sector rises automatically, not because production alters, but because there are fewer mouths to share the product. After a while the change actually becomes noticeable, and the capitalist wage begins to be forced up. Secondly, the increase in the size of the capitalist sector relatively to the subsistence sector may turn the terms of trade against the capitalist sector (if they are producing different things) and so force the capitalists to pay workers a higher percentage of their product, in order to keep their real income constant. Thirdly, the subsistence sector may also become more productive in the technical sense. For example, it may begin to imitate the techniques of the capitalist sector; the peasants may get hold of some of the new seeds, or hear about new fertilisers or rotations. They may also benefit directly from some of the capitalist investments, *e.g.*, in irrigation works, in transport facilities, or in electricity. Anything which raises the productivity of the subsistence sector (average per person) will raise real wages in the capitalist sector, and will therefore reduce the capitalist surplus and the rate of capital accumulation, unless it at the same time more than correspondingly moves the terms of trade against the subsistence sector. Alternatively, even if the productivity of the capitalist sector is unchanged, the workers in the capitalist sector may imitate the capitalist way of life, and may thus need more to live on. The subsistence level is only a conventional idea, and conventions change. The effect of this would be to widen the gap between earnings in the subsistence sector, and wages in the capitalist sector. This is hard to do, if labour is abundant, but it may be achieved by a combination of trade union pressure and capitalist conscience. If it is achieved, it will reduce the capitalist surplus, and also the rate of capital accumulation.

The most interesting of these possibilities is that the terms of trade may move against the capitalist sector. This assumes that the capitalist and subsistence sectors are producing different things. In practice this is a question of the relationship between industry and agriculture. If the capitalists are investing in plantation agriculture side by side with their investment in industry, we can think of the capitalist sector as self-contained. The expansion of this sector does not then generate any demand for anything produced in the subsistence sector, and there are therefore no terms of trade to upset the picture we have drawn. To bring the terms of trade in, the simplest assumption to make is that the subsistence sector consists of peasants producing food, while the capitalist sector produces everything else.

Now if the capitalist sector produces no food, its expansion increases the demand for food, raises the price of food in terms of capitalist products, and so reduces profits. This is one of the senses in which industrialisation is dependent upon agricultural improvement; it is not profitable to produce a growing volume of manufactures unless agricultural production is growing simultaneously. This is also why industrial and agrarian revolutions always go together, and why economies in which agriculture is stagnant do not show industrial development. Hence, if we postulate that the capitalist sector is not producing food, we must either postulate that the subsistence sector is increasing its output, or else conclude that the expansion of the capitalist sector will be brought to an end through adverse terms of trade eating into profits. (Ricardo's problem of increasing rents is first cousin to this conclusion; he worried about rents increasing *inside* the capitalist sector, whereas we are dealing with rents *outside* the sector).

On the other hand, if we assume that the subsistence sector is producing more food, while we escape the Scylla of adverse terms of trade we may be caught by the Charybdis of real wages rising because the subsistence sector is more productive. We escape both Scylla and Charybdis if rising productivity in the subsistence sector is more than offset by improving terms of trade. However, if the subsistence sector is producing food, the elasticity of demand for which is less than unity, increases in productivity will be more than offset by reductions in price. A rise in the productivity of the subsistence sector hurts the capitalist sector if there is no trade between the two, or if the demand of the capitalist sector for the subsistence sector's product is elastic. On the assumptions we have made, a rise in food productivity benefits the capitalist sector. Nevertheless, when we take rising demand into account, it is not at all unlikely that the price of food will not fall as fast as productivity increases, and this will force the capitalists to pay out a larger part of their product as wages.

If there is no hope of prices falling as fast as productivity increases (because demand is increasing), the capitalists' next best move is to prevent the farmer from getting all his extra production. In Japan this was achieved by raising rents against the farmers, and by taxing them more heavily, so that a large part of the rapid increase in productivity which occurred (between 1880 and 1910 it doubled) was taken away from the farmers and used for capital formation; at the same time the holding down of the farmers' income itself held down wages, to the advantage of profits in the capitalist sector. Much the same happened in the U.S.S.R., where farm incomes per head were held down, in spite of farm mechanisation and the considerable release of labour to the towns; this was done jointly by raising the prices of manufactures relatively to farm products, and also by levying heavy taxes upon the collective farms.

This also defines for us the case in which it is true to say that it is agriculture which finances industrialisation. If the capitalist sector is self-contained, its expansion is in no way dependent upon the peasants. The surplus is wholly "at the expense" of the workers in the capitalist sector. But if the capitalist sector depends upon the peasants for food, it is essential to get the peasants to produce more, while if at the same time they can be prevented from enjoying the full fruit of their extra production, wages can be reduced relatively to the capitalist surplus. By contrast a state which is ruled by peasants may be happy and prosperous, but it is not likely to show such a rapid accumulation of capital. (*E.g.*, will China and the U.S.S.R. diverge in this respect?).

We conclude, therefore, that the expansion of the capitalist sector may be stopped because the price of subsistence goods rises, or because the price is not falling as fast as subsistence productivity per head is rising, or because capitalist workers raise their standard of what they need for subsistence. Any of these would raise wages relatively to the surplus. If none of these processes is enough to stop capital accumulation, the capitalist sector will continue to expand until there is no surplus labour left. This can happen even if population is growing. For example, if it takes 3 per cent. of annual income invested to employ 1 per cent. more people, an annual net investment of 12 per cent. can cope with as much as a 4 per cent. increase in population. But population in Western Europe at the relevant times grew only by 1 per cent. or so per annum (which is also the present rate of growth in India), and rates of growth exceeding $2\frac{1}{2}$ per cent. per annum are even now rather rare. We cannot say that capital will always grow faster than labour (it obviously has not done so in Asia), but we can say that if conditions are favourable for the capitalist surplus to grow more rapidly than population, there must come a day when capital accumulation has caught up with labour supply. Ricardo and Malthus did not provide for this in their models, because they over-estimated the rate of growth of population. Marx did not provide for it either, because he had persuaded himself that capital accumulation increases unemployment instead of reducing it (he has a curious model in which the short run effect of accumulation is to reduce unemployment, raise wages and thus provoke a crisis, while the long run effect is to increase the reserve army of unemployed). Of the classical economists only Adam Smith saw clearly that capital accumulation would eventually create a shortage of labour, and raise wages above the subsistence level.

When the labour surplus disappears our model of the closed economy no longer holds. Wages are no longer tied to a subsistence level. Adam Smith thought they would then depend upon the degree of monopoly (a doctrine which was re-presented in the 1930's as one of the novelties of modern economic analysis). The neo-classicists invented the doctrine of marginal productivity. The problem is not yet solved to anyone's satisfaction, except in static models which take no account of capital accumulation and of technical progress. It is, however, outside the terms of reference of this essay and we will not pursue it here.

Our task is not, however, finished. In the classical world all countries have surplus labour. In the neo-classical world labour is scarce in all countries. In the real world, however, countries which achieve labour scarcity continue to be surrounded by others which have abundant labour. Instead of concentrating on one country, and examining the expansion of its capitalist sector, we now have to see this country as part of the expanding capitalist sector of the world economy as a whole, and to enquire how the distribution of income inside the country and its rate of capital accumulation, are affected by the fact that there is abundant labour available elsewhere at a subsistence wage.

II. The Open Economy

9. When capital accumulation catches up with the labour supply, wages begin to rise above the subsistence level, and the capitalist surplus is adversely affected. However, if there is still surplus labour in other countries, the capitalists can avoid this in one of two ways, by encouraging immigration or by exporting their capital to countries where there is still abundant labour at a subsistence wage. We must examine each of these in turn.

10. Let us first clear out of the way the effects of the immigration of skilled workers, since our main concern is with an abundant immigration of unskilled workers released by the subsistence sectors of other countries. It is theoretically possible that the immigration of skilled workers may reduce the demand for the services of native unskilled workers, but this is most unlikely. More probably it will make possible new investments and industries which were not possible before, and will thus increase the demand for all kinds of labour, relatively to its supply.

We must also get out of the way relatively small immigrations. If 100,000 Puerto Ricans emigrate to the United States every year, the effect on U.S. wages is negligible. U.S. wages are not pulled down to the Puerto Rican level; it is Puerto Rican wages which are then pulled up to the U.S. level.

Mass immigration is quite a different kettle of fish. If there were free immigration from, India and China to the U.S.A., the wage level of the U.S.A. would certainly be pulled down towards the Indian and Chinese levels. In fact in a competitive model the U.S. wage could exceed the Asian wage only by an amount covering migration costs plus the "cliff" to which we have already referred. The result is the same whether one assumes increasing or diminishing returns to labour. Wages are constant at subsistence level plus. All the benefit of increasing returns goes into the capitalist surplus.

This is one of the reasons why, in every country where the wage level is relatively high, the trade unions are bitterly hostile to immigration, except of people in special categories, and take steps to have it restricted. The result is that real wages are higher than they would otherwise be, while profits, capital resources, and total output are smaller than they would otherwise be.

11. The export of capital is therefore a much easier way out for the capitalists, since trade unions are quick to restrict immigration, but much slower in bringing the export of capital under control.

The effect of exporting capital is to reduce the creation of fixed capital at home, and therefore to reduce the demand for labour. Labour will still be required to create the capital (*e.g.* to make machines for export), but domestic labour will no longer be required to work with the capital, as it would also be if the capital were invested at home.

This, however, is only one side of the picture, for the capital may be used in foreign countries in ways which raise the standard of living of the capital exporting country (and so offset wholly or partly the first effect), or in ways which lower it (thus aggravating the first effect). The result depends on the type of competition which there is between the capital exporting and the capital importing countries.

12. Let us assume, to begin with, that there is no competition, and even no trade. Both countries are self-sufficient. Wages however are rising in country *A*, while labour is abundant in country *B*. *A's* capitalists therefore invest their capital in *B*. Trade returns show first the export surplus from *A*, representing the transfer of capital, and later the import surplus representing the return home of dividends. There is no effect on the workers in *A* other than that their wages cease to rise, as they would have if the capital were invested instead at home. If *A's* resources and *B's* resources are exactly the same, wages cannot rise in *A* until capital accumulation in *B* has wiped out *B's* labour surplus.

Now in the real world the resources of two countries are not exactly alike, and it cannot be taken for granted that it will be more profitable to invest in *B* if profits are falling in *A* (which also cannot be taken for granted). The profitability of investing in a country depends upon its natural resources, upon its human material, and upon the amount of capital already invested there.

The most productive investments are those which are made to open up rich, easily accessible natural resources, such as fertile soil, ores, coal or oil. This is the principal reason why most of the capital exported in the last hundred years went to the Americas and to Australasia rather than to India or to China, where the known resources were already being used. In the well developed parts of the world (in the resource sense) the main opportunity for productive investment lies in improving techniques—these countries are well (even over-) developed in the resource sense, but under-developed in their techniques. It is profitable to use capital to introduce new techniques, but this is not as profitable as using capital to make available both new techniques and also new resources. This also explains why the United Kingdom rapidly became a capital exporting country (the limits of its natural resources were soon reached), whereas the United States is very late in reaching this stage, since its natural resources are so extensive that capital investment at home is still very profitable even though wages are very high.

Productivity depends also on the human material. Even though the genetic composition of peoples may be much the same, as far as potential productivity may be concerned, their cultural inheritance is very different. Differences in literacy, forms of government, attitudes to work, and social relations generally may make a big difference to productivity. Capitalists naturally find it more profitable and safer to invest in countries where the atmosphere is capitalist than they do in widely different cultures.

But this is not all. For the productivity of investment in *B* depends not only upon *B's* natural resources and its human institutions, but also upon the efficiency of all other industries whose services the new investment would require to use. This depends partly upon how highly capitalised these other industries are. The productivity of one investment depends upon other investments having been made before. Hence it may be more profitable to invest capital in countries which already have a lot of capital than to invest it in a new country. If this were always so, no capital would be exported, and the gap between wages in the surplus (labour) and non-surplus countries would not diminish but would widen. In practice capital export is small, and the gap does widen, and we cannot at all exclude the possibility that there is a natural tendency for capital to flow towards the capitalised, and to shun the un-capitalised.

If we could assume that there is a natural tendency for the rate of profit to fall in a closed economy, we could say that however low the rate may be in other countries, the rate in the closed economy must ultimately fall towards the level elsewhere, after which capital export must begin. Practically all the best known economists of every school, in every century, have affirmed that such a tendency exists, though their reasons have varied widely. The most notable exception is Marshall, who gave the right answer, which is that increasing capital per head tends to lower the yield of capital, while increasing technical knowledge tends to raise it. Thus, said Marshall, the yield fell from 10 per cent. in the Middle Ages to 3 per cent. in the middle of the eighteenth century—a long period of slow technical growth—after which the decline was arrested by the great increase in opportunities for using capital. This being so, the natural tendency for the yield of capital to fall is nothing but a popular myth. The yield may fall or it may not; we cannot foretell.

We get a different answer, however, if we turn from the rate of profit on capital in general to the rate in particular lines of investment. In any particular line the possibilities of further expansion are soon exhausted, or at any rate greatly reduced. All industries develop on a logistic pattern, growing fairly slowly at first, then rapidly, and later on growing again quite slowly. Hence the investors in any particular line sooner or later come to a point where there is not much more scope for investment in that line at home. It is open to them to put their accumulating profits into quite different industries. But there is also the temptation to stick to the field in which they have specialised knowledge, and to use their profits to take the industry into new countries.

What brings about the exportation of capital is not inevitably falling home profits, or rising wages at home, but simply the fact that [in] foreign countries having different resources unutilised in different degrees there are some profitable opportunities for investment abroad. This is not even dependent on capital accumulation having caught up with surplus labour at home; for even if there is still surplus labour at home, available at subsistence wages, investment opportunities abroad may be more profitable. Many capitalists residing in surplus labour countries invest their capital in England or the United States.

We must therefore beware of saying that a country will begin to export capital as soon as capital accumulation at home catches up with labour supply. All the same, countries do export capital, and we can say that if labour is scarce in those countries, the effect is to reduce the demand for labour in those countries and thus to prevent wages from rising as much as they otherwise would.

13. Let us now assume that the two countries do not compete, but trade with each other. There are two variants of this case. One where the two countries produce only one good, but a different good in each. Here wage levels are not determined in relation to each other. In the second case, each country produces two or more goods, one of which is common to both, and is the good produced in the subsistence sector.

Suppose that in the first case country A produces wheat, and country B produces peanuts. Relative prices are determined solely by supply and demand. Assume that a capitalist sector develops in A, applying new techniques to wheat production. At first it may get unlimited labour at an average wage in wheat related to average subsistence wheat production. In due course, however, the surplus is eliminated and wheat wages start to rise. If the capitalist techniques which fructified wheat production are equally applicable to peanuts, it will pay to export capital to B, where unlimited labour is available at a wage related to average subsistence output of peanuts.

As in the case discussed before, wages in A will be held down by the profitability of investing capital in B. A new element, however enters into consideration, because of the effects of investment on the terms of trade. When capital is being invested in A, and raising the output of wheat, the price of peanuts will rise relatively. Hence the capitalist workers in A as well as subsistence workers in A will be worse off in terms of peanuts, though earning the same real wage in wheat. And the workers in B will be better off in terms of wheat, while earning the same in peanuts. Where capital is invested in B the opposite happens: the terms of trade are moved against the B workers in favour of the A workers.

The moral is that capital export may benefit the workers on balance if it is applied to increasing the supply of things they import. For example, in the Britain of 1850 exclusive investment at home in the cotton industry, while tending to raise wages, might also still more have depressed the terms of trade against the cotton industry.

When we pass to the second case, the result is the same, except that the terms of trade are now determinate. Assume that both countries produce food, but do not trade in it. Country A also produces steel, and country B also produces rubber. If B can release unlimited supplies of labour from subsistence food production, wages in *B* will equal average (not marginal) product in food (abstracting from the difference between subsistence and capitalist wages). In *A* also the wage cannot fall below productivity in the food industry. We may simplify by assuming in the first instance that labour is the sole sector of production and that one day's labour

in *A* produces 3 food or 3 steel

in *B* " 1 food or 1 rubber.

Earnings in *A* will then be three times earnings in *B* (the difference in food productivity). And the rate of exchange will be 1 food = 1 steel = 1 rubber. Suppose now that productivity increases in *B*'s rubber industry only, so that one day's labour produces instead 3 rubber. This is excellent for the workers in *A*, since 1 steel will now buy 3 rubber. But it will do the workers in *B* no good whatsoever (except in so far as they purchase rubber), since their wage will continue to be 1 food. If on the other hand the subsistence economy became more productive, wages would rise correspondingly. Suppose that 1 day's labour in *B* now produced 3 food or 1 rubber, wages would be as high in *B* as in *A*, and the price of rubber would now be 1 rubber = 3 steel. Workers in *A* are benefitted if productivity in *B* increases in what they buy, and are worse off if productivity in *B* increases in *B*'s subsistence sector. Workers in *B* are benefitted only if productivity increases in their subsistence sector; all other increases in productivity are lost in the terms of trade.

We have here the key to the question why tropical produce is so cheap. Take for example the case of sugar. This is an industry in which productivity is extremely high by any biological standard. It is also an industry in which output per acre has about trebled over the course of the last 75 years, a rate of growth of productivity which is unparalleled by any other major industry in the world—certainly not by the wheat industry. Nevertheless workers in the sugar industry continue to walk barefooted and to live in shacks, while workers in wheat enjoy among the highest living standards in the world. The reason is that wages in the sugar industry are related to the fact that the subsistence sectors of tropical economies are able to release however many workers the sugar industry may want, at wages which are low, because tropical food production per head is low. However vastly productive the sugar industry may become, the benefit accrues chiefly to industrial purchasers in the form of lower prices for sugar. (The capitalists who invest in sugar do not come into the argument because their earnings are determined not by productivity in sugar but by the general rate of profit on capital; this is why our leaving capital out of this and subsequent analysis of the effects of changing productivity upon wages and the terms of trade simplifies the analysis without significantly affecting its results.) To raise the price of sugar, you must increase the productivity of the tropical subsistence food economies. Now the contribution of the temperate world to the tropical world, whether in capital or in knowledge, has in the main been confined to the commercial crops for export, where the benefit mainly accrues to the temperate world in lower prices. The prices of tropical commercial crops will always permit only subsistence wages until, for a change, capital and knowledge are put at the disposal of the subsistence producers to increase the productivity of tropical food production for home consumption.

The analysis applies to all tropical commercial products of which an unlimited supply can be produced because unlimited natural resources exist, in relation to demand—*e.g.*, land of suitable quality. It does not apply where natural resources of a particular kind are scarce. For example, the lands suitable for cultivating sugar or peanuts are very extensive. But mineral bearing lands, or lands with just the right suitability for cocoa, are relatively scarce. Hence the price of a mineral, or of cocoa, may rise to any level consistent with demand. If the lands are owned by capitalists, employing workers, this will make little difference to their wages. But if these scarce lands are owned by peasants, the peasants may of course become rich. In general the peasants have got little out of their mineral bearing lands, especially when these have been expropriated by imperial governments (or declared to be Crown property) and sold to foreign capitalists for a song. Cocoa is the only case (a doubtful one) where it seems that a world scarcity of suitable land may now permanently bring to the peasants earnings higher than they could obtain from subsistence food production.

This is not to say that the tropical countries gain *nothing* from having foreign capital invested in commercial production for export. They gain an additional source of employment, and of taxation. The accumulation of fixed capital in their midst also brings nearer the day when the demand for labour will catch up with the supply (though even this will not raise wages in any one tropical country until they start to rise in all, since capital would otherwise merely transfer itself to the countries where there is still a surplus). What they do not gain is rising real wages; the whole benefit of increasing productivity in the commercial sector goes to the foreign consumer, at least in the early stages. In the latest stages they may also gain if their peasants imitate the capitalist techniques, so that subsistence productivity rises; or if the continual increase in the output of commercial crops moves the terms of trade in favour of subsistence food production; either of these changes would react upon real wages (see section 8), but would do so effectively only when the changes have extended throughout the tropical world.

14. In the next case we assume that the two countries can produce the same things, and trade with each other. *A* is the country where labour is scarce, *B* the country where unlimited labour is available in the subsistence (food) sector. Using the classical framework for the Law of Comparative Costs we write that one day's labour

in *A* produces 3 food or 3 cotton manufactures
in *B*   "   2   " or 1   "   "

This, of course, gives the wrong answer to the question "who should specialise in which," since we have written the average instead of the marginal products. We can assume that these coincide in A, and also in cotton manufacture in B. Then we should write, in marginal terms,

in A produces 3 food or 3 cotton manufactures
in B "   0   " or 1   "   "

B should specialise in cotton manufacture and import food. In practice, however, wages will be 2 food in B and between 3 food and 6 food in A, at which levels it will be "cheaper" for B to export food and import cotton.

This divergence between the actual and what it ought to be is the most serious difference which the existence of surplus labour makes to the neo-classical theory of international trade. It has caught out many economists, who have wrongly advised under-developed countries on the basis of current money costs, instead of lifting the veil to see what lies beneath. It has also caught out many countries, which have allowed (or been forced to allow) their industries to be destroyed by cheap foreign imports, with the sole effect of increasing the size of the labour surplus, when the national income would have been increased if the domestic industries had instead been protected against imports. The fault is not that of the Law of Comparative Costs, which remains valid if written in real marginal terms but of those who have forgotten that money costs are entirely misleading in economies where there is surplus labour at the ruling wage.

Of course if labour is a free good but the two industries use some scarce resource, such as land or capital, the comparison has to be made not in terms of labour cost but in terms of the scarce resource. Thus, even though labour is unemployed, it may be more economic to use capital to increase the production of food than to use it in creating new manufacturing industries. Adam Smith was as usual on the ball; this was the substance of his argument that a tariff could not raise the national income even if it increased employment, since it would simply be diverting capital from more to less productive uses. (The Keynesian model doesn't help, since it assumes unlimited capital as well as unemployment.) All the same, there may be cases where it is more economic to use capital to create new industries, rather than to fructify old ones, and where this is nevertheless not the most profitable thing to do, in the financial sense, because labour has to be paid a wage when its marginal productivity is really zero. Moreover, many manufacturing activities do not in fact use any other scarce resource but labour. The handicraft and cottage industries especially, which may provide employment for up to 10 per cent. of the people in backward countries, use no capital resources to speak of. Yet these are the very first industries to be destroyed by cheap imports of manufactures (*e.g.* the havoc wrought to the Indian cotton industry in the first half of the nineteenth century).

The Law of Comparative Costs, rightly applied, enables us to predict the pattern of international trade. We can say that those countries which have inadequate agricultural resources in relation to their populations (*e.g.* India, Japan, Egypt, Great Britain, Jamaica) must live by importing agricultural products and exporting manufactures; metal manufactures if they have the coal and ores (India, Great Britain) and light manufactures if they have not (Japan, Egypt, Jamaica). Correspondingly countries which are rich in agricultural land (U.S.A., Argentina), should be net exporters of agricultural products at relatively good terms of trade. Currently this pattern is distorted by the divergence between money and real costs. But if world population continues to grow at its current rate, this pattern must emerge in due course, unless there are revolutionary developments in agricultural science.

Let us, however continue to examine this case, assuming that no distortion is taking place. As before A is developed while B has surplus labour in food. Suppose that one day's labour

in A produces 5 food or 5 cotton manufactures
in B "   1   "   or 3   "   "   (average)

B ought to specialise in cotton, and will actually do so. Wages and prices are determinate. The wage in B will be 1 food, the price of cotton will be 1 cotton equals $\frac{1}{3}$ food, the wage in A will be 5 food, and A will get all the benefit of the exchange. Suppose now that productivity increases in B's cotton industry. B's wage is unchanged, and the whole benefit accrues to A. But if productivity increases in B's food industry (the average rising say from 1 to 2) B's wage will rise (from 1 food to 2 food). A's wage will still be 5 food, but cotton will now be dearer (1 cotton equals $\frac{2}{3}$ food), to the advantage of B and disadvantage of A. B's wage is determinate because there is unlimited labour available at a subsistence wage; and all the benefit of the exchange goes to A because B is producing both commodities).

15. It is time to say a word about the effect of increasing the subsistence productivity in countries with surplus labour. The analysis is the same as we made for the (section 8), except that we must now think of the world as a whole as the closed economy. We must also think of the commercial sector of these economies as being a part of the world capitalist sector.

Then, if the world capitalist sector is not dependent on the peasants for food, even to feed its plantation and mining labourers in the surplus countries, an increase in the productivity of the peasants must raise wages against the capitalists. To have this effect, however, productivity must rise in all these countries, otherwise the capitalists will simply transfer from those countries where subsistence productivity has risen to those where it has not.

If, on the other hand, we assume that the capitalists need the peasants' food, and that the demand for food is inelastic, then increased productivity reduces the price of food even more, and so reduces the share of capitalist workers in the capitalist product. This again assumes that the changes are world-wide; if one country raises its productivity, the price of food will not fall; wages will rise in that country, and capitalists will move elsewhere. However, even if the price of food falls, the peasants eat most of their output, and will still be better off. For example, suppose a peasant produces 100 food, eats 80 food, and sells 20 food for 20 manufactures. Suppose now that his productivity increases to 200, reducing the price of food by more than half, say to 0.4. The peasant can now have 30 manufactures, costing 75 food, and still eat 125 food instead of 80. The standard of living in the surplus countries is thus raised nearer to that of the advanced countries, but the terms of trade move against both the food and the commercial products of the surplus countries (would move in favour of the commercial products if the elasticity of demand for food were 1.0 or more).

In practice, food production in tropical countries with surplus labour is only a small part of world food production (Asia and Africa together produce less than 20 per cent. of the world's food). Hence increases in food productivity in the tropics could not reduce the price of food *pari passu*. Real wages would therefore rise, and the terms of trade would move in favour of tropical commercial products. This would hurt labour in the industrial countries in so far as it was buying such products, and benefit it in so far as tropical countries were competing in industrial production.

16. This brings us finally to the case where the two countries *A* and *B* produce competing goods to sell in third markets. This need not detain us long. If capital is exported in ways which raise subsistence productivity in the capital importing country, the workers in the capital exporting country will benefit, since the wages of their rivals will be raised. If, however, it is exported to increase productivity in the exporting sector of the capital importing country, the workers in the capital exporting country will be doubly hit, first by the reduced capital accumulation at home, and then again by the fall in their rivals' prices.

17. We may conclude as follows. Capital export tends to reduce wages in capital exporting countries. This is wholly or partly offset if the capital is applied to cheapening the things which the workers import, or to raising wage costs in countries which compete in third markets (by raising productivity in their subsistence sectors). The reduction in wages is however aggravated if the capital is invested in ways which raise the cost of imports (by increasing productivity in subsistence sectors), or which increase the productivity of competing exports. We have also seen that capital importing countries with surplus labour do not gain an increase in real wages from having foreign capital invested in them, unless this capital results in increased productivity in the commodities they produce for their own consumption.

III. Summary

18. We may summarise this article as follows:
   1. In many economies an unlimited supply of labour is available at a subsis-

tence wage. This was the classical model. The neo-classical model (including the Keynesian) when applied to such economies gives erroneous results.

2. The main sources from which workers come as economic development proceeds are subsistence agriculture, casual labour, petty trade, domestic service, wives and daughters in the household, and the increase of population. In most but not all of these sectors, if the country is overpopulated relatively to its natural resources, the marginal productivity of labour is negligible, zero, or even negative.

3. The subsistence wage at which this surplus labour is available for employment may be determined by a conventional view of the minimum required for subsistence; or it may be equal to the average product per man in subsistence agriculture, plus a margin.

4. In such an economy employment expands in a capitalist sector as capital formation occurs.

5. Capital formation and technical progress result not in raising wages, but in raising the share of profits in the national income.

6. The reason why savings are low in an undeveloped economy relatively to national income is not that the people are poor, but that capitalist profits are low relatively to national income. As the capitalist sector expands, profits grow relatively, and an increasing proportion of national income is re-invested.

7. Capital is formed not only out of profits but also out of credit creation. The real cost of capital created by inflation is zero in this model, and this capital is just as useful as what is created in more respectable fashion (*i.e.* out of profits).

8. Inflation for the purpose of getting hold of resources for war may be cumulative; but inflation for the purpose of creating productive capital is self-destructive. Prices rise as the capital is created, and fall again as its output reaches the market.

9. The capitalist sector cannot expand in these ways indefinitely, since capital accumulation can proceed faster than population can grow. When the surplus is exhausted, wages begin to rise above the subsistence level.

10. The country is still, however, surrounded by other countries which have surplus labour. Accordingly as soon as its wages begin to rise, mass immigration and the export of capital operate to check the rise.

11. Mass immigration of unskilled labour might even raise output per head, but its effect would be to keep wages in all countries near the subsistence level of the poorest countries.

12. The export of capital reduces capital formation at home, and so keeps wages down. This is offset if the capital export cheapens the things which workers import, or raises wage costs in competing countries. But it is aggravated if the capital export raises the cost of imports or reduces costs in competing countries.

13. The importation of foreign capital does not raise real wages in countries which have surplus labour, unless the capital results in increased productivity in the commodities which they produce for their own consumption.

14. The main reason why tropical *commercial* produce is so cheap, in terms of the standard of living it affords, is the inefficiency of tropical *food* production per man. Practically all the benefit of increasing efficiency in export industries goes to the foreign consumer; whereas raising efficiency in subsistence food production would automatically make commercial produce dearer.

15. The Law of Comparative Costs is just as valid in countries with surplus labour as it is in others. But whereas in the latter it is a valid foundation of arguments for free trade, in the former it is an equally valid foundation of arguments for protection.

4

W. W. ROSTOW

The Five Stages-of-Growth—
A Summary

It is possible to identify all societies, in their economic dimensions, as lying within one of five categories: the traditional society, the preconditions for take-off, the take-off, the drive to maturity, and the age of high mass-consumption.

The Traditional Society

First, the traditional society. A traditional society is one whose structure is developed within limited production functions, based on pre-Newtonian science and technology, and on pre-Newtonian attitudes towards the physical world. Newton is here used as a symbol for that watershed in history when men came widely to believe that the external world was subject to a few knowable laws, and was systematically capable of productive manipulation.

The conception of the traditional society is, however, in no sense static; and it would not exclude increases in output. Acreage could be expanded; some *ad hoc* technical innovations, often highly productive innovations, could be introduced in trade, industry and agriculture; productivity could rise with, for example, the improvement of irrigation works or the discovery and diffusion of a new crop. But the central fact about the traditional society was that a ceiling existed on the level of attainable output per head. This ceiling resulted from the fact that the potentialities which flow from modern science and technology were either not available or not regularly and systematically applied.

EDITOR'S NOTE: *Another classic, of sorts, though more for its anticommunist propaganda than for its theoretical innovations, Rostow's treatise on (non-Marxian) stages was a cold war propaganda triumph, despite its irrelevance to any positive policy effort to "cure" underdevelopment other than an expressive optimism (on the basis of the "history-repeats-itself" idea) about the eventual outcome of development efforts.*

Both in the longer past and in recent times the story of traditional societies was thus a story of endless change. The area and volume of trade within them and between them fluctuated, for example, with the degree of political and social turbulence, the efficiency of central rule, the upkeep of the roads. Population— and, within limits, the level of life—rose and fell not only with the sequence of the harvests, but with the incidence of war and of plague. Varying degrees of manufacture developed; but, as in agriculture, the level of productivity was limited by the inaccessibility of modern science, its applications, and its frame of mind.

Generally speaking, these societies, because of the limitation on productivity, had to devote a very high proportion of their resources to agriculture; and flowing from the agricultural system there was an hierarchical social structure, with relatively narrow scope—but some scope—for vertical mobility. Family and clan connexions played a large role in social organization. The value system of these societies was generally geared to what might be called a long-run fatalism; that is, the assumption that the range of possibilities open to one's grandchildren would be just about what it had been for one's grandparents. But this long-run fatalism by no means excluded the short-run option that, within a considerable range, it was possible and legitimate for the individual to strive to improve his lot, within his lifetime. In Chinese villages, for example, there was an endless struggle to acquire or to avoid losing land, yielding a situation where land rarely remained within the same family for a century.

Although central political rule—in one form or another—often existed in traditional societies, transcending the relatively self-sufficient regions, the centre of gravity of political power generally lay in the regions, in the hands of those who owned or controlled the land. The landowner maintained fluctuating but usually profound influence over such central political power as existed, backed by its entourage of civil servants and soldiers, imbued with attitudes and controlled by interests transcending the regions.

In terms of history then, with the phrase "traditional society" we are grouping the whole pre-Newtonian world: the dynasties in China; the civilization of the Middle East and the Mediterranean; the world of medieval Europe. And to them we add the post-Newtonian societies which, for a time, remained untouched or unmoved by man's new capability for regularly manipulating his environment to his economic advantage.

To place these infinitely various, changing societies in a single category, on the ground that they all shared a ceiling on the productivity of their economic techniques, is to say very little indeed. But we are, after all, merely clearing the way in order to get at the subject of this book; that is, the post-traditional societies, in which each of the major characteristics of the traditional society was altered in such ways as to permit regular growth: its politics, social structure, and (to a degree) its values, as well as its economy.

The Preconditions for Take-Off

The second stage of growth embraces societies in the process of transition; that is, the period when the preconditions for take-off are developed; for it takes time to transform a traditional society in the ways necessary for it to exploit the fruits of modern science, to fend off diminishing returns, and thus to enjoy the blessings and choices opened up by the march of compound interest.

The preconditions for take-off were initially developed, in a clearly marked way, in Western Europe of the late seventeenth and early eighteenth centuries as the insights of modern science began to be translated into new production functions in both agriculture and industry, in a setting given dynamism by the lateral expansion of world markets and the international competition for them. But all that lies behind the break-up of the Middle Ages is relevant to the creation of the preconditions for take-off in Western Europe. Among the Western European states, Britain, favoured by geography, natural resources, trading possibilities, social and political structure, was the first to develop fully the preconditions for take-off.

The more general case in modern history, however, saw the stage of preconditions arise not endogenously but from some external intrusion by more advanced societies. These invasions—literal or figurative—shocked the traditional society and began or hastened its undoing; but they also set in motion ideas and sentiments which initiated the process by which a modern alternative to the traditional society was constructed out of the old culture.

The idea spreads not merely that economic progress is possible, but that economic progress is a necessary condition for some other purpose, judged to be good: be it national dignity, private profit, the general welfare, or a better life for the children. Education, for some at least, broadens and changes to suit the needs of modern economic activity. New types of enterprising men come forward—in the private economy, in government, or both—willing to mobilize savings and to take risks in pursuit of profit or modernization. Banks and other institutions for mobilizing capital appear. Investment increases, notably in transport, communications, and in raw materials in which other nations may have an economic interest. The scope of commerce, internal and external, widens. And, here and there, modern manufacturing enterprise appears, using the new methods. But all this activity proceeds at a limited pace within an economy and a society still mainly characterized by traditional low-productivity methods, by the old social structure and values, and by the regionally based political institutions that developed in conjunction with them.

In many recent cases, for example, the traditional society persisted side by side with modern economic activities, conducted for limited economic purposes by a colonial or quasi-colonial power.

Although the period of transition—between the traditional society and the take-off—saw major changes in both the economy itself and in the balance of social values, a decisive feature was often political. Politically, the building of an effective centralized national state—on the basis of coalitions touched with a new nationalism, in opposition to the traditional landed regional interests, the colonial power, or both—was a decisive aspect of the preconditions period; and it was, almost universally, a necessary condition for take-off.

There is a great deal more that needs to be said about the preconditions period, but we shall leave it for chapter 3,* where the anatomy of the transition from a traditional to a modern society is examined.

The Take-Off

We come now to the great watershed in the life of modern societies: the third stage in this sequence, the take-off. The take-off is the interval when the old blocks and resistances to steady growth are finally overcome. The forces making for economic progress, which yielded limited bursts and enclaves of modern activity, expand and come to dominate the society. Growth becomes its normal condition. Compound interest becomes built, as it were, into its habits and institutional structure.

In Britain and the well-endowed parts of the world populated substantially from Britain (the United States, Canada, etc.) the proximate stimulus for take-off was mainly (but not wholly) technological. In the more general case, the take-off awaited not only the build-up of social overhead capital and a surge of technological development in industry and agriculture, but also the emergence to political power of a group prepared to regard the modernization of the economy as serious, high-order political business.

During the take-off, the rate of effective investment and savings may rise from, say, 5 per cent of the national income to 10 per cent or more; although where heavy social overhead capital investment was required to create the technical preconditions for take-off the investment rate in the preconditions period could be higher than 5 per cent, as, for example, in Canada before the 1890's and Argentina before 1914. In such cases capital imports usually formed a high proportion of total investment in the preconditions period and sometimes even during the take-off itself, as in Russia and Canada during their pre-1914 railway booms.

During the take-off new industries expand rapidly, yielding profits a large proportion of which are reinvested in new plant; and these new industries, in turn, stimulate, through their rapidly expanding requirement for factory workers, the services to support them, and for other manufactured goods, a further expansion in urban areas and in other modern industrial plants. The whole

---

*Not in this volume. See W. W. Rostow, *The Stages of Economic Growth: A Non-Communist Manifesto* (Cambridge, England: Cambridge University Press, 1960).

process of expansion in the modern sector yields an increase of income in the hands of those who not only save at high rates but place their savings at the disposal of those engaged in modern sector activities. The new class of entrepreneurs expands; and it directs the enlarging flows of investment in the private sector. The economy exploits hitherto unused natural resources and methods of production.

New techniques spread in agriculture as well as industry, as agriculture is commercialized, and increasing numbers of farmers are prepared to accept the new methods and the deep changes they bring to ways of life. The revolutionary changes in agricultural productivity are an essential condition for successful take-off; for modernization of a society increases radically its bill for agricultural products. In a decade or two both the basic structure of the economy and the social and political structure of the society are transformed in such a way that a steady rate of growth can be, thereafter, regularly sustained.

As indicated in chapter 4,* one can approximately allocate the take-off of Britain to the two decades after 1783; France and the United States to the several decades preceding 1860; Germany, the third quarter of the nineteenth century; Japan, the fourth quarter of the nineteenth century; Russia and Canada the quarter-century or so preceding 1914; while during the 1950's India and China have, in quite different ways, launched their respective take-offs.

The Drive to Maturity

After take-off there follows a long interval of sustained if fluctuating progress, as the now regularly growing economy drives to extend modern technology over the whole front of its economic activity. Some 10–20 per cent of the national income is steadily invested, permitting output regularly to outstrip the increase in population. The make-up of the economy changes unceasingly as technique improves, new industries accelerate, older industries level off. The economy finds its place in the international economy: goods formerly imported are produced at home; new import requirements develop, and new export commodities to match them. The society makes such terms as it will with the requirements of modern efficient production, balancing off the new against the older values and institutions, or revising the latter in such ways as to support rather than to retard the growth process.

Some sixty years after take-off begins (say, forty years after the end of take-off) what may be called maturity is generally attained. The economy, focused during the take-off around a relatively narrow complex of industry and technology, has extended its range into more refined and technologically often more

---

*Not in this volume. See W. W. Rostow, op. cit.

complex processes; for example, there may he a shift in focus from the coal, iron, and heavy engineering industries of the railway phase to machine-tools, chemicals, and electrical equipment. This, for example, was the transition through which Germany, Britain, France, and the United States had passed by the end of the nineteenth century or shortly thereafter. But there are other sectoral patterns which have been followed in the sequence from take-off to maturity, which are considered in chapter 5.*

Formally, we can define maturity as the stage in which an economy demonstrates the capacity to move beyond the original industries which powered its take-off and to absorb and to apply efficiently over a very wide range of its resources—if not the whole range—the most advanced fruits of (then) modern technology. This is the stage in which an economy demonstrates that it has the technological and entrepreneurial skills to produce not everything, but anything that it chooses to produce. It may lack (like contemporary Sweden and Switzerland, for example) the raw materials or other supply conditions required to produce a given type of output economically; but its dependence is a matter of economic choice or political priority rather than a technological or institutional necessity.

Historically, it would appear that something like sixty years was required to move a society from the beginning of take-off to maturity. Analytically the explanation for some such interval may lie in the powerful arithmetic of compound interest applied to the capital stock, combined with the broader consequences for a society's ability to absorb modern technology of three successive generations living under a regime where growth is the normal condition. But, clearly, no dogmatism is justified about the exact length of the interval from take-off to maturity.

The Age of High Mass-Consumption

We come now to the age of high mass-consumption, where, in time, the leading sectors shift towards durable consumers' goods and services: a phase from which Americans are beginning to emerge; whose not unequivocal joys Western Europe and Japan are beginning energetically to probe; and with which Soviet society is engaged in an uneasy flirtation.

As societies achieved maturity in the twentieth century two things happened: real income per head rose to a point where a large number of persons gained a command over consumption which transcended basic food, shelter, and clothing; and the structure of the working force changed in ways which increased not only the proportion of urban to total population, but also the proportion of the popula-

---

*Not in this volume. See W. W. Rostow, op. cit.

tion working in offices or in skilled factory jobs—aware of and anxious to acquire the consumption fruits of a mature economy.

In addition to these economic changes, the society ceased to accept the further extension of modern technology as an overriding objective. It is in this post-maturity stage, for example, that, through the political process, Western societies have chosen to allocate increased resources to social welfare and security. The emergence of the welfare state is one manifestation of a society's moving beyond technical maturity; but it is also at this stage that resources tend increasingly to be directed to the production of consumers' durables and to the diffusion of services on a mass basis, if consumers' sovereignty reigns. The sewing-machine, the bicycle, and then the various electric-powered household gadgets were gradually diffused. Historically, however, the decisive element has been the cheap mass automobile with its quite revolutionary effects—social as well as economic—on the life and expectations of society.

For the United States, the turning point was, perhaps, Henry Ford's moving assembly line of 1913–14; but it was in the 1920's, and again in the post-war decade, 1946–56, that this stage of growth was pressed to, virtually, its logical conclusion. In the 1950's Western Europe and Japan appear to have fully entered this phase, accounting substantially for a momentum in their economies quite unexpected in the immediate post-war years. The Soviet Union is technically ready for this stage, and, by every sign, its citizens hunger for it; but Communist leaders face difficult political and social problems of adjustment if this stage is launched.

Beyond Consumption

Beyond, it is impossible to predict, except perhaps to observe that Americans, at least, have behaved in the past decade as if diminishing relative marginal utility sets in, after a point, for durable consumers' goods, and they have chosen, at the margin, larger families—behaviour in the pattern of Buddenbrooks dynamics.* Americans have behaved as if, having been born into a system that provided economic security and high mass-consumption, they placed a lower valuation on acquiring additional increments of real income in the conventional form as opposed to the advantages and values of an enlarged family. But even in this adventure in generalization it is a shade too soon to create—on the basis of one case—a new stage-of-growth, based on babies, in succession to the age of consumers' durables: as economists might say, the income-elasticity of demand for

---

*In Thomas Mann's novel of three generations, the first sought money; the second, born to money, sought social and civic position; the third, born to comfort and family prestige, looked to the life of music. The phrase is designed to suggest, then, the changing aspirations of generations, as they place a low value on what they take for granted and seek new forms of satisfaction.

babies may well vary from society to society. But it is true that the implications of the baby boom along with the not wholly unrelated deficit in social overhead capital are likely to dominate the American economy over the next decade rather than the further diffusion of consumers' durables.

Here then, in an impressionistic rather than an analytic way, are the stages-of-growth which can be distinguished once a traditional society begins its modernization: the transitional period when the preconditions for take-off are created generally in response to the intrusion of a foreign power, converging with certain domestic forces making for modernization; the take-off itself; the sweep into maturity generally taking up the life of about two further generations; and then, finally, if the rise of income has matched the spread of technological virtuosity (which, as we shall see, it need not immediately do) the diversion of the fully mature economy to the provision of durable consumers' goods and services (as well as the welfare state) for its increasingly urban—and then suburban—population. Beyond lies the question of whether or not secular spiritual stagnation will arise, and, if it does, how man might fend it off: a matter considered in chapter 6.*

---

*Not in this volume. See W. W. Rostow, op. cit.

5

A. GERSCHENKRON

Reflections on the Concept of "Prerequisites" of Modern Industrialization

The concept of historical prerequisites of modern industrialization is a rather curious one. Certain major obstacles to industrialization *must* be removed and certain things propitious to it *must* be created before industrialization can begin. Both in its negative and its positive aspects, the concept seems to imply, if not the historical inevitability of industrialization, at least the notion that it must proceed in a certain manner; that is to say, through certain more or less discrete stages. Along with it goes the idea of the uniformity of industrial development in the sense that every industrialization necessarily must be based on the same set of preconditions. What is meant, of course, is not the common-sense notion that in order to start an industrial plant certain very concrete things are needed. The concept refers to long-run historical changes.

It would be easy to reject the concept out of hand as a classic example of historical determinism and to leave it at that. This however, might be regrettable. To be sure, determinism, historical or other, is beyond the boundary line that circumscribes scientific endeavors. It is quite possible that complete knowledge of the world would reveal to us that every event has been inevitably preordained. It may not reveal that at all. How can we know what we would know if we knew? At the same time, however, we cannot approach historical reality except through a search of regularities and deviations from regularities, by conceiving events and sequences of events in terms of constructs of our mind, of patterns, of

EDITOR'S NOTE: *A cautious work by a Russian expatriate economist with memories of the Soviet experience, Gerschenkron's essay leans toward the "Big Spurt" idea as the inevitable pattern in history despite divergences in the causation underlying such dialectical leaps and against the sins of "historicism" (read: Marx and Rostow) prevalent in traditional Eurocentered discourse.*

models. There is an infinite variety of possible models, each one of them subject to change and rejection. And yet, as long as we think in terms of a given model, we are all determinists in the sense that we pose a certain interrelation, or sequence, of events and phenomena which is "inevitable." Within this "denaturalized" meaning all scholarly work is deterministic, except that we remain determinists subject to notice, as it were, in the never-ending process of constructing models and discarding them.

Therefore, it may be quite worthwhile to look more closely into the question of prerequisites of industrial development, however rigid the concept may appear on the face of it. It is precisely the purpose of the following pages to discuss the connotations of the concept and to see whether or not it can be divested of its dogmatic character and perhaps be placed within some broader and less stringent explanatory patterns.

I

Although the concept of prerequisites seems to have rather firm connotations, the individual factors that have been considered prerequisites have been rather loosely defined. Very frequently, a rather curious procedure has been followed. One first takes a look at something like an "ideal type" of preindustrial economy, say, the medieval economy in Western Europe of the fourteenth century, and emphasizes a social framework within which the opportunities for growth were rather restricted. Thereupon, in a cinematographic shift, attention is moved to a modern industrial economy. The change in landscape naturally is striking. The inventory of economic progress is enormous: a large politically and economically unified territory; a legal system assuring the rights of the individual and satisfactory protection for property; a store of technological lore; increase in productivity in agriculture rendered possible by the elimination of the open-field system and distribution of common pastures; availability of labor supply of various skills; an entrepreneurial group willing and able to calculate and to innovate; availability of capital for long-term investment; nonexistence of guild restrictions; wide and absorptive markets; and so forth and so on.

Then, with a slight twist of the pen, all those basic traits of a modern economy are declared to be "prerequisites" of industrial development. This, no doubt, has rather discouraging implications as far as development of backward countries is concerned. Have they really to create all those conditions *before* they can embark upon the process of industrialization? Obviously, some of the factors listed are not prerequisites at all, but rather something that developed in the course of industrial development. Moreover, what can be reasonably regarded as a prerequisite in some historical cases can be much more naturally seen as a product of industrialization in others. The line between what is a precondition of, and what is a response to industrial development seems to be a rather flexible one. It might be possible to indicate some regularities according to which the relevant phenomena might be found on the one or the other side of that line.

As was said before, the idea that there are some fundamental prerequisites of industrial development implies a view of that development characterized both by a high degree of generality and by specific discontinuities. Let us select from the rather hybrid listing of various prerequisites the one of "capital availability" and try, with the help of this example, to discuss at some length the nature, the validity, and the usefulness of the concept.

When availability of capital is turned into a prerequisite it assumes the form of "original accumulation of capital," a concept given currency in Marx's famous Chapter 24 in Volume One of *Das Kapital*. There, Adam Smith's concept of previous accumulation hitched to the period of production of the firm, so matter-of-fact and so short-run, was turned into a magnificent historical generalization. It referred to an accumulation of capital continuing over long historical periods—perhaps over several centuries—until one day the tocsin of the industrial revolution was to summon it to the battlefields of factory construction.

The concept found a considerable resonance in terms of a large body of literature. Perhaps its last faint echo, mainly designed "to amuse the curious," was Keynes's reference to Drake's booty as the fount and origin of England's foreign investment.[1] We are concerned here neither with the specific treatment of the problem by Marx nor with the further discussions and controversies in which Sombart's somewhat grandiloquent and, alas, so thoroughly unsuccessful attempt to "solve the riddle of bourgeois wealth"[2] played such a large part. It matters little that Marx chose to connect his concept so intimately with the early land-enclosing movements in England, to place so much emphasis upon the redistribution of *existing* wealth, and to allow himself to be deflected into the question of preindustrial accumulation of labor. Modern research has cast a good deal of doubt on some of Marx's empirical findings, particularly on his evaluation of the English enclosures in the sixteenth century. The relative significance of the alleged sources of original accumulation—piracy and wars, exploitation of colonies, trade, enclosures, urban rents, influx of precious metals—is rather immaterial for our purpose, except of course for one basic fact: industrial profits could *not* be regarded as a source of original accumulation without negating the very nature of the concept. And this is indeed the problem.

If for the moment we consider original accumulation analytically rather than historically, and try to perceive the pattern of industrial development of which the concept is an integral part, the pertinent question is: why should development proceed in this fashion at all? Why should a long period of capital accumulation *precede* the period of rapid industrialization? Why is not the capital as it is being accumulated also invested in industrial ventures, so that industry grows *pari passu* with the accumulation of capital? To the extent that this happened, Marxian "originality" of accumulation would be reduced to the modest size of Smithian "previousness." In other words, nothing would remain of the specifically Marxian concept. Therefore, if one wishes to defend it one must exclude the contingency of a gradual industrialization and assume that, for one reason or another, industrialization either comes as a big spurt or does not come at all. There must be a certain specific discontinuity about the development which makes it possible to discern with reasonable clarity the beginning of the process.

In the light of the discussions in recent years, it is not difficult to think of conditions which would make for a "rapid spurt or nothing" situation. One can either argue technologically, as it were, from the point of view of the minimum capital needs of an industrializing economy, having in mind the technologically required minimum size of the individual industrial firm and the availability of technologically required inputs which represent outputs of other firms. These considerations of indivisibility *cum* complementarity appear on the supply side and were presented with particular clarity and ingenuity in Dahmén's concept of development blocks.[3] Alternatively, or conjointly, one can argue from the demand side, postulating an industrial development along a broad front as the necessary condition of successful industrialization; the new enterprises created in the process in different branches of the industrial economy sustain their growth by the mutual demand for each other's products. If industrialization comes as a spurt, it must demand considerable capital and is therefore predicated upon the existence of sizable "preindustrial" accumulations of capital. In the spurt these accumulations appear essentially as claims on current output and render possible a deflection of resources from consumption to investment which is sufficiently large to sustain the high rate of industrial growth. This is a rather self-contained view in which the prerequisite and the resulting industrialization are indeed logically connected.

On the other hand, the idea that a conjunction of many different factors is necessary for successful industrialization lies on a somewhat different, though obviously related, plane. It may make sense to say that industrialization cannot begin as long as, say, most of the population is held away from industrial employment by a rigid system of serfdom. The sudden abolition of the institution may indeed adumbrate the beginning of industrial development. Such a beginning may be marked clearly enough. But one could not on the basis of such a reasoning *alone* argue that the capital requirements of such an industrial development will be particularly high. One would have to introduce some additional considerations in order to make this plausible. The abolition of serfdom may have released some latent entrepreneurial talent, some pent-up demand, and the like. But discontinuities of this sort do not stem from the nature of the process of industrialization.

One would look in vain in Marx's discussion for any explicit mention of the fundamental connection between preindustrial accumulation of capital and the subsequent industrialization. Curiously enough, the only explanation provided refers to the abolition of feudal restrictions, that is to say, to a rather incidental circumstance (incidental from the point of view of the concept). But this is of little interest. It cannot be gainsaid that the concept of original accumulation, if properly restated, has a rather modern touch. It testifies to the brilliance of Marx's intuition.

Moreover, the intuition is not just analytical. It is also historical. The more we learn about the nature of the industrialization process in a number of now advanced countries, the greater becomes the assurance with which we can assert that in very many cases the industrial development, after a certain period of preparation, assumed the form of a big spurt, during which for a fairly considerable length of time the development proceeded at an unusually rapid pace. Whether we look at the history of modern industrialism in England, France, Germany, Russia, or Italy, we can discern such upsurges in the growth of industrial output. Actual historical cases cannot, of course, conform with precision to the postulates of an analytical pattern. It is only with a grain of salt that those spurts of industrialization can be regarded as truly "initial." And still, bearing the necessary qualification in mind, it does make sense to say that most of the important industrializations in Europe started in the form of more or less violent industrial revolutions.

Perhaps a few words on that controversial term may be in order. The concept of the Industrial Revolution in England has been frequently criticized. What happened was very much in the nature of what Huizinga once called "inflation of historical concepts." Just as the concept of the Renaissance, originally securely anchored in the sixteenth century, was torn away from its moorings and allowed to drift backward into the preceding centuries, so also the start of the Industrial Revolution began to be shifted from the eighteenth to the seventeenth century, and further on into still earlier periods, the original meaning melting away in the process. All this was done in veneration of historical continuity which was, and perhaps still is, a fashionable concept with some writers. Now, historical continuity is used rather confusedly in at least three different senses. Continuity may mean that the historical roots of a given phenomenon reach very far back into the past. That, of course, is indubitably true as a general proposition and is, in fact, the basic justification of all historical work. Yet it says little about the actual course of historical processes, in particular whether such a course is revolutionary or evolutionary. To give an example from political history: Peter Struve, the great Russian economic historian, once remarked that the Russian political revolutions of this century occurred *because* Empress Anne, in 1730, had torn to shreds the draft of a constitution presented to her for signature by members of the high aristocracy.[4] This view may or may not be valid, but, assuming for a moment that it is, the fact that the roots of an event must be sought in a remote past does not necessarily make it evolutionary. As revolutions go, the Russian revolutions of 1905 and 1917 were revolutionary indeed. At the same time, continuity is used to indicate periodic recurrence of events on a broad historical scale. It is in this sense that one—again rightly or wrongly—operates with concepts like neomercantilism, particularly when, as in the case of Lipson,[5] it connotes the return to the "normalcy of planning," a fulfillment of a natural pattern in the course of which the wind returneth according to its circuits. Finally, continuity is also made to imply a very gradual change, the degree of which is hardly perceptible, in the sense of the motto, *natura non facit saltus*, Alfred Marshall chose for his *Principles*. Now, one may abhor revolutions and any rapid change; alternatively, one may find history without revolutions insufferably dull. The problem, however, is not one of personal likes and dislikes. Nor is it simply one of ascertaining the correct facts. In a sense, speed and changes in speed are arbitrary concepts. To the extent that we deal with measurable phenomena, they depend on the specific averaging techniques used in determining the rate of speed and acceleration. They depend on the length of the period chosen. These choices in turn must depend on the requirements of the problems under study. What is a revolution for one purpose may be seen as a very gradual change in another. A concept is as good as what can be discovered with its help. If by "revolution" we understand in the first instance nothing more than a sudden upward change in the rate of growth of industrial output and if, in addition, such accelerations in speed as we do ascertain can be regarded as an independent factor in the process of growth because important characteristics in the process of industrialization tend to vary significantly with changes in speed, then economic historians can ill afford to ignore the existence of industrial revolutions. And indeed the revolutions which stare out at the historian from many of the long-term indices of industrial output in Western Europe cannot be ignored precisely because so many important factors of industrial development are so peculiarly correlated with those big spurts of early industrialization.

So far so good. But perhaps not good enough as far as the concept of original accumulation is concerned. True, the existence of initial periods of rapid growth *prima facie* speaks in favor of the concept. If no such periods were ascertainable, the concept could have been dismissed out of hand. As it is, further discussion is in order. There is still the question of whether in actual fact original accumulation can be considered as having materially aided the countries concerned during the period of their rapid industrial growth.

II

Before we touch on this crucial aspect of the problem, a few specific difficulties with the concept of original accumulation might be briefly mentioned. Also, this concept has been subject to "inflation," the beginnings of the process being shifted farther and farther back to the very start of the modern era and, with some writers, even farther back to the high noon of the Middle Ages.

A good deal of historical material assembled in support of the concept actually purports to show that in some earlier historical periods some people managed to become quite wealthy. But over long historical periods wealth is not only created but also destroyed. The Fuggers had acquired an amount of wealth that was unprecedented in the history of Europe. That wealth was largely acquired through connections with political powers but it was also destroyed by these connections. The South German wealth accumulated at the turn of the fifteenth and sixteenth centuries had written an important page in the story of European economic development. Export of technology and of modes of business organization from South Germany fertilized far-away areas. Those activities broke the period of deflationary pressures that had greatly contributed to the economic stagnation of Europe in the preceding period. But all this hardly fits any reasonably understood concept of original accumulation. The wealth of the Fuggers, dissipated in power politics and war finance, went up in the smoke of innumerable battlefields and was given the *coup de grâce* in the Spanish bankruptcies.

If we could assume for a rash moment that Sombart was right in his theory of urban rents as a source of medieval wealth, one still would have to ask: "What of it?" There would be still an obligation to follow through the history of that wealth up till the time of the great upsurge of German industrialization in the second half of the nineteenth century. Naturally, no one has attempted to do that, and one may be right in supposing that we know what the answer would be without too much investigating. In other words, the concept of original accumulation is not just a magnificent generalization; it is *too* magnificent a generalization, in the sense that in order to accept it one has to make abstraction from equally magnificent details, such as the economic impact of the Thirty Years' War upon Germany.

It is extremely doubtful, therefore, whether thinking in terms of very long historical periods of preparation for the industrial spurt makes good historical sense. On the other hand, when the period of original accumulation is foreshortened and reduced to a less extravagant length, other difficulties remain. It is easy to say that a wealthy country will find it easier to launch the period of rapid industrialization. As an abstract statement such a proposition is unexceptionable. In historical reality, however, simple availability of wealth will be helpful for industrialization only if it is assembled in the hands of the people who either will be willing to invest it in industrial ventures themselves or, alternatively, are willing and able to pass it on in one form or another to those who are immediately engaged in industrialization. In any case, it must be wealth in a form which either directly or through some financial transformation is capable of being so passed on. One can think of many historical cases where wealth, even though potentially available and available in an appropriate form, will not in fact reach the industrial entrepreneurs. An inveterate tradition of hoarding may constitute an effective barrier. Apprehensions on the part of the landowning classes lest industrial development deprive them of their position of pre-eminence within the community may have similar effects. Merchants who have a good deal of liquid capital at their disposal may be quite unwilling to make their capital available for industrial ventures because such ventures would disrupt the putting-out system in which they may have direct and important interests. In short, there is no assurance at all that previously accumulated wealth will in fact be made available for industrial investment finance.

The problem, however, is not so much that "original accumulation" must be further qualified before it can serve as a historical prerequisite of modern industrialization. It is rather to find out under what special conditions the concept, even when duly qualified and deprived of its original magnificence, can be regarded as a true prerequisite of industrial development, and under what conditions it may be difficult, impossible, or unnecessary to attribute a great deal of significance to it. With this question we approach the second previously mentioned implication in the concept of prerequisites of industrial development: namely, the assumption of a uniform process of industrialization evolving in such a way that the industrialization, when it occurs anywhere on the globe, repeats in all essential characteristics a process of industrialization that had taken place previously in some other country or region. It would seem that such an assumption leads to a much too simplified view of industrial processes in general, and particularly in their initial phases.

This, of course, is not to raise once more the specter of the "unique and individual" in history. Enough has been said before to suggest that the point is not to reject broad patterns as such, but to select patterns appropriate to the problem. Moreover, up to a point, a uniform pattern of industrial development is quite reasonable. Industrialization everywhere means increase in the volume of fixed capital; it means changes in technology, economies of scale, transformation of agricultural laborers and small artisans into factory workers; it means appearance of men, willing and able to exercise the entrepreneurial function.

Time and again the industrial development of Europe has been described in terms of a general pattern constructed upon the empirical material gleaned from English economic history. Such an approach is not without merit. Precisely because there are common features in all industrializations, it possessed and still possesses some explanatory and even predictive value. To concentrate upon these general aspects of industrialization may be quite useful for some purposes. But it is equally true, as always when the level of generality is pitched very high, that as one moves deeper and deeper into the subject one is bound to come across things in one area or another that do not fit the general model. When that happens, the historian, after he has refused to ignore the uncomfortable irregularities, is faced with two alternatives. He may regard those things as exceptions and treat them as such. Or else he can attempt to systematize the deviations from the original pattern by bringing them into a new, although necessarily more complicated, pattern. This is not something peculiar to economic history; rather, it is the path along which all scientific progress must move. Perhaps the historian who deals with broad and important phenomena has reason to be particularly aware of the problem and to remember that in principle every historical event that takes place changes the course of all subsequent events. The Industrial

Revolution in England, and for that matter in other countries, affected the course of all subsequent industrializations.

This writer has felt for some time that some additional insights and a more profound understanding of the processes of European industrializations can be obtained if, instead of working with an undifferentiated uniform pattern of industrialization, one would consider the processes of industrial development in relation to the degree of backwardness of the areas concerned on the eve of their great spurts of industrialization. Such a view has distinct advantages in as much as it makes it possible to regard crucial features in the industrial evolution of the individual areas not as specific peculiarities, idiosyncrasies, or exceptions to the norm, but as part and parcel of a system of gradations of backwardness. Such a view has a direct bearing on the question of preindustrial accumulation and the problem of prerequisites of industrial development in general.

It is not necessary to present here more than the briefest possible outline of this general conception, and the reader may find a fuller treatment elsewhere. But two relevant points may precede such a summary. The question as to what is "an intelligible area of study" is faced in any attempt at interpretive history. Intelligibility, of course, must be defined in terms of the problem at hand. Simon Kuznets once detailed the reasons for which a country, taken as a political unit, should be regarded as a basic area of observation in studies of economic development. He referred to the fact that neither the subdivisions within the country nor blocs of several countries constituted more significant units; he mentioned that data are usually available in terms of "states," and he clinched his argument by saying that a country presented a compact "bundle of historical experience." All this is indubitably correct.

Yet it is equally true that one cannot understand the industrial development of any country, as long as it be considered in isolation. Backwardness, of course, is a relative term. It presupposes the existence of more advanced countries. Moreover, it is only by comparing industrialization processes in several countries at various levels of backwardness that one can hope to separate what is accidental in a given industrial evolution from what can be reasonably attributed to the historical lags in a country's development. And, finally, it is only because a backward country is part of a larger area which comprises more advanced countries that the historical lags are likely to be overcome in a specifically intelligible fashion.

The other point refers to the measurability of backwardness. Is it an operational term? If the levels of output or income per capita of the population could be regarded as a satisfactory measure of backwardness, one would not be too far away from a satisfactory solution. In fact, one would be just as far away as the availability and quality of the data *and* the index-number problem would allow. Even so, serious problems of measurement must be encountered. Projecting outputs of different countries against the screen of the price system of one given country may lead to a widely different ranking of countries as compared with the ranking that would result from the use of the price system of another country. In practice, only the price system of the most advanced country in the group could be chosen because of the more limited range of output and accordingly of available price data in a more backward country.

But can a definition in terms of per-capita output suffice? Obviously, the level of per-capita output may be the result of unfavorable climatic conditions or of poor endowment with natural resources. While not impossible, it would be hazardous indeed to weigh the output data by the reciprocals of resource endowment and climatic propitiousness. Moreover, such conditions which make for high or low output in a preindustrial branch of the economy may, within limits, become more or less relevant after the big structural change has been ushered in and the industrialization launched.

Finally, it is not clear that output, however measured, is a fully satisfactory gauge of the degree of backwardness. One might want to define the degree of backwardness in more dynamic terms. And that would involve asking to what degree a country at a certain moment had developed the preconditions for subsequent economic development. Assume a country A where, say, per-capita output and resource endowment are equal to those of country B, but in the latter country a much larger percentage of the active population is illiterate, thus creating an obstacle to a rapid acquisition of industrial skills; or assume that in country B, for religious reasons, the people consider urban ways of life displeasing to the Lord and are deeply rooted in the soil, while such sentiments are quite alien to the inhabitants of country A, where there is a great and widespread willingness to respond to the call of pecuniary incentives. Would it not make good sense to include such factors, and many others of similar importance and bearing, in the concept of degree of backwardness? Obviously, this would be a hopeless enterprise. There is no precise system of weights by virtue of which disparate factors could be brought together over a common denominator; nor could we possibly determine the precise quantities of the pertinent factors to which those weights could be applied. One has to conclude, however reluctantly, that "degree of backwardness" defies exact measurement. But just how discouraging is a conclusion of this nature? It is important to have drawn it to prevent misleading notions and false hopes. On the other hand, it is far from clear that a high degree of precision is required for the purposes of historical analysis.

The purpose of such analysis is to associate certain differences in the historical process with the absence or presence of certain features in the economies concerned. If the cases with which we have to deal are sufficiently discrete and if, in addition, the individual factors on the whole tend to point in the same direction, then we may hope, without aspiring to any exact measurement, to be able to wield our material in such a fashion as to glean from it some meaningful and not altogether unimportant answers. And, indeed, as we look upon the economic scenery of nineteenth-century Europe, riveting our attention, say, to the midpoint of that century, few would disagree that Germany was more backward economically than France; that Austria was more backward than Germany; that Italy was more backward than Austria; and that Russia was more backward than any of the countries just mentioned. Similarly, few would deny England the position of the most advanced country of the time. Whether we think of levels of output, the degree of technological progress achieved, the skill of the population, the degree of its literacy, the standards of honesty and the time horizon of the entrepreneurs, or a number of other similar factors, we get roughly identical answers. In practice, we *can* rank the countries according to their backwardness and even discern groups of similar degree of backwardness.

The main proposition we can then make with regard to countries so ranked is that, the more delayed the industrial development of a country, the more explosive was the great spurt of its industrialization, if and when it came. Moreover, the higher degree of backwardness was associated with a stronger tendency toward larger scale of plant and enterprise and greater readiness to enter into monopolistic compacts of various degrees of intensity. Finally, the more backward a country, the more likely its industrialization was to proceed under some organized direction; depending on the degree of backwardness, the seat of such direction could be found in investment banks, in investment banks acting under the aegis of the state, or in bureaucratic controls. So viewed, the industrial history of Europe appears not as a series of mere repetitions of the "first" industrialization but as an orderly system of graduated deviations from that industrialization.

III

To return at length to the main problem of this essay, we may ask what happens to the concept of uniform prerequisites of industrial development in a world that is far from being uniform. In particular, what happens to the concept of preindustrial accumulation of capital? We have seen that what makes preindustrial accumulation of capital potentially meaningful is the discontinuity of industrial development. We have suggested that, the higher the degree of backwardness, the more discontinuous the development is likely to be. Does this mean that, the more backward a country, the more important was the previously accumulated wealth? Could this conclusion be further strengthened if one considers that in nineteenth-century Europe the capital-output ratios tended upward and, accordingly, the later a country industrialized, the higher was the rate of growth during its big upsurge of industrialization and the greater were its capital requirements per one percent of increase in output?

There is little doubt that in reality the opposite seems to have taken place. The building of factories in England no doubt benefited considerably from the existence of manifold sources of private wealth. One of the characteristics of the English development was that, in conditions of considerable antecedent progress, there was much willingness on the part of individuals to invest in industrial pursuits. But, in the more backward countries on the European continent, neither the size of previous accumulations nor the sympathy with industrial development was consonant with the much greater capital requirements of a delayed industrialization. The focal role in capital provision in a country like Germany must be assigned not to any original capital accumulation but to the role of credit-creation policies on the part of the banking system. It is true that the banks also collected and passed on to entrepreneurs both current savings and some previously created assets that could be converted into claims on current output, but this is much less significant.

When one moves on to even more backward areas where the spurts of industrialization were even more delayed and even more violent, such as Russia in the last decade of the century, one again would find it difficult to attribute a crucial role to any preindustrial accumulations of capital. There it was the budgetary policies of the state that must be considered as the strategic factor in capital supply. This is not to say that this was the only available source. Capital imports were considerable. Preindustrial wealth played some part. Plowed-back profits could not be denied all importance even in the early stages of the process. Much remains to be done in the study of capital formation in Russia in the nineteenth century. But this much seems clear: all the other sources do tend to pale into insignificance compared with the role of budgetary finance of the new and growing industrial enterprises. If a somewhat sweeping expression is permissible, one might say that original accumulation of capital was not a prerequisite of industrial development in major countries on the European continent.

It would appear, therefore, that not very much has remained of the concept of original accumulation of capital. First, it had to be reduced temporally by limiting the length of the periods to which it could be reasonably applied. Then, it had to be further reduced, this time spatially. One might want to conclude that there is no general set of prerequisites valid for all times and climes and that each case must be studied independently. Yet it would be unfortunate if this negative conclusion were taken as a renunciation of a comparative approach to the problem. The framework which has been sketched out in the preceding paragraphs would seem to open up different possibilities. As has been intimated before, one way of defining the degree of backwardness is precisely in terms of absence, in a more backward country, of factors which in a more advanced country served as prerequisites of industrial development. Accordingly, one of the ways of approaching the problem is by asking what substitutions and what patterns of substitutions for the lacking factors occurred in the process of industrialization in conditions of backwardness.

One thing is obvious. Illiteracy and low standards of education, and the resulting difficulty in training skilled labor and efficient engineers, can be overcome to some extent by immigration from more advanced countries and to some extent by using the training facilities of those countries. The same is true, even more importantly, of the lack of a store of technical knowledge. It can be imported from abroad. In this sense, however, one can say that in a backward country there exists a "prerequisite" to industrial development which "the" advanced country did not have at its disposal, that is, the existence of the more advanced countries as sources of technical assistance, skilled labor, and capital goods. In addition, the existence of capital-abundant areas abroad has a bearing on the problem of original accumulation. To the extent that capital can be imported from abroad, the importance of previously created domestic wealth is *pro tanto* reduced. It is true, however, that the *tantum* never was excessively large. Even in Russia of the 1890s, according to this writer's computations, capital imports constituted but a relatively small portion of total capital made available for the purposes of industrialization; this is true even if very low capital-output ratios are assumed for calculating total capital formation during the period. On the other hand, capital import, unlike transformation of previously created wealth into titles on current output, implies the possibility to invest without lowering the rate of current consumption; similarly, the opportunities for imports of capital goods from abroad, if they are financed by such previous accumulations of bullion and plate as may exist in the backward country, also avoid reduction in levels of consumption. That is something which neither the credit-creating policies of banks nor the government policies of tax-financed expenditures can achieve. It is another question that a government engaged in the policy of vigorous industrialization, as was the Russian government in the 1890s, was in a position to tap otherwise inaccessible founts of credit.

Considerations of this sort, however, do not begin to exhaust the range of possible substitution patterns. The question as to why industrialization occurred under the aegis of the banks in the moderately backward areas in Central Europe and under that of the state in the more backward areas farther east can at least partly be answered in terms of absence or presence of certain prerequisites. What effectively prevented banks from engaging in industrial investment in Russia of the nineteenth century was *inter alia* the impossibility of building up an effective system of long-term bank credit in a country where the standards of commercial honesty had been so low and where economic, and particularly mercantile, activities and deceit were regarded as inseparably connected. "He who does not cheat does not sell," taught the economic wisdom of the folklore. Well-staged and repeated bankruptcies were regarded as almost normal steps on the road to wealth. In these circumstances, the government even felt impelled to issue specific injunctions against involvement of banks in long-term credit operations.

In a sense, in Russia the activities of the government effectively substituted for the lacking prerequisite of minimum acceptable standards of commercial honesty. The existence of the prerequisite in Central Europe made possible a different, much more decentralized type of industrialization finance. But one could go further and inquire into the reasons of the differences in standards of commercial honesty in, say, Germany and Russia. To be sure, many an answer to such a question could be found. For instance, the badly delayed emancipation of the Russian peasantry must have had a good deal to do with it. The institution of labor services bred mendacity and deception. The serf-entrepreneurs had many excellent reasons to deceive their owners. The legal uncertainty with regard to peasants' property rights was hardly designed to educate the mass of the population in the spirit of respect for contractual obligations. Yet probably no less important was the absence in Russia of a tradition of urban independence. A sociology of economic honesty still remains to be written, but there is little doubt that over large areas of Europe the historical experience of the craft guilds, with their attempts to increase and to maintain standards of quality and reliability, was of considerable importance in forming the business ethics of the community. One could argue, therefore, that in a country like Germany it was the historical training school of the craft guilds that served as a prerequisite to industrial development by making it possible to substitute the prerequisite of original accumulation by the more efficient banking policies rather than by the less efficient and more costly bureaucratic controls. When in the seventeenth century a keen foreign observer, Yuri Krizhanich, cogitated on the ways and means to reform the sloth and dishonesty of the Russian artisans and traders, the introduction of craft guilds suggested itself to his mind as the most natural remedy.[6] An attempt to create the guilds by government fiat, as was later tried by Peter the Great, could not yield the same positive results as did their spontaneous evolution in Western Europe. One might say, then, that in Russia the government's policies of industrialization also had to function as a substitute for the missing prerequisite of craft-guild experience.

To give another example: cause and effect are usually intermingled in the discussion of the relationship between the enclosure movement and the industrial progress in England. But it is clear that the latter was materially aided by the growth of productivity in English agriculture that took place during the eighteenth century. But here again government action may be regarded as a substitute, however unpleasant, for the prerequisite of increases in food supplies. To be sure, the transformation of virgin steppes in the south of Russia into arable [land] widened the food basis somewhat. Still, the period of the rapid industrial spurt in Russia in the last decade of the century occurred in conditions of a grave crisis in agriculture. To some extent, the crisis was caused by the fact that industrialization was financed, and, among other things, food supplies to the cities and for export were made available, through confiscation of peasant income and to some extent even through capital depletion. It is true, of course, that all such processes were later dwarfed by the agrarian policies of the Soviet government and its incomparably more ruthless exploitation of the Russian peasantry. Yet the Soviet case is a very peculiar one, and for many reasons prerevolutionary Russia seems to provide a much more "normal" case for a discussion of specific patterns of substitution in the process of industrialization.

Along with increases in food supplies, the increase in supply of labor for the needs of the nascent industries is usually mentioned as the factor which imparts to agrarian reforms the character of a prerequisite. The deliberate preservation and even strengthening of the Russian village commune through the emancipation procedure of the 1860s and several subsequent measures certainly tended to inhibit the formation of an industrial labor force in Russia. Permanent renunciation of the right to land allotment involved considerable financial losses; a member of the village commune working in cities was subject to recall to the village; for decades, departures for work in towns required permissive action on the part of village authorities and family heads. All these were serious impediments to a movement which in any circumstances had to overcome a good deal of ingrained reluctance and inertia.

The finality which attended the move of a landless laborer from the East Elbian estates to the Ruhr Valley was more seldom reproduced in Russia. As a result, a labor force permanently committed to the factory increased much more slowly than might have been the case otherwise. But, to some extent, this deficiency was substituted for by specific entrepreneurial decisions with regard to the volume and character of capital investment in Russian factories. The difficulties in creating a reliable and steady labor force were at least partly compensated for by a choice of more labor-saving equipment in a number of industrial branches. At the same time, in other branches of industry the large labor-force turnover was met by the introduction of more modern machinery, simpler in operation, for which the necessary learning time was shorter and therefore more reasonably related to the prospective duration of employment. In this way, what might be called the basic propensity of a backward country to concentrate on the areas of most recent technological progress, and thus to utilize a specific advantage of backwardness, was further intensified.

IV

It has not been the purpose of the foregoing pages to present more than a few examples; nor has it been intended to qualify and elaborate the relationships touched upon. The purpose rather has been to point out the great elasticity and variability in the industrialization processes that are known from historical experience. It would seem that the lack of something that might be regarded as a *general* set of prerequisites of industrial development does not necessarily diminish the heuristic value of the concept of prerequisites. It is precisely by starting from that concept and by trying to understand how a given country managed to start its process of industrialization despite the lack of certain prerequisites that one can arrive at some differentiated and still coordinated view of industrialization in conditions of graduated backwardness. As we look at the later stages of the process, we find that what may have functioned as a prerequisite and, in a sense, as a "cause" of industrialization in one country appears as an effect of industrialization in another. This serves to reinforce and to complete the present approach to industrial development. This process of a belated "normalization" of the development is also likely to be understood more clearly if it is related to the degree of backwardness of the areas concerned.

On the other hand, there is, of course, no intention to infer that absence of certain "prerequisites" should be regarded in any way as "advantages of backwardness." It is largely the existence of such advantages that makes it possible to overcome the lack of preconditions for economic progress. But the process as a rule was a costly one. It would be a fruitful undertaking in research to explore and perhaps to measure and compare the difficulties, the strains, and the cost which were involved in the various processes of substitution which have been discussed in the preceding pages. The sovereign disregard for the human cost of such substitutions has been perhaps the most characteristic feature of Soviet industrialization over some three decades.

At the same time, however, it may be in order to suggest that past historical experience may justify a measure of optimism with regard to the general prospects of industrialization of backward countries. What is meant is not simply that past industrializations occurred in the face of considerable obstacles and deficiencies. In viewing the historical record one cannot fail to be impressed with the ingenuity, originality, and flexibility with which backward countries tried to solve the specific problems of their industrial development. There is no *a priori* reason to suppose that the underdeveloped countries which today stand on the threshold of their industrial revolutions will show less creative adaptation in compensating for the absence of factors which in more fortunate countries may be said to have "preconditioned" the initial spurts of rapid industrial growth. One can only hope that in drafting the maps of their own industrial progress they will be eager to select those paths along which they will be able to keep down the cost and to increase the yield in terms of human welfare and human happiness.

Notes

1. John M. Keynes, *A Treatise on Money* (London, 1930), II, 156–157.
2. Werner Sombart, *Der moderne Kapitalismus: Die vorkapitalische Wirtschaft* (Munich-Leipzig, 1928), I:2, 581f.
3. Erik Dahmén, *Svensk industriell företagarversksamhet* (Stockholm, 1950), I, 70.
4. *Sotsial'naya i ekonomicheskaya istoriya Rossii* (Social and Economic History of Russia) (Paris, 1952), p. 314.
5. E. Lipson, *A Planned Economy or Free Enterprise* (London, 1946).
6. *Russkoye gosudarstvo v polovine XVII veka* (The Russian State in the Middle of the Seventeenth Century) (Moscow, 1859), pp. 28f.

Part II

Early Critical Challenges

6

P. BARAN

On the Roots of Backwardness

We have been concerned thus far with highly developed capitalist societies over-flowing with economic surplus and incapable of its rational utilization. They represent, however, only one aspect of the general landscape of contemporary capitalism. Its other and no less significant component is the large segment of the "free world" that is usually referred to as underdeveloped. Just as the advanced sector includes a multitude of areas as far apart in economic, social, political, and cultural characteristics as the United States and Japan, Germany and France, Britain and Switzerland, so the underdeveloped sector is composed of a wide variety of countries with tremendous differences between them. Nigeria and Greece, Brazil and Thailand, Egypt and Spain all belong in the group of the backward areas.

Nevertheless in attempting to comprehend the laws of motion of both the advanced and the backward parts of the capitalist world, it is possible, and indeed mandatory, to abstract from the peculiarities of the individual cases and to con-centrate on their essential common characteristics. In fact, no scientific world is conceivable if this method is not to be applied; and whether it be Marx's "pure capitalism," Marshall's "representative firm," or Weber's "ideal type," abstrac-tion from the secondary attributes of a phenomenon and concentration on its basic scaffolding have always been the primary tools of all analytical effort.[1] That the resulting "model" of whatever happens to be studied does not do full justice to any particular case, does not adequately accommodate all its peculiarities and specifications, matters very little, and does not represent a valid censure of the method itself or of its immediate results. If the model lives up to its aim, if it

EDITOR'S NOTE: *In this neo-Marxist classic Baran, a great Third World partisan, reversed classical Marxian ideas about the civilizing mission of European capitalism in the periph-ery by pointing out the great reverse flow of resources that made the Western industrial triumph possible (deemed the "surplus drain" hypothesis in the literature), thus carrying forward Lenin's theory of imperialism.*

succeeds in capturing the dominant features of the real process, it will contribute more to its understanding than any quantity of detailed information, any amount of particular data. What is more, it is only with the help of such a model, only with the contours of the "ideal type" clearly in mind, that meaning can be attached to all the information and data continually assembled by organized research that more frequently serve as a substitute for insight than as an aid to it.

The relevance of this to the study of the conditions prevailing in the underdeveloped countries and to the comprehension of the problems confronting them was recognized in a recent United Nations report: ". . . while it may be true that no two countries face identical difficulties in their industrialization process, it is also true that countries at a similar developmental stage face difficulties of much the same kind and, being subjected to much the same economic forces, often find themselves in very similar situations."[2] Thus in what follows no attempt is made to present a photographic picture of any *particular* underdeveloped capitalist country nor to analyze the obstacles to industrialization under capitalism existing in *specific* geographic areas. It is rather the purpose of this . . . [chapter] to identify what I consider to be the essential elements of the matter, and to assemble as it were the bare skeleton of the issue—without concern for the concrete setting and form in which it may appear in any individual case.

With this reservation in mind we may proceed *in medias res*. What characterizes all underdeveloped countries, indeed what accounts for their designation as underdeveloped, is the paucity of their per capita output. Although international comparisons of national income estimates are beset by a host of well-known difficulties, a notion of the situation existing in underdeveloped countries is adequately conveyed by the following table:

World Income Distribution in 1949[3]

	World income (percent)	World population (percent)	Income Per capita
High-income countries	67	18	$915
Middle-income countries	18	15	310
Low-income countries	15	67	54

It can be seen that approximately two-thirds of the human race have an average per capita income equivalent to some 50 to 60 dollars a year; it needs no explanation that for nearly all areas to which this statistic applies it signifies chronic starvation, abysmal squalor, and rampant disease. Nor has there been any appreciable change in this condition for a century or two; in some underdeveloped countries matters may even have deteriorated in the course of the last hundred years. Since during this period living standards in the advanced countries have markedly improved, "the distribution of per capita income among the countries of the world has grown less rather than more equal."[4]

The question that immediately arises is, why is it that in the backward capitalist countries there has been no advance along the lines of capitalist development that are familiar from the history of other capitalist countries, and why is it that forward movement there has been either slow or altogether absent? A correct answer to this question is of foremost importance. It is indeed indispensable if one is to grasp what at the present time stands in the way of economic and social progress in underdeveloped countries, and if one is to understand the direction and the form which their future development is likely to assume.

The problem may best be approached by recalling the conditions from which capitalism evolved in both the now advanced and the now underdeveloped part of the world. These were everywhere a mode of production and a social and political order that are conveniently summarized under the name feudalism. Not that the structure of feudalism was everywhere the same. Quite on the contrary, just as "one would be right in talking, not of a single history of capitalism, and of the general shape which this has, but of a collection of histories of capitalism, all of them having a general similarity of shape, but each of them separately dated as regards its main stages,"[5] so one has to bear in mind the tremendous difference between the histories of the feudal systems in different parts of the world. Indeed, the far-reaching divergences between the pre-capitalist structure of China, the society founded upon the village communities of India, and the social order rooted in serfdom that was characteristic of much of the pre-capitalist development of Europe have led many historians to doubt the general applicability of the term "feudalism." Without having to enter this debate, we may confine ourselves to a proposition on which there would seem to be fairly wide consensus: that the pre-capitalist order, be it in Europe or be it in Asia, had entered at a certain state of its development a period of disintegration and decay. In different countries this decomposition was more or less violent, the period of decline was shorter or longer—the general *direction* of the movement was everywhere the same. At the risk of extreme oversimplification the following distinct, if closely interrelated, processes may be considered to have been its salient features. First, there was a slow but nevertheless appreciable increase in agricultural output accompanied by intensified feudal pressure upon the underlying agricultural population as well as ever more massive displacement and rebellion of peasants and consequently emergence of a potential industrial labor force. Secondly, there was a more or less far-reaching and more or less general propagation of division of labor and with it the evolution of the class of merchants and artisans accompanied by the growth of towns. And thirdly there was a more or less spectacular accumulation of capital in the hands of the more or less steadily expanding and rising class of merchants and wealthy peasants.

It is the confluence of all these processes (and of a number of other secondary developments) that forms the indispensable precondition for the emergence of capitalism. In the words of Marx, "what enables money wealth to become capital is on one hand its meeting with free workers; is secondly its meeting with equally free and available for sale means of subsistence, materials etc. that were otherwise d'une manière ou d'une autre the property of the now dispossessed masses."[6] Yet it is the third—the primary accumulation of capital—to which, as the term "capitalism" clearly suggests, strategic significance must undoubtedly be assigned. To be sure, the mere accumulation of merchant capital does not per se lead to the development of capitalism.[7] What warrants nonetheless its being singled out for particular attention are two considerations. In the first place, other conditions determining the transition from feudalism to capitalism were maturing nearly everywhere—if at different times and with different speed—under the impact of the internal stresses and strains of the feudal order. Secondly, it was the scope and the speed of the accumulation of merchant capital and of the ascent of the merchant class that played itself a major part in corroding the structure of feudal society, in creating the prerequisites for its ultimate demise. To quote Marx again: "It is determined by the very nature of capital . . . by its genesis that it stems from *money* and therefore from wealth which exists in the form of money. For the same reasons it makes its appearance as emerging from circulation, as its *product*. Capital formation does not stem therefore from landed property (here at best from the *tenant* to the extent to which he is a trader in agricultural produce); nor from the guild (although there is a possibility)—but from merchant and usurer wealth."[8]

In Western Europe, mercantile accumulations were particularly large, and, what is of considerable significance, highly concentrated. This was partly due to the geographical location of the Western European countries which gave them the possibility for an early development of navigation, and with it of a rapid expansion of maritime and riparian commerce. It was caused secondly—paradoxically enough—by Western Europe's being in terms of natural resources poorer and in terms of its economic development at the relevant time in many respects more backward rather than more advanced than the parts of the world which were the objects of its commercial penetration. Hence the drive to procure tropical produce of all kinds (spices, tea, ivory, indigo, etc.) that could not be obtained nearby, hence also the effort to import valuable products of Oriental skills (high quality cloth, ornaments, pottery, and the like), and hence finally the wild scramble to bring back precious metals and stones that were in short supply at home. The resulting far-flung trade, combined with piracy, outright plunder, slave traffic, and discovery of gold, led to a rapid formation of vast fortunes in the hands of Western European merchants.[9]

This wealth had the usual tendency to snowball. The requirements of navigation gave a strong stimulus to scientific discovery and technological progress. Shipbuilding, outfitting of overseas expeditions, the manufacturing of arms and other supplies required by them for protection as well as for the conduct of "negotiations" with their overseas trading partners—all provided a mighty impulse to the development of capitalist enterprise. The principle that "one thing gives another" came in full operation, external economies of various kinds became increasingly available, and further development could proceed at an accelerated rate. We need not trace here in any detail the varied ways by which the accumulated capital turned gradually to industrial pursuits. Wealthy merchants entered manufacturing to assure themselves of steady and cheap supplies. Artisans grown rich or in partnership with moneyed tradesmen expanded the scale of their operations. Not infrequently even rich landowners became involved in industry (particularly mining) and thus laid the foundation for large capitalist enterprises. But most important of all, the state, ever more under the control of capitalist interests, became increasingly active in aiding and advancing the budding entrepreneurs. "They all employ the power of the State, the concentrated and organized force of society, to hasten, hothouse fashion, the transformation of the feudal mode of production into the capitalist mode, and to shorten the transition."[10]

Western Europe's large leap forward need not necessarily have prevented economic growth in other countries. Though they might not have been able to narrow down, let alone to eliminate, the gap between themselves and the Western European pioneers, they could nevertheless have entered a growth process of their own, attaining more or less advanced levels of productivity and output. Indeed, the expanding contact with the scientifically and technologically leading Western European nations might have been expected to facilitate the forward movement of the countries with which Western Europe came into contact. So it actually appeared during the latter seventeenth and the eighteenth centuries, in the beginnings of modern capitalism; and such developments as took place at that time in a number of now underdeveloped countries lent ample support to this expectation. The primary accumulation of capital was making rapid progress, crafts and manufacturing expanded, and mounting revolts of the peasantry combined with increasing pressure from the rising bourgeoisie everywhere shook the foundations of the pre-capitalist order. This can be seen whether we consider the early history of capitalism in Russia and in Eastern and Southeastern Europe or whether we retrace the beginning of capitalism in India, the Near East, or even China. Not that all these and other countries would necessarily have moved along a road identical to that traveled by Britain, Holland, Germany, or France. Differences not only in the natural prerequisites of economic development, in geographic location and climate, but also in political, cultural, and religious background were bound to create divergences in levels and rates of increase of productivity. Similarly these differences could not but cause wide variations in the amounts of capital accumulation in the hands of the capitalist classes of individual nations as well as in the degrees of cohesion and resilience of their respective pre-capitalist political and social structures. Still, whatever its speed and whatever its zigzags, the general direction of the historical movement seems to have been the same for the backward echelons as for the forward contingents.

"The country that is more developed industrially only shows to the less developed the image of its own future."[11]

That in reality things have not developed in this way, that Western Europe left the rest of the world far behind was, however, by no means a matter of fortuitous accident or of some racial peculiarities of different peoples. It was actually determined by the nature of Western European development itself. For the effects of Western European capitalist penetration of the outside world were enormously complex. They depended on the exact nature of that penetration. They depended no less on the stage of development reached by the societies that were exposed to the foreign contacts. Therefore one cannot distinguish sharply enough between the impact of Western Europe's entrance into North America (and Australia and New Zealand) on one side, and the "opening up" by Western capitalism of Asia, Africa, or Eastern Europe. In the former case Western Europeans entered more or less complete societal vacua, and *settled* in those areas establishing themselves as their permanent residents. Whether such were their original intentions or not; whether they were merchant-adventurers seeking quick profits to take home and refugees from political and religious persecutions as in the case of North America, or deportees of all kinds as in the case of Australia; whether they brought with them some capital or merely aggressiveness, skills, and ingenuity—this matters very little. They came to the new lands with "capitalism in their bones" and meeting no resistance worth the name—the exploits of Davy Crockett notwithstanding—they succeeded in a short time in establishing on virtually virgin (and exceptionally fertile) soil an indigenous society of their own. From the outset capitalist in its structure, unencumbered by the fetters and barriers of feudalism, that society could single-mindedly devote itself to the development of its productive resources. Its social and political energies were neither sapped by a protracted struggle against feudal rule nor dissipated in overcoming the conventions and traditions of the feudal age. The only obstacle to accumulation and capitalist expansion was foreign domination. Yet, although by no means free of internal tensions and conflicts of considerable intensity—Benedict Arnold!—the newly emerging bourgeois societies were at an early stage cohesive and strong enough to overthrow that domination and to create a political framework conducive to the growth of capitalism.

This is a far cry from what occurred in other parts of the world. What is decisive is not so much that the Western European enterprisers breaking into India, China, the countries of Southeast Asia, the Near East, and Africa were in many respects different from those who had directed themselves to North America. Equally products of the capitalist development in the West, they nurtured aspirations that were nothing but self-seeking and engaged in activities that were nothing but predatory. Where the crucial difference lay was in what they found upon their arrival in Asia and Africa. That was indeed a world apart from what was encountered in America or in Australia.

Where climate and the natural environment were such as possibly to invite

Western European settlers, they were faced by established societies with rich and ancient cultures, still pre-capitalist or in the embryonic state of capitalist development. Where the existing social organizations were primitive and tribal, the general conditions and in particular the climate were such as to preclude any mass settlement of Western European arrivals. Consequently in both cases the Western European visitors rapidly determined to extract the largest possible gains from the host countries, and to take their loot home. Thus they engaged in outright plunder or in plunder thinly veiled as trade, seizing and removing tremendous wealth from the places of their penetrations. "In the cruel rapacity of its exploitation colonial policy in the seventeenth and eighteenth centuries differed little from the methods by which in earlier centuries Crusaders and the armed merchants of Italian cities had robbed the Byzantine territories of the Levant."[12] And "the treasures captured outside Europe by undisguised looting, enslavement and murder flowed back to the mother-country and transformed themselves into capital."[13]

The importance of these "unilateral transfers" of wealth from the non-European countries to those of Western Europe is commonly obscured by focusing attention merely on their magnitude in terms of the *aggregate outputs* of the countries to which they accrued or of those from which they were taken. Not that they were not large even by that standard. However, what lent them their crucial significance to the development of Western Europe and to that of the now under-developed countries is the nature, so to speak, the economic *locus* of the resources involved. Indeed whatever may have been the fractional increase of Western Europe's *national income* derived from its overseas operations, they *multiplied the economic surplus* at its disposal. What is more: the increment of the economic surplus appeared immediately in a concentrated form and came largely into the hands of capitalists who could use it for investment purposes. The intensity of the boost to Western Europe's development resulting from this "exogenous" contribution to its capital accumulation can hardly be exaggerated.[14]

This transfusion itself and in particular the methods by which it was perpetrated had perhaps an even more telling impact on the reluctant—to say the least—"donor" countries. They violently jolted their entire development and affected drastically its subsequent course. They burst with explosive force into the glacial movement of their ancient societies and tremendously accelerated the process of decomposition of their pre-capitalist structures. By breaking up the age-old patterns of their agricultural economy, and by forcing shifts to the production of exportable crops, Western capitalism destroyed the self-sufficiency of their rural society that formed the basis of the pre-capitalist order in all countries of its penetration, and rapidly widened and deepened the scope of commodity circulation. By outright—in many countries, massive—seizure of peasant-occupied land for plantation purposes and other uses by foreign enterprise and by exposing their rural handicrafts to the withering competition of its industrial exports, it created a vast pool of pauperized labor.[15] Enlarging thus the area of capitalist activities, it advanced the evolution of legal and property relations attuned to the needs of a market economy and established administrative institutions required for their enforcement. If only in order to expand and to tighten the economic and political grip on the areas of its domination, it forced the diversion of some of their economic surplus to the improvement of their systems of communication, to the building of railroads, harbors, and highways, providing thereby as a by-product the facilities needed for profitable investment of capital.

This is, however, only one side of the ledger. Accelerating with irresistible energy the maturing of *some* of the basic prerequisites for the development of a capitalist system, the intrusion of Western capitalism in the now underdeveloped countries blocked with equal force the ripening of others. The removal of a large share of the affected countries' previously accumulated and currently generated surplus could not but cause a serious setback to their primary accumulation of capital. Their being exposed to ruinous competition from abroad could not but smother their fledgling industries. Although the expansion of commodity circulation, the pauperization of large numbers of peasants and artisans, the contact with Western technology, provided a powerful impetus to the development of capitalism,this development was forcibly shunted off its normal course, distorted and crippled to suit the purposes of Western imperialism.

Thus the peoples who came into the orbit of Western capitalist expansion found themselves in the twilight of feudalism and capitalism enduring the worst features of both worlds, and the entire impact of imperialist subjugation to boot. To oppression by their feudal lords, ruthless but tempered by tradition, was added domination by foreign and domestic capitalists, callous and limited only by what the traffic would bear. The obscurantism and arbitrary violence inherited from their feudal past was combined with the rationality and sharply calculating rapacity of their capitalist present. Their exploitation was multiplied, yet its fruits were not to increase their productive wealth; these went abroad or served to support a parasitic bourgeoisie at home. They lived in abysmal misery, yet they had no prospect of a better tomorrow. They existed under capitalism, yet there was no accumulation of capital. They lost their time-honored means of livelihood, their arts and crafts, yet there was no modern industry to provide new ones in their place. They were thrust into extensive contact with the advanced science of the West, yet remained in a state of the darkest backwardness.

II

The outstanding case in point is obviously India. The record of India from the days of the East India Company is well known and calls for no elaboration. On few historical subjects is there so much agreement among students of widely differing persuasions as on what happened to India after Western capitalism appended her to its chariot. It is well expressed by an authority surely not suspect of anti-British prejudice who summarizes her findings as follows: ". . . up to the eighteenth century, the economic condition of India was relatively advanced, and Indian methods of production and of industrial and commercial organization could stand comparison with those in vogue in any other part of the world. . . . A country which has manufactured and exported the finest muslins and other luxurious fabrics and articles, at a time when the ancestors of the British were living an extremely primitive life, has failed to take part in the economic revolution initiated by the descendants of those same wild barbarians."[16] Nor was that "failure" something accidental or due to some peculiar inaptitude of the Indian "race."[17] It was caused by the elaborate, ruthless, systematic despoliation of India by British capital from the very onset of British rule. So stupendous was the extent of plunder, so utterly fantastic the amount of what was extracted from India that in 1875 the Marquess of Salisbury—then Secretary of State for India—warned that "as India must be bled, the bleeding should be done judiciously."[18] The volume of wealth that Britain derived from India and that was added to Britain's capital accumulations has to my knowledge never been fully assessed. Digby notes that estimates had been made according to which between Plassey and Waterloo—a period of crucial importance for the development of British capitalism—between £500,000,000 and £1,000,000,000 worth of treasure was taken by Britain from India. The vastness of this sum can be visualized when it is considered that at the turn of the nineteenth century the aggregate capital of all joint stock companies operating in India amounted to £36,000,000. The authoritative Indian statisticians, K. T. Shah and K. J. Khambata, calculated that in the early decades of the current century Britain appropriated annually under one title or another over 10 percent of India's gross national income.[19] And it can be safely assumed that this drain was smaller in the twentieth century than in the eighteenth and nineteenth centuries. It can moreover be considered as certain that this ratio understates the extent of Britain's encroachment on India's resources since it refers merely to *direct* transfers and does not include India's losses due to unfavorable terms of trade imposed upon her by the British.

Looking at the matter in terms of what it meant to Britain, Brooks Adams paints a vivid picture that is worth citing at some length:

> Upon the plundering of India there can be no better authority than Macaulay, who held high office at Calcutta . . . and who less than any of the writers who have followed him was a mouth-piece of the official class. He has told how after Plassey "the shower of wealth" began to fall, and he has described Clive's own gains: "We may safely affirm that no Englishman who started with nothing has ever, in any line of life, created such a fortune at the early age of thirty-four! But the takings of Clive, either for himself or for the government, were trifling compared to the wholesale robbery and spoliation which followed his departure, when Bengal was surrendered a helpless prey to a myriad of greedy officials. These officials were absolute, irresponsible, and rapacious, and they emptied the private hoards. Their only thought was to wring some hundreds of thousands of pounds out of the

natives as quickly as possible, and hurry home to display their wealth. Enormous fortunes were thus rapidly accumulated at Calcutta, while thirty millions of human beings were reduced to the extremity of wretchedness. . . . The misgovernment of the English was carried to a point such as seems hardly compatible with the very existence of society. The Roman proconsul, who, in a year or two, squeezed out of a province the means of rearing marble palaces and baths on the shore of Campania, of drinking from amber, of feasting on singing birds, of exhibiting armies of gladiators and flocks of camelopards; the Spanish viceroy, who, leaving behind him the curses of Mexico or Lima, entered Madrid with a long train of gilded coaches, and of sumpter-horses trapped and shod with silver, were now outdone."[20] . . . Very soon after Plassey the Bengal plunder began to arrive in London, and the effect appears to have been instantaneous, for all authorities agree that the "industrial revolution," the event which has divided the nineteenth century from all antecedent time, began with the year 1760. Prior to 1760 . . . the machinery used for spinning cotton in Lancashire was almost as simple as in India; while about 1750 the English iron industry was in full decline. . . . To the capitalist then, rather than to the inventor, civilization owes the steam-engine as a part of daily life."[21]

A comprehensive analysis of the impact of this frantic orgy of primary accumulation of capital upon the development of India is presented in the standard work by Romesh Dutt, *The Economic History of India*,[22] and we can do no better than borrow his words:

It is, unfortunately, a fact, that in many ways, the sources of national wealth in India have been narrowed under the British rule. India in the eighteenth century was a great manufacturing as well as a great agricultural country, and the products of the Indian loom supplied the markets of Asia and of Europe. It is, unfortunately, true that the East Indian Company and the British Parliament, following the selfish commercial policy of a hundred years ago, discouraged Indian manufacturers in the early years of British rule in order to encourage the rising manufactures of England. Their fixed policy, pursued during the last decades of the eighteenth century and the first decades of the nineteenth, was to make India subservient to the industries of Great Britain, and to make the Indian people grow raw produce only, in order to supply material for the looms and manufactures of Great Britain. This policy was pursued with unwavering resolution and with fatal success; orders were sent out, to force Indian artisans to work in the Company's factories; commercial residents were legally vested with extensive powers over villages and communities of Indian weavers; prohibitive tariffs excluded Indian silk and cotton goods from England; English goods were admitted into India free of duty or on payment of a nominal duty. . . . The invention of the power-loom in Europe completed the decline of the Indian industries; and when in recent years the power-loom was set up in India, England once more acted towards India with unfair jealousy. An excise duty has been imposed on the production of cotton fabrics in India which . . . stifles the new steam-mills of India. Agriculture is now virtually the only remaining source of national wealth of India . . . but what the British Government . . . take as Land Tax at the present day sometimes approximates to the whole of the economic rent. . . . This . . . paralyses agriculture, prevents saving, and keeps the tiller of the soil in a state of poverty and indebtedness. . . . In India the State virtually interferes with the accumulation of wealth from the soil, intercepts the incomes and gains of the tillers . . . leaving the cultivators permanently poor. . . . In India, the State has fostered no new industries and revived no old industries for the people. . . . In one shape or another all that could be raised in India by an excessive taxation flowed to Europe, after paying for a starved administration. . . . Verily the moisture of India blesses and fertilizes other lands.

The catastrophe that was brought upon India by the invasion of British capitalism thus assumed staggering proportions. To be sure, the process of transition from feudalism to capitalism, and of the diversion of resources to capital formation that forms its integral part, has caused a vast amount of suffering, misery, and destitution wherever it has taken its inexorable course. Society's economic surplus was not only transferred from one use to another with all the attendant upheavals, struggles, and hardships; more of it was squeezed from the underfed, underclad, underhoused, and overworked masses. Yet this surplus—albeit only incompletely and irrationally—was used for productive investment, and served to lay the foundations for the eventual expansion of productivity and output. Indeed, there can be no doubt that had the amount of economic surplus that Britain has torn from India been *invested in India*, India's economic development to date would have borne little similarity to the actual somber record. It is idle to speculate whether India by now would have reached a level of economic advancement commensurate with its fabulous natural resources and with the potentialities of its people. In any case the fate of the successive Indian generations would not have resembled even remotely the chronic catastrophe of the last two centuries.

But the harm done to India's economic potential is exceeded only by the crippling, and perhaps even more lasting, damage inflicted upon its people. "All the civil wars, invasions, revolutions, conquests, famines strangely complex, rapid and destructive as the successive action in Hindustan may appear, did not go deeper than its surface. England has broken down the entire framework of Indian society, without any symptoms of reconstitution yet appearing. This loss of his old world, with no gain of a new one, imparts a particular kind of melancholy to the present misery of the Hindu and separates Hindustan, ruled by Britain, from all its ancient traditions, and from the whole of its past history."[23]

For British policy in India was patterned very closely upon the practice followed by some Indian tyrants eloquently described by Macaulay: "When they dreaded the capacity and spirit of some distinguished subject, and yet could not venture to murder him, [they used] . . . to administer to him a daily dose of the pousta, a preparation of opium, the effect of which was in a few months to destroy all the bodily and mental powers of the wretch who was drugged with it, and to turn him into a helpless idiot. The detestable artifice, more horrible than assassination itself, was worthy of those who employed it."[24] Thus the British administration of India systematically destroyed all the fibres and foundations of

Indian society. Its land and taxation policy ruined India's village economy and substituted for it the parasitic landowner and moneylender. Its commercial policy destroyed the Indian artisan and created the infamous slums of the Indian cities filled with millions of starving and diseased paupers. Its economic policy broke down whatever beginnings there were of an indigenous industrial development and promoted the proliferations of speculators, petty businessmen, agents, and sharks of all descriptions eking out a sterile and precarious livelihood in the meshes of a decaying society. "British rule thus consolidated itself by creating new classes and vested interests who were tied up with that rule and whose privileges depended on its continuance. There were the landowners and the princes, and there were a large number of subordinate members of the services in various departments of the government, from the patwari, the village headman, upward. . . . To all these methods must be added the deliberate policy, pursued throughout the period of British rule, of creating divisions among Indians, of encouraging one group at the cost of the other."[25] And reference has already been made to British policies with regard to education. In the chapter of Nehru's book from which the above passage was taken, the following is quoted from Kaye's *Life of Metcalfe*: ". . . this dread of the free diffusion of knowledge became a chronic disease . . . continually afflicting the members of Government with all sorts of hypochondriacal day-dreams and nightmares, in which visions of the Printing Press and the Bible were making their flesh creep, and their hair stand erect with horror. It was our policy in those days to keep the natives of India in the profoundest state of barbarism and darkness, and every attempt to diffuse the light of knowledge among the people, either of our own or of the independent states, was vehemently opposed and resented."

It is thus a fair assessment of the effects on India of two centuries of domination by Western capitalism as well as a correct analysis of the causes of India's present backwardness when Nehru says: ". . . nearly all our major problems today have grown up during British rule and as a direct result of British policy: the princes; the minority problem; various vested interests, foreign and Indian; the lack of industry and the neglect of agriculture; the extreme backwardness in the social services; and, above all, the tragic poverty of the people."[26]

It is hardly necessary to add that all this is not to idealize India's pre-British past and to portray it romantically as a Paradise Lost. As Marx stressed in a magnificent passage of one of his previously cited articles on India:

> . . . we must not forget that these idyllic village communities, inoffensive though they may appear, had always been the solid foundation of Oriental despotism, that they restricted the human mind within the smallest possible compass, making it the unresisting tool of superstition, enslaving it beneath traditional rules, depriving it of all grandeur and historical energies. We must not forget the barbarian egotism which, concentrating on some miserable patch of land, had quietly witnessed the ruin of empires, the perpetration of unspeakable cruelties, the massacre of the population of large towns with no other consideration bestowed upon them than on

natural events, itself the helpless prey of any aggressor who deigned to notice it at all. We must not forget that this undignified, stagnatory, and vegetative life, that this passive sort of existence evoked on the other part, in contradistinction, wild, aimless, unbounded forces of destruction and rendered murder itself a religious rite in Hindustan. We must not forget that these little communities were contaminated by a distinction of caste and by slavery, that they subjugated man to external circumstances, instead of elevating man the sovereign of circumstances, that they transformed a self-developing social state into never changing natural destiny, and thus brought about a brutalizing worship of nature.[27]

At the same time it should not be overlooked that India, if left to herself, might have found in the course of time a shorter and surely less tortuous road toward a better and richer society. That on that road she would have had to pass through the purgatory of a bourgeois revolution, that a long phase of capitalist development would have been the inevitable price that she would have had to pay for progress, can hardly be doubted. It would have been, however, an entirely different India (and an entirely different world), had she been allowed—as some more fortunate countries were—to realize her destiny in her own way, to employ her resources for her own benefit, and to harness her energies and abilities for the advancement of her own people.

III

This is speculation to be sure, but a legitimate one. For the alternative to the massive removal of their accumulated wealth and current output, to the ruthless suppression and distortion of all indigenous economic growth, to the systematic corruption of their social, political, and cultural life that were inflicted by Western capitalism upon all of the now underdeveloped countries is by no means purely hypothetical.[28]

This can be clearly seen in the history of the only Asian country that succeeded in escaping its neighbors' fate and in attaining a relatively high degree of economic advancement. For in the period under consideration—when Western capitalism was ruining India, establishing its grip over Africa, subjugating Latin America, and opening up China—conditions in Japan were as conducive, or rather as unfavorable, to economic development as anywhere else in Asia. Indeed, Japan "with its purely feudal organization of landed property and its developed small peasant economy" (Marx), while torn by all the internal tensions and conflicts of a feudal society, was perhaps even more tightly locked in the straitjacket of feudal constraints and restrictions than any other pre-capitalist country. "Every effort was made for over two hundred years to suppress growth and change. . . . society was frozen into a legally immutable class mold. . . . Maintenance of the warrior class continued to take the surplus of society, leaving little for investment. . . . the closed class system smothered creative energies and tended to freeze labor and talent in traditional occupations. To sweep away these obstacles to industrial development was unthinkable."[29]

At the same time, however, under the rigid crust of feudal rule, there was a rapid accumulation of capital in the hands of urban and rural merchants.[30] As a measure of the magnitude of the wealth that was being amassed by the prosperous bourgeoisie, the following may serve: "In 1760 the Bakufu 'borrowed' from members of the great trading guilds as much as 1,781,000 *ryo*, a sum of the same order of magnitude as the total ordinary expenditure of the government for one year."[31] Since such "borrowing" was frequently not followed by repayment, this sum conveys not merely an indication of the affluence of the mercantile class, but also a notion of the extent of the exactions to which the government forced it to submit. Those exactions were not merely financial.[32] "The authorities hedged [the merchant class] . . . about with numerous restrictions; their style of clothing, use of foot-gear, umbrellas, all these and a thousand other petty details were regulated by law. The government would not even allow a merchant to have a name which resembled a *daimyo* name, nor would it permit tradesmen to live in the *samurai* district. In fact no feudal aristocracy could express greater distaste for money-making and money-makers than the Tokugawa moralists and legislators."[33]

While there seems to be some disagreement among the historians of Japan on the share of "credit" due to different classes for their part in overthrowing the Tokugawa rule, there is no doubt that the pressure of the rapidly developing capitalist relations against the barriers of the feudal order was the basic force that brought about the Meiji Restoration. This is intended neither to belittle the tremendous *political* significance of the mounting opposition of the (lower) *samurai* or of the rising wave of peasant uprisings that during the first half of the nineteenth century shook the very foundations of the Tokugawa regime, nor to exaggerate the political role played by the merchant class as such in establishing the new order.[34] As in all revolutions, it was a combination of heterogeneous social groups that accomplished the overturn of the *ancien régime*. But while the most active and most conspicuous among them were the *déclassé* warriors and the frustrated intellectuals, the embittered feudal lords and the disgruntled courtiers who were left out by the Tokugawa ruling group, yet it was the rising bourgeoisie that determined both the direction and the outcome of the movement, and it was the capitalist class that reaped the political and economic fruits of the Revolution. "Less dramatic than the political and military exploits of the *samurai*, but more far-reaching in accomplishing both the overthrow of the *Bakufu* and the stabilization of the new regime, was the financial support of the great *chonin*, especially of Osaka, where it is said 70 percent of Japan's wealth was concentrated. . . . the decisive battles in the war for the Restoration . . . were fought and won with funds supplied by the *chonin*."[35]

It would take us too far afield, and would be unnecessary for our present purpose, to trace in any detail the changes in Japan that were brought about by the Meiji Revolution. Suffice it to say that it succeeded in creating the political and economic framework indispensable for capitalist development. Providing a striking example of how "*governments*, f.i. Henry VII, VIII etc. enter as instrumentalities of the process of historical dissolution and as creators of conditions for the existence of capital,"[36] the regime emerging from the Restoration drastically shifted the country's economic gears and provided a tremendous impetus both to the still incomplete primary accumulation of capital and to its transfer from purely mercantile to industrial pursuits.

As far as the former is concerned, no effort was spared to squeeze as much as possible out of the hard-pressed direct producers. The economy being predominantly agrarian, with between 70 and 75 percent of the population engaged in agriculture, the bulk of the economic surplus could not but continue to come out of the peasantry.[37] This was assured by what constituted the outstanding trait of the Japanese development: the blending of feudal relations in agriculture with a strong, centralized, capitalist-dominated state furthering by all available means the growth of capitalist enterprise.[38] In fact, the combined pressure of the reorganized and "streamlined" state and the now dominant new "bourgeois" landowning class of the *jinushi* led to a marked increase of the burden imposed on the peasantry. If the share of the agricultural output retained by the direct producer was 39 percent during the first half of the nineteenth century, it fell to 32 percent after the agrarian reform promulgated by the Meiji government, not to exceed 42 percent until 1933–1935.[39] It is thus no exaggeration to say that the main source of primary accumulation of capital in Japan was the village which in the course of its entire modern history played for Japanese capitalism the role of an internal colony.[40]

The traditional policy of ruthless direct extractions from the peasants was supplemented by a number of other devices calculated to maximize the aggregate economic surplus. Wages of workers employed in non-agricultural activities were rigorously held down to rock bottom—a principle that was easy to enforce in a labor market glutted with agricultural surplus population. Even more important was the systematic inflationary policy initiated by the Meiji administration, which resulted not merely in further redistribution of income in favor of capital accumulation but also in expansion of the economic surplus through the utilization of previously unemployed resources.[41] The most significant contribution to the primary accumulation of capital resulted, however, from the issuance of government debentures in payment of indemnities to the dislodged feudal lords, and the assumption of their debts by the government. "The feudal lord ceased to be a *territorial* magnate drawing his income from the peasant and became instead, by virtue of the commutation of his pension, a *financial* magnate investing his freshly capitalized wealth in banks, stocks, industries or landed estates, and so joined the small financial oligarchy."[42] Similarly the settlement of the claims of the *samurai* to a regular government stipend that was effected by their capitalization in the form of interest-bearing bonds resulted in further swelling of the stock of available capital. This capital, centralized and administered by the rapidly growing banking system, became the basis for a massive expansion of credit. Direct government borrowing from the banks, indeed the nearly complete amalgamation of the Treasury with some of the leading banking houses of the time—Mitsui, Ono, Simada, Yasuda, and others—and the lavish profits earned by the latter in the process of this cooperation, boosted further the spectacular agglomeration of capital in the hands of a small number of financial establishments.[43]

Yet although the utmost was done in this way to fill the coffers of the bourgeoisie, to create new and vast fortunes, and to increase the capital available to the existing and prospective business class, this effort per se failed to induce a spurt of investment in *industrial* development. Just as during the last stages of the Tokugawa rule, so after the Meiji Restoration the mere concentration of tremendous wealth in the hands of the merchants, combined even as it was with a plethora of cheap manpower, did not suffice to call forth a shift from mercantile to industrial activities on the part of the entrepreneurs. "Many ... merchant families, most notably Mitsui, did ... take a leading role in the development of industry, but in the early years of the Meiji period ... merchants almost to a man stuck resolutely to traditional fields of activity—commodity speculation, trade, and moneylending."[44] The process of primary accumulation of capital was still far from completed; Japan was still going through the mercantile phase of capitalism.

It was stressed before that the mercantile bourgeoisie never accomplished by itself the transition to industrial capitalism. It always required energetic and openhanded support on the part of the state, brought under the control of the rising capitalist class. Such an impetus was indeed provided by the modernized, capitalist state created by the Meiji Revolution, an impetus that moved the Japanese economy off dead center, that launched it on the road of industrial capitalism. What Marx observed in general terms about the genesis of industrial capitalism precisely describes Japanese conditions at the time of the Meiji Restoration. "The minimum of the sum of value that the individual possessor of money or commodities must command in order to metamorphose himself into a capitalist, changes with the different stages of development of capitalist production, and is on any given stage different in different spheres of production, depending on their specific technical conditions. Certain spheres of production demand, even at the very outset of capitalist production, a minimum of capital that is not as yet found in the hands of single individuals. This gives rise partly to state subsidies to private persons, as in France in the time of Colbert, and as in many German states up to our own epoch; partly to the formation of societies with legal monopoly for the exploitation of certain branches of industry and commerce."[45]

The Meiji state went much further; it invested heavily in railway construction, in shipbuilding, in the development of a communications system, in basic industries, in production of machinery, and the like. The story of the early industrialization of Japan has been told many times: through it runs like a red thread the dominant part played by the government in accelerating the development of industrial capitalism. How this government policy was carried out is relatively unimportant. Some of the government investment was financed directly with what was no longer required to pay the stipends of the *samurai*—an amount that in earlier days used to absorb nearly all of the government's ordinary revenues. Other ventures were made possible by far-reaching government guarantees to the investors. Still others were promoted by the government's commitments to purchase many years' output of the newly established enterprises. Whichever way was chosen, the result was invariably a tremendous enhancement of the power of industrial capital. The profits earned by the Mitsui, Mitsubishi, Sumitomo, Okura, and other future "Zaibatsu" on various government contracts were truly fabulous. They were perhaps overshadowed only by the gains provided these concerns by the government's eventual policy of "re-privatization" of the state-owned industrial enterprises. "There is no doubt that this policy greatly enhanced the power of the financial oligarchy, especially in view of the ridiculously low prices at which the government sold its model factories."[46]

Thus in the early history of industrial development in Japan (as for that matter in other countries) there is not much to be seen of the daring and innovating entrepreneur whom our modern rewriters of history present, for only too transparent reasons, as the original creators and promoters of all economic progress.[47] Indeed, if anything is obvious, it is the exorbitant amount of protection and bribery on the part of the state that was required to pull capital away from its favorite speculation and usury to investment in productive enterprise.

And this brings us back to the question which was raised at the outset of the present discussion and which encompasses its central theme. What was it that enabled Japan to take a course so radically different from that of all the other countries in the now underdeveloped world? Or, in other words, what was the historical constellation that left room for a bourgeois revolution in Japan which in turn led to the establishment of a bourgeois-dominated regime serving from its very inception as a vigorous and relentless engine of Japanese capitalism?

The answer to this question is extraordinarily complex and at the same time extraordinarily simple. It is simple because, reduced to its core, it comes down to the fact that Japan is the only country in Asia (and in Africa and in Latin America) that escaped being turned into a colony or dependency of Western European or American capitalism, that had a chance of independent national development. It is complex because it was only a felicitous confluence of a large number of more or less independent factors that gave Japan its lucky break.

Basic among them—reminiscent of the paradox presented by Western Europe and in particular by Great Britain—was the backwardness and poverty of the Japanese people and the paucity of their country's natural resources.[48] "Japan had very little to offer either as a market for foreign manufactures or as a granary of raw materials for Western industry."[49] Consequently the lure of Japan to Western European capitalists and governments came nowhere near the irresistible attraction exercised by the gold of Latin America, the flora, fauna, and minerals of

Africa, the fabulous riches of the Indies, or the supposedly bottomless markets of China.

No less important was the fact that in the middle of the nineteenth century, when Western penetration of Asia reached the highest degree of intensity, the resources of the leading Western European countries were already severely taxed by other undertakings. Especially Great Britain, the world's leading colonial power, had enough on its hands in Europe, the Near East, India, and China without becoming involved in a militarily most uninviting campaign for the conquest of Japan. This strain on Britain's expansionist capabilities accelerated the far-reaching change in the nature and orientation of its colonial policy that was afoot from the middle of the nineteenth century. Although veiled by a political debate that appeared to be mere shadow boxing—with the Tories fully accepting the essence of Palmerston's foreign policies—it actually implied the transition from old-fashioned piracy characteristic of the mercantile phase of capitalism and of primary accumulation of capital to the more subtle and complex strategy of modern imperialism.[50]

But what decisively affected the position of Japan was another characteristic of modern imperialism: the growing rivalry among the established imperialist whales, and the arrival on the world stage of a new imperialist power, the United States. It was that rivalry, with the resulting checks and balances in international power politics, that had much to do with preventing Britain from meting out to China all of the punishment that was suffered by India; and it was this very same international jealousy that rendered it impossible for any one imperialist power to attempt the conquest of Japan.[51] Although in the case of Japan it was the United States that carried out the initial opening-up and that imposed upon it its first unequal treaty, neither the stage reached in the development of American capitalism nor its international status allowed the United States as yet to try to establish exclusive control over Japan. "The proximity to China gave Japan extraordinary strategic importance. The powers that forced upon Japan the unequal treaties watched jealously lest any one of them gain predominant influence in Japan, let alone be able to convert it into its colony and thus into a staging area for further advance into China."[52]

Both the possibility and the necessity of staving off the Western menace exercised a powerful impact on the speed and direction of Japan's subsequent development. It was not only allowed to invest its economic surplus in its own economy; its being spared the mass invasion of Western fortune hunters, soldiers, sailors, and "civilizers" saved it also from the extremes of xenophobia which so markedly retarded the spread of Western science in other countries of Asia. The exceptional Japanese receptiveness to Western knowledge, so frequently referred to and so warmly commended by Western writers, was largely due to the fortunate circumstance that Western civilization was not brought to Japan at the point of a gun, that Western thought and Western technology were in Japan not directly associated with plunder, arson, and murder as they were in

India, China, and other now underdeveloped countries. This permitted the retention in Japan of a socio-psychological "climate" not inimical to the adoption of Western science both through the importation of Western technicians and through dispatching young men to Western centers of learning.

On the other hand the threat of Western penetration acted as an ever-present stimulant to Japan's economic development. Toward the end of the Tokugawa period it appeared as an essentially military danger, and was treated accordingly by the feudal rulers. Considerable efforts were undertaken by them to establish strategic industries such as iron, armaments, and shipbuilding.[53] Yet superimposed upon a feudal, backward society, without a basis for growth in its socioeconomic structure, those modern industrial enclaves remained insignificant alien bodies in a pre-capitalist, pre-industrial economy.

Matters took an altogether different turn in the '60s. The foreign threat was no longer "merely" a threat to Japan's national independence. Japan's markets, rendered defenseless by the unequal treaties, were flooded by foreign wares. The very existence of Japan's rising capitalism was gravely endangered. The policy of the government that emerged from the Meiji Revolution was fully attuned to the interests that it represented and to the issues that it had to solve. Neither foreign competition nor foreign aggression could be deterred by building a few armaments factories or by piling up a stock of weapons. What was called for was the rapid development of an integrated industrial economy capable of supporting modern warfare and at the same time able to meet the onslaught of foreign competition.

This correspondence of the vital interests of Japanese capitalism with the military requirements for national survival was of momentous importance in determining the speed of Japan's economic and political development after the Meiji Revolution. It greatly accelerated its economic growth by directing investment into basic industries, shipbuilding, communications, and the like rather than solely to armaments factories. At the same time it enabled the new bourgeois government to harness the patriotic and martial fervor of the *déclassé* military castes to its quest for a modern economy. Less than half a century had to pass before the concentrated, monopolistically controlled industry provided a firm basis for an impressive military potential which, combined with the purposefully nurtured chauvinism of the *samurai* and their descendants, turned Japan from an object of imperialist intrigues into one of Western imperialism's most successful junior partners. In the words of Lenin, "by their colonial looting of Asian countries the Europeans managed to harden one of them—Japan— for great military exploits that assured it of an independent national development."[54]

IV

It is obviously impossible even to conjecture on the speed with which the now backward countries would have gone the way of Japan and would have autonomously generated a process of capitalist development and economic growth, in the absence of Western invasion and exploitation. Indeed, the rapidity of Japan's transformation into a capitalist, industrialized country was due to a large extent to the military and economic threat from the West. Yet whatever might have been the tempo and the specific circumstances of the forward movement, there is ample evidence in the history of all the countries in question to indicate the nature of its general trend. Regardless of their national peculiarities, the pre-capitalist orders in Western Europe and in Japan, in Russia and in Asia were reaching at different times and in different ways their common historical destiny.[55] By the eighteenth and nineteenth centuries they were universally in a state of disintegration and decay. Peasants' revolts and the rise of the bourgeoisie shattered everywhere their very foundations. Depending on specific historical conditions, on the internal strength of their pre-capitalist social orders and on the intensity of the anti-feudal pressures, bourgeois revolutions and the development of capitalism were more or less effectively resisted and retarded. Nowhere would they have been indefinitely prevented. Indeed, if the most advanced countries' contact with the backward world had been different from what it was, if it had consisted of genuine cooperation and assistance rather than of oppression and exploitation, then the progressive development of the now underdeveloped countries would have proceeded with incomparably less delay, less friction, less human sacrifice and suffering. A peaceful transplantation of Western culture, science, and technology to the less advanced countries would have served everywhere as a powerful catalyst of economic progress. The violent, destructive, and predatory opening up of the weaker countries by Western capitalism immeasurably distorted their development. A comparison of the role played by British science and British technology in the development of the United States with the role played by British opium in the development of China fully epitomizes this difference.

Notes

1. This is not to say that the knowledge of what *are* the essential characteristics of a phenomenon is given by God to "His own in their sleep." It cannot be attained except as the result of a thorough and detailed study of the subject matter, with this research forming the basis for the decision as to what is to be abstracted from and what is to be included in the theoretical model. In this sense social sciences no less than other sciences convey *cumulative* knowledge; not each and every investigator needs to start from scratch. There are available wholly adequate guideposts to what constitutes the essential elements of a socioeconomic process. As in all scientific work, the adequacy of these guideposts can be established in no other way than by practice, that is, in their theoretical and empirical application to concrete historical material.

2. *Processes and Problems of Industrialization of Under-developed Countries* (1955), pp. 6 ff.

3. Ragnar Nurkse, *Problems of Capital Formation in Underdeveloped Countries* (Oxford, 1953), p. 63, where the source for this calculation is indicated.

4. E. S. Mason, *Promoting Economic Development* (Claremont, California, 1955), p. 16.

5. Maurice Dobb, *Studies in the Development of Capitalism* (London, 1946), p. 21.

6. *Grundrisse der Kritik der Politischen Ökonomie* (Rohentwurf) (Berlin, 1953), p. 404.

7. As Dobb points out, "one feature of this new merchant bourgeoisie that is at first as surprising as it is universal, is the readiness with which this class compromised with feudal society once its privileges had been won." *Op. cit.*, p. 120.

8. *Loc. cit.*

9. Cf. Dobb, *op. cit.*, pp. 207 ff. On the role played by slavery and slave traffic in the primary accumulation of capital, cf. Eric Williams, *Capitalism and Slavery* (Chapel Hill, North Carolina, 1944).

10. Marx, *Capital* (Kerr ed.), Vol. I, p. 823. Of the role played by the capitalist-dominated state in the early development of capitalism, even in a country with proverbially little government participation in economic affairs, there is a useful reminder by Professor E. S. Mason: "Most Americans are unaware of the extent to which the Federal and State governments promoted the early economic development of the United States through the provision of social capital in the form of canals, river development, turnpikes, railways, port facilities and the like. The provision of public works of this sort by government was, of course, essential to the expansion of private investment." *Promoting Economic Development* (Claremont, California, 1955), p. 47.

11. Marx, *Capital* (Kerr ed.), Vol. I, p. 13.

12. Dobb, *Studies in the Development of Capitalism* (London, 1946), p. 208.

13. Marx, *Capital* (Kerr ed.), Vol. I, p. 826.

14. This is not to say that on balance the effect on the "beneficiary" countries was an unmixed blessing. The corruption of social and political life in Western Europe, the growth of chauvinism and racism, the eventual development of imperialism and jingoism, all owe much to the heinous rape of non-European peoples that accompanied the early development of Western capitalism.

15. Cf. W. E. Moore, *Industrialization and Labor* (Ithaca and New York, 1951), p. 52.

16. Vera Anstey, *The Economic Development of India* (London, New York, Toronto, 1929; cited from 4th edition, 1952), p. 5.

17. As was noted by an earlier observer of India, "the great mass of the Indian people possesses a great *industrial energy*, is well fitted to accumulate capital, and remarkable for a mathematical clearness of head, and talent for figures and exact sciences. Their intellects are excellent." Quoted in Marx, "The Future Results of the British Rule in India," in Marx and Engels, *On Britain* (Moscow, 1953), p. 390. (Italics in the original.) That at the same time the British-organized-and-supervised educational system did all it could not to promote but to repress the growth of scientific and industrial aptitude among the Indians has been attested by a number of students of India. In the words of Vera Anstey: ". . . should we not inquire how far the system of education introduced by the British has helped to generate the scientific spirit and the spread of scientific knowledge? Do we not find that, instead of teaching the people to understand the world about them and how natural forces can best be utilized and controlled, they have been taught to write notes on archaic phrases in the works of sixteenth- and seventeenth-century Englishmen and to learn by rote the personal history of obscure rulers of a foreign land?" *Op. cit.*, p. 4.

18. William Digby, *"Prosperous" British India* (London, 1901), p. xii.

19. Referred to in R. Palme Dutt, *India Today* (Bombay, 1949), p. 32. This ratio should be considered in the light of the share of income that could be expected to constitute *economic surplus* in a country as poor as India.

20. The above passage is from Macaulay's *Lord Clive*.

21. *The Law of Civilization and Decay, An Essay on History* (NewYork, 1896; cited from 1943 reprint), pp. 294 ff.

22. London, 1901; quoted from the 7th edition, 1950, pp. viii ff. This writer, a high-ranking civil servant in the British administration of India and Lecturer in Indian History at University College, London, is not to be confused with R. Palme Dutt, the author of the important book on India, *India Today* (London, 1940; 2nd edition, Bombay, 1949).

23. Marx, "British Rule in India," in Marx and Engels, *Selected Works* (Moscow, 1949–1950), Vol. I, p. 313.

24. *Speeches*, quoted in Digby, *"Prosperous" British India* (London, 1901), p. 63.

25. Jawaharlal Nehru, *The Discovery of India* (New York, 1946), pp. 304 ff.

26. *Ibid.*, pp. 306 ff.

27. "British Rule in India," *op. cit.*, p. 317.

28. We have treated India at some length, but what applies to India applies *mutatis mutandis* to all the other backward areas. For comprehensive surveys of the experience of Burma and the Dutch East Indies (as well as for an excellent discussion of the entire colonial policy of the Western powers), see the books by J. S. Furnivall, in particular *Netherlands Indies* (Cambridge, England, 1944) and *Colonial Policy and Practice* (Cambridge, England, 1948). Very useful is also J. H. Boeke, *The Evolution of the Netherlands Indies Economy* (New York, 1946). The literature on China is vast. In the context of the present discussion most illuminating are Michael Greenberg, *British Trade and the Opening of China 1800–1842* (Cambridge, England, 1951), and G. E. Efimov, *Ocherki po Novoy i Noveyshey Istorii Kitaya* (Essays on the Recent and Most Recent History of China) (Moscow, 1951). A good survey of what has happened to Africa will be found in Leonard Woolf, *Empire and Commerce in Africa* (London, N.D.), while of the truly unbelievable catastrophe that befell the Caribbean region the classic book by Bishop Bartolomeo de las Casas, *The Tears of the Indians* (reprint, Stanford, California, N.D.), is probably still the best account.

29. Thomas C. Smith, *Political Change and Industrial Development in Japan: Government Enterprise, 1868–1880* (Stanford, California, 1955), Chapter II. I am greatly indebted to Professor Smith for letting me see the galley proofs of this excellent monograph.

30. It is most important to note that already in the eighteenth century powerful feudal clans, in particular that of Satsuma in southern Kyushu, engaged in far-flung trading and accumulated large amounts of capital. E. Herbert Norman, *Japan's Emergence as a Modern State* (New York, 1946), p. 15. The early orientation toward mercantile activities on the part of some feudal lords had probably much to do with the fact that belonging to the 86 *tozama* or "outside" lords, they were excluded by the ruling Tokugawa group from all participation in government and were thus forced to seek outlets for their energies in other pursuits.

31. G. B. Sansom, *The Western World and Japan* (New York, 1950), p. 240.

32. They are described in some detail by G. B. Sansom, *loc. cit.*

33. E. Herbert Norman, *Japan's Emergence as a Modern State* (New York, 1946), p. 17.

34. It is in general rather questionable how much importance should be attached to the class background of *individuals* participating in revolutionary events. Too many random factors influencing the decisions and behavior of individual members of different classes are at work for a close relation to be found between the class content of a historical movement and the class origin of possibly even significant numbers of its participants and leaders. A bourgeois revolution is rendered no less bourgeois by the fact that it is joined by a great number of noblemen who, precisely because of their background and education, may have risen above the vantage point of their own class, and to a position of leadership in a progressive movement: nor is a proletarian revolution less proletarian

because its leading echelons may contain, for similar reasons, many individuals of bour-geois or aristocratic background. Therefore, I would not give much weight to the informa-tion presented by Thomas C. Smith *(op. cit.,* Chapter II) on the class origins of the Restoration leaders given court rank posthumously, presumably in recognition of the part they played in the Restoration. The striking smallness of the number of merchants so rewarded would seem to suggest that the merchant class played only a minor part in the revolutionary movement. This impression would be, however, highly misleading. Tradi-tionally, bourgeois *as individuals* have nowhere taken active part in *revolutionary politics.* Indeed, it is probably one of the outstanding characteristics of the capitalist class and is closely related to its economic and ideological habitat that it customarily operates on the political stage—particularly in times of upheaval—through retainers, agents, and allies, rather than directly through its own members. And surely in Japan, in a political environ-ment entirely dominated by the feudal tradition and with hungry and eager *samurai* and *ronin* in superabundant supply, the merchants of Yedo and Osaka readily discerned the better part of wisdom in substituting their money for their persons in the struggle for freedom. "The descendants of the wealthy shopkeepers of Yedo and Osaka played an important, indeed an indispensable part in the movement which ended by overthrowing the Shogunate in 1868, because it could scarcely have succeeded without their financial backing." G. B. Sansom, *op. cit.,* p. 189.

35. E. Herbert Norman, *op. cit.,* p. 49.

36. Marx, *Grundrisse der Kritik der Politischen Ökonomie* (Rohentwurf) (Berlin, 1953), p. 406. (Italics and abbreviation of "for instance" in the original.)

37. "The Japanese merchant . . . lacked such opportunities for the accumulation of capital through trade and plunder as were enjoyed by his counterpart in 16th-17th century Europe." Norman, *op. cit.,* p. 51.

38. "The Meiji Revolution, far from suppressing them, incorporated in the new capi-talist society of Japan and legally sanctified the essential relations of feudal property." H. Kohachiro Takahashi, "La Place de la Révolution de Meiji dans l'histoire agraire du Japon," *Revue Historique* (October-November 1953), p. 248.

39. *Ibid.,* p. 262, where the work of the well-known Japanese statistician and historian M. Yamada is referred to as the source of these data.

40. Ya. A. Pevsner, *Monopolisticheski Kapital Yaponii* (Monopoly Capital of Japan) (Moscow, 1950), p. 11.

41. The scope and methods of the deficit financing involved are surveyed in Thomas C. Smith, *Political Change and Industrial Development in Japan: Government Enter-prise, 1868–1880* (Stanford, California, 1955), Chapter VII.

42. Norman, *op. cit.,* p. 94. Takahashi makes an additional important observation: "These measures taken by the government of the Restoration on one hand relieved the magnates *(daimyo)* of their ancient debts to usurers, and on the other hand transformed the capitalists-usurers who were often compelled to lend them money under feudal coercion into bearers of debentures redeemable by the nation. What only yesterday was valueless paper now became capital with a modern function." *Op. cit.,* p. 252 n.

43. From 1875 to 1880 the aggregate capital of banks expanded from 2,450,000 yen to 43,040,000 yen. "The increase was very largely the result of the issuance of pension funds to *samurai* and *daimyo* in 1876; these bonds could be exchanged at the treasury for bank notes to be used in the establishment of national banks." Thomas C. Smith, *op. cit.,* Chapter IV. Cf. also Pevsner, *op. cit.,* p. 20.

44. Thomas C. Smith, *op. cit.,* Chapter IV.

45. *Capital* (Kerr ed.), Vol. 1, p. 338. (The translation has been slightly changed in the light of the German original.) The first part of this passage, incidentally, is of consid-erable relevance to our earlier discussion of monopoly capitalism; cf. p. 76 above. [Not in

this volume. See P. Baran, *The Political Economy of Growth* (New York: Monthly Review Press, 1957).]

46. Norman, *Japan's Emergence as a Modern State* (New York, 1946), p. 131. "The factories were sold, as a rule, for 15 to 30 percent of the amounts which they cost the government and so that the buyers were permitted to pay the purchase price over long periods of time, sometimes as long as two to three decades." Pevsner, *op. cit.*, p. 23.

47. On the currently rampant research in "entrepreneurial history" lavishly supported by corporations and learned foundations the purpose of which is the glorification of the robber baron, cf. Leo Huberman, "The 'New' History or the Crowning of Mammon," *Monthly Review* (August 1952), as well as Herbert Aptheker, *Laureates of Imperialism* (New York, 1954).

48. Even now, after nearly one hundred years of intensive explorations, the known natural wealth of Japan cannot be compared with that of most other industrial countries. It has no oil, no bauxite, no nonferrous metals, very little coal and iron, the only saving feature being its large capacity for generating hydroelectric power. Cf. E. W. Zimmerman, *World Resources and Industries* (revised edition, New York, 1951), in particular pp. 456, 525, 718.

49. Norman, *op cit.*, p. 46.

50. "The old Imperialism levied tribute; the new Imperialism lends money at interest." H. N. Brailsford, *The War of Steel and Gold* (London, 1914), p. 65. The waning importance of merchant capital and the waxing of industrial and financial interests leading to a marked cooling off of the enthusiasm for additional commitments to the conquest of rather doubtful Far Eastern markets rejected itself in the progressive decline of the influence of the so-called Old China Hands. Cf. the excellent account in N. A. Pelcovits, *Old China Hands and the Foreign Office* (New York, 1948).

51. "The peculiar complexity of the international situation from 1850 right through to the end of the American Civil War and the outbreak of the Franco-Prussian War, and the stalemate resulting from the Anglo-French intrigues in Japan . . . gave Japan the vitally necessary breathing-space in which to shake off the restricting fetters of feudalism which had caused the country to rot economically and to be exposed to the dangers of commercial and military domination from abroad." Norman, *op. cit.*, p. 46.

52. Kh. Eydus, *Yaponia ot Pervoy do Vtoroy Mirovoy Voiny* (Japan from the First to the Second World War) (Moscow, 1946), p. 4.

53. Thomas C. Smith, *Political Change and Industrial Development in Japan: Government Enterprise, 1868–1880* (Stanford, California, 1955), Chapter I.

54. *Sochinenya* (Works) (4th edition, Moscow, 1947), Vol. 15, p. 161.

55. "In the commodity production unfolding in the depths of Chinese feudal society there were nascent already the first beginnings of capitalism. China would have therefore even without the impact of foreign capitalism gradually developed into a capitalist country." Mao Tse-tung, *Isbrannye Proizvedenia* (Selected Works) (Moscow, 1953), Vol. III, p. 142.

7

ANDRÉ GUNDER FRANK

The Development of Underdevelopment

We cannot hope to formulate adequate development theory and policy for the majority of the world's population who suffer from underdevelopment without first learning how their past economic and social history gave rise to their present underdevelopment. Yet most historians study only the developed metropolitan countries and pay scant attention to the colonial and underdeveloped lands. For this reason most of our theoretical categories and guides to development policy have been distilled exclusively from the historical experience of the European and North American advanced capitalist nations.

Since the historical experience of the colonial and underdeveloped countries has demonstrably been quite different, available theory therefore fails to reflect the past of the underdeveloped part of the world entirely, and reflects the past of the world as a whole only in part. More important, our ignorance of the underdeveloped countries' history leads us to assume that their past and indeed their present resembles earlier stages of the history of the now developed countries. This ignorance and this assumption lead us into serious misconceptions about contemporary underdevelopment and development. Further, most studies of development and underdevelopment fail to take account of the economic and other relations between the metropolis and its economic colonies throughout the history of the world-wide expansion and development of the mercantilist and capitalist system. Consequently, most of our theory fails to explain the structure and development of the capitalist system as a whole and to account for its simultane-

EDITOR'S NOTE: *One of the firm classics of dependency theory, Frank's article provided the solid rejoinder to the mainstream rhetoric of Lewis and Rostow (and many varieties of EuroMarxism) with its brilliantly original separation of "undevelopment" (a natural state) from "underdevelopment" (a forcibly created retardation), thereby boosting the Baran hypothesis and providing a powerful radical countercurrent to mainstream and Marxian orthodoxy.*

ous generation of underdevelopment in some of its parts and of economic development in others.

It is generally held that economic development occurs in a succession of capitalist stages and that today's underdeveloped countries are still in a stage, sometimes depicted as an original stage of history, through which the now developed countries passed long ago. Yet even a modest acquaintance with history shows that underdevelopment is not original or traditional and that neither the past nor the present of the underdeveloped countries resembles in any important respect the past of the now developed countries. The now developed countries were never *under*developed, though they may have been *un*developed. It is also widely believed that the contemporary underdevelopment of a country can be understood as the product or reflection solely of its own economic, political, social, and cultural characteristics or structure. Yet historical research demonstrates that contemporary underdevelopment is in large part the historical product of past and continuing economic and other relations between the satellite underdeveloped and the now developed metropolitan countries. Furthermore, these relations are an essential part of the structure and development of the capitalist system on a world scale as a whole. A related and also largely erroneous view is that the development of these underdeveloped countries and, within them of their most underdeveloped domestic areas, must and will be generated or stimulated by diffusing capital, institutions, values, etc., to them from the international and national capitalist metropoles. Historical perspective based on the underdeveloped countries' past experience suggests that on the contrary in the underdeveloped countries economic development can now occur only independently of most of these relations of diffusion.

Evident inequalities of income and differences in culture have led many observers to see "dual" societies and economies in the underdeveloped countries. Each of the two parts is supposed to have a history of its own, a structure, and a contemporary dynamic largely independent of the other. Supposedly, only one part of the economy and society has been importantly affected by intimate economic relations with the "outside" capitalist world; and that part, it is held, became modern, capitalist, and relatively developed precisely because of this contact. The other part is widely regarded as variously isolated, subsistence-based, feudal, or precapitalist, and therefore more underdeveloped.

I believe on the contrary that the entire "dual society" thesis is false and that the policy recommendations to which it leads will, if acted upon, serve only to intensify and perpetuate the very conditions of underdevelopment they are supposedly designed to remedy.

A mounting body of evidence suggests, and I am confident that future historical research will confirm, that the expansion of the capitalist system over the past centuries effectively and entirely penetrated even the apparently most isolated sectors of the underdeveloped world. Therefore, the economic, political, social, and cultural institutions and relations we now observe there are the products of the historical development of the capitalist system no less than are the seemingly more modern or capitalist features of the national metropoles of these underdeveloped countries. Analogously to the relations between development and underdevelopment on the international level, the contemporary underdeveloped institutions of the so-called backward or feudal domestic areas of an underdeveloped country are no less the product of the single historical process of capitalist development than are the so-called capitalist institutions of the supposedly more progressive areas. In this paper I should like to sketch the kinds of evidence which support this thesis and at the same time indicate lines along which further study and research could fruitfully proceed.

II

The Secretary General of the Latin American Center for Research in the Social Sciences writes in that Center's journal: "The privileged position of the city has its origin in the colonial period. It was founded by the Conqueror to serve the same ends that it still serves today; to incorporate the indigenous population into the economy brought and developed by that Conqueror and his descendants. The regional city was an instrument of conquest and is still today an instrument of domination."[1] The Instituto Nacional Indigenista (National Indian Institute) of Mexico confirms this observation when it notes that "the mestizo population, in fact, always lives in a city, a center of an intercultural region, which acts as the metropolis of a zone of indigenous population and which maintains with the underdeveloped communities an intimate relation which links the center with the satellite communities."[2] The Institute goes on to point out that "between the mestizos who live in the nuclear city of the region and the Indians who live in the peasant hinterland there is in reality a closer economic and social interdependence than might at first glance appear" and that the provincial metropoles "by being centers of intercourse are also centers of exploitation."[3]

Thus these metropolis-satellite relations are not limited to the imperial or international level but penetrate and structure the very economic, political, and social life of the Latin American colonies and countries. Just as the colonial and national capital and its export sector become the satellite of the Iberian (and later of other) metropoles of the world economic system, this satellite immediately becomes a colonial and then a national metropolis with respect to the productive sectors and population of the interior. Furthermore, the provincial capitals, which thus are themselves satellites of the national metropolis—and through the latter of the world metropolis—are in turn provincial centers around which their own local satellites orbit. Thus, a whole chain of constellations of metropoles and satellites relates all parts of the whole system from its metropolitan center in Europe or the United States to the farthest outpost in the Latin American countryside.

When we examine this metropolis-satellite structure, we find that each of the satellites, including now-underdeveloped Spain and Portugal, serves as an instrument to suck capital or economic surplus out of its own satellites and to channel part of this surplus to the world metropolis of which all are satellites. Moreover, each national and local metropolis serves to impose and maintain the monopolistic structure and exploitative relationship of this system (as the Instituto Nacional Indigenista of Mexico calls it) as long as it serves the interests of the metropoles which take advantage of this global, national, and local structure to promote their own development and the enrichment of their ruling classes.

These are the principal and still surviving structural characteristics which were implanted in Latin America by the Conquest. Beyond examining the establishment of this colonial structure in its historical context, the proposed approach calls for study of the development—and underdevelopment—of these metropoles and satellites of Latin America throughout the following and still continuing historical process. In this way we can understand why there were and still are tendencies in the Latin American and world capitalist structure which seem to lead to the development of the metropolis and the underdevelopment of the satellite and why, particularly, the satellized national, regional, and local metropoles in Latin America find that their economic development is at best a limited or underdeveloped development.

III

That present underdevelopment of Latin America is the result of its centuries-long participation in the process of world capitalist development, I believe I have shown in my case studies of the economic and social histories of Chile and Brazil.[4] My study of Chilean history suggests that the Conquest not only incorporated this country fully into the expansion and development of the world mercantile and later industrial capitalist system but that it also introduced the monopolistic metropolis-satellite structure and development of capitalism into the Chilean domestic economy and society itself. This structure then penetrated and permeated all of Chile very quickly. Since that time and in the course of world and Chilean history during the epochs of colonialism, free trade, imperialism, and the present, Chile has become increasingly marked by the economic, social, and political structure of satellite underdevelopment. This development of underdevelopment continues today, both in Chile's still increasing satellization by the world metropolis and through the ever more acute polarization of Chile's domestic economy.

The history of Brazil is perhaps the clearest case of both national and regional development of underdevelopment. The expansion of the world economy since the beginning of the sixteenth century successively converted the Northeast, the Minas Gerais interior, the North, and the Center-South (Rio de Janeiro, São Paulo, and Paraná) into export economies and incorporated them into the structure and development of the world capitalist system. Each of these regions experienced what may have appeared as economic development during the period of its respective golden age. But it was a satellite development which was neither self-generating nor self-perpetuating. As the market or the productivity of the first three regions declined, foreign and domestic economic interest in them waned; and they were left to develop the underdevelopment they live today. In the fourth region, the coffee economy experienced a similar though not yet quite as serious fate (though the development of a synthetic coffee substitute promises to deal it a mortal blow in the not too distant future). All of this historical evidence contradicts the generally accepted theses that Latin America suffers from a dual society or from the survival of feudal institutions and that these are important obstacles to its economic development.

IV

During the First World War, however, and even more during the Great Depression and the Second World War, São Paulo began to build up an industrial establishment which is the largest in Latin America today. The question arises whether this industrial development did or can break Brazil out of the cycle of satellite development and underdevelopment which has characterized its other regions and national history within the capitalist system so far. I believe that the answer is no. Domestically the evidence so far is fairly clear. The development of industry in São Paulo has not brought greater riches to the other regions of Brazil. Instead, it converted them into internal colonial satellites, de-capitalized them further, and consolidated or even deepened their underdevelopment. There is little evidence to suggest that this process is likely to be reversed in the foreseeable future except insofar as the provincial poor migrate and become the poor of the metropolitan cities. Externally, the evidence is that although the initial development of São Paulo's industry was relatively autonomous it is being increasingly satellized by the world capitalist metropolis and its future development possibilities are increasingly restricted.[5] This development, my studies lead me to believe, also appears destined to limited or underdeveloped development as long as it takes place in the present economic, political, and social framework.

We must conclude, in short, that underdevelopment is not due to the survival of archaic institutions and the existence of capital shortage in regions that have remained isolated from the stream of world history. On the contrary, underdevelopment was and still is generated by the very same historical process which also generated economic development: the development of capitalism itself. This view, I am glad to say, is gaining adherents among students of Latin America and is proving its worth in shedding new light on the problems of the area and in affording a better perspective for the formulation of theory and policy.[6]

V

The same historical and structural approach can also lead to better development theory and policy by generating a series of hypotheses about development and underdevelopment such as those I am testing in my current research. The hypotheses are derived from the empirical observation and theoretical assumption that within this world-embracing metropolis-satellite structure the metropoles tend to develop and the satellites to underdevelop. The first hypothesis has already been mentioned above: that in contrast to the development of the world metropolis which is no one's satellite, the development of the national and other subordinate metropoles is limited by their satellite status. It is perhaps more difficult to test this hypothesis than the following ones because part of its confirmation depends on the test of the other hypotheses. Nonetheless, this hypothesis appears to be generally confirmed by the non-autonomous and unsatisfactory economic and especially industrial development of Latin America's national metropoles, as documented in the studies already cited. The most important and at the same time most confirmatory examples are the metropolitan regions of Buenos Aires and São Paulo whose growth only began in the nineteenth century, was therefore largely untrammelled by any colonial heritage, but was and remains a satellite development largely dependent on the outside metropolis, first of Britain and then of the United States.

A second hypothesis is that the satellites experience their greatest economic development and especially their most classically capitalist industrial development if and when their ties to their metropolis are weakest. This hypothesis is almost diametrically opposed to the generally accepted thesis that development in the underdeveloped countries follows from the greatest degree of contact with and diffusion from the metropolitan developed countries. This hypothesis seems to be confirmed by two kinds of relative isolation that Latin America has experienced in the course of its history. One is the temporary isolation caused by the crises of war or depression in the world metropolis. Apart from minor ones, five periods of such major crises stand out and seem to confirm the hypothesis. These are: the European (and especially Spanish) Depression of the seventeenth century, the Napoleonic Wars, the First World War, the Depression of the 1930's, and the Second World War. It is clearly established and generally recognized that the most important recent industrial development—especially of Argentina, Brazil, and Mexico, but also of other countries such as Chile—has taken place precisely during the periods of the two World Wars and the intervening Depression. Thanks to the consequent loosening of trade and investment ties during these periods, the satellites initiated marked autonomous industrialization and growth. Historical research demonstrates that the same thing happened in Latin America during Europe's seventeenth-century depression. Manufacturing grew in the Latin American countries, and several of them such as Chile became exporters of manufactured goods. The Napoleonic Wars gave rise to independence movements in Latin America, and these should perhaps also be interpreted as confirming the development hypothesis in part.

The other kind of isolation which tends to confirm the second hypothesis is the geographic and economic isolation of regions which at one time were relatively weakly tied to and poorly integrated into the mercantilist and capitalist system. My preliminary research suggests that in Latin America it was these regions which initiated and experienced the most promising self-generating economic development of the classical industrial capitalist type. The most important regional cases probably are Tucumán and Asunción, as well as other cities such as Mendoza and Rosario, in the interior of Argentina and Paraguay during the end of the eighteenth and the beginning of the nineteenth centuries. Seventeenth and eighteenth century São Paulo, long before coffee was grown there, is another example. Perhaps Antioquia in Colombia and Puebla and Querétaro in Mexico are other examples. In its own way, Chile was also an example since, before the sea route around the Horn was opened, this country was relatively isolated at the end of the long voyage from Europe via Panama. All of these regions became manufacturing centers and even exporters, usually of textiles, during the periods preceding their effective incorporation as satellites into the colonial, national, and world capitalist system.

Internationally, of course, the classic case of industrialization through non-participation as a satellite in the capitalist world system is obviously that of Japan after the Meiji Restoration. Why, one may ask, was resource-poor but unsatellized Japan able to industrialize so quickly at the end of the century while resource-rich Latin American countries and Russia were not able to do so and the latter was easily beaten by Japan in the War of 1904 after the same forty years of development efforts? The second hypothesis suggests that the fundamental reason is that Japan was not satellized either during the Tokugawa or the Meiji period and therefore did not have its development structurally limited as did the countries which were so satellized.

VI

A corollary of the second hypothesis is that when the metropolis recovers from its crisis and re-establishes the trade and investment ties which fully re-incorporate the satellites into the system, or when the metropolis expands to incorporate previously isolated regions into the world-wide system, the previous development and industrialization of these regions is choked off or channelled into directions which are not self-perpetuating and promising. This happened after each of the five crises cited above. The renewed expansion of trade and the spread of economic liberalism in the eighteenth and nineteenth centuries choked off and reversed the manufacturing development which Latin America had experienced during the seventeenth century, and in some places at the beginning of the nineteenth. After the First World War, the new national industry of Brazil suffered serious consequences from American economic invasion. The increase in the growth rate of Gross National Product and particularly of industrialization throughout Latin America was again reversed and industry became increasingly satellized after the Second World War and especially after the post–Korean War recovery and expansion of the metropolis. Far from having become more developed since then, industrial sectors of Brazil and most conspicuously of Argentina have become structurally more and more underdeveloped and less and less able to generate continued industrialization and/or sustain development of the economy. This process, from which India also suffers, is reflected in a whole gamut of balance-of-payments, inflationary, and other economic and political difficulties, and promises to yield to no solution short of far-reaching structural change.

Our hypothesis suggests that fundamentally the same process occurred even more dramatically with the incorporation into the system of previously unsatellized regions. The expansion of Buenos Aires as a satellite of Great Britain and the introduction of free trade in the interest of the ruling groups of both metropoles destroyed the manufacturing and much of the remainder of the economic base of the previously relatively prosperous interior almost entirely. Manufacturing was destroyed by foreign competition, lands were taken and concentrated into latifundia by the rapaciously growing export economy, intraregional distribution of income became much more unequal, and the previously developing regions became simple satellites of Buenos Aires and through it of London. The provincial centers did not yield to satellization without a struggle. This metropolis-satellite conflict was much of the cause of the long political and armed struggle between the Unitarists in Buenos Aires and the Federalists in the provinces, and it may be said to have been the sole important cause of the War of the Triple Alliance in which Buenos Aires, Montevideo, and Rio de Janeiro, encouraged and helped by London, destroyed not only the autonomously developing economy of Paraguay but killed off nearly all of its population which was unwilling to give in. Though this is no doubt the most spectacular example which tends to confirm the hypothesis, I believe that historical research on the satellization of previously relatively independent yeoman-farming and incipient manufacturing regions such as the Caribbean islands will confirm it further.[7] These regions did not have a chance against the forces of expanding and developing capitalism, and their own development had to be sacrificed to that of others. The economy and industry of Argentina, Brazil, and other countries which have experienced the effects of metropolitan recovery since the Second World War are today suffering much the same fate, if fortunately still in lesser degree.

VII

A third major hypothesis derived from the metropolis-satellite structure is that the regions which are the most underdeveloped and feudal-seeming today are the ones which had the closest ties to the metropolis in the past. They are the regions which were the greatest exporters of primary products to and the biggest sources of capital for the world metropolis and which were abandoned by the metropolis when for one reason or another business fell off. This hypothesis also contradicts the generally held thesis that the source of a region's underdevelopment is its isolation and its pre-capitalist institutions.

This hypothesis seems to be amply confirmed by the former super-satellite development and present ultra-underdevelopment of the once sugar-exporting West Indies, Northeastern Brazil, the ex-mining districts of Minas Gerais in Brazil, highland Peru, and Bolivia, and the central Mexican states of Guanajuato, Zacatecas, and others whose names were made world famous centuries ago by their silver. There surely are no major regions in Latin America which are today more cursed by underdevelopment and poverty; yet all of these regions, like Bengal in India, once provided the life blood of mercantile and industrial capitalist development—in the metropolis. These regions' participation in the development of the world capitalist system gave them, already in their golden age, the typical structure of underdevelopment of a capitalist export economy. When the market for their sugar or the wealth of their mines disappeared and the metropolis abandoned them to their own devices, the already existing economic, political, and social structure of these regions prohibited autonomous generation of economic development and left them no alternative but to turn in upon themselves and to degenerate into the ultra-underdevelopment we find there today.

VIII

These considerations suggest two further and related hypotheses. One is that the latifundium, irrespective of whether it appears as a plantation or a hacienda today, was typically born as a commercial enterprise which created for itself the institutions which permitted it to respond to increased demand in the world or national market by expanding the amount of its land, capital, and labor and to increase the supply of its products. The fifth hypothesis is that the latifundia which appear isolated, subsistence-based, and semi-feudal today saw the demand for their products or their productive capacity decline and that they are to be found principally in the above-named former agricultural and mining export regions whose economic activity declined in general. These two hypotheses run counter to the notions of most people, and even to the opinions of some historians and other students of the subject, according to whom the historical roots and socio-economic causes of Latin American latifundia and agrarian institutions are to be found in the transfer of feudal institutions from Europe and/or in economic depression.

The evidence to test these hypotheses is not open to easy general inspection and requires detailed analyses of many cases. Nonetheless, some important confirmatory evidence is available. The growth of the latifundium in nineteenth-century Argentina and Cuba is a clear case in support of the fourth hypothesis and can in no way be attributed to the transfer of feudal institutions during colonial times. The same is evidently the case of the post-revolutionary and contemporary resurgence of latifundia particularly in the North of Mexico, which produce for the American market, and of similar ones on the coast of Peru and the new coffee regions of Brazil. The conversion of previously yeoman-farming Caribbean islands, such as Barbados, into sugar exporting economies at various times between the seventeenth and twentieth centuries and the resulting rise of the latifundia in these islands would seem to confirm the fourth hypothesis as well. In Chile, the rise of the latifundium and the creation of the institutions of servitude which later came to be called feudal occurred in the eighteenth century and have been conclusively shown to be the result of and response to the opening of a market for Chilean wheat in Lima.[8] Even the growth and consolidation of the latifundium in seventeenth-century Mexico—which most expert students have attributed to a depression of the economy caused by the decline of mining and a shortage of Indian labor and to a consequent turning in upon itself and ruralization of the economy—occurred at a time when urban population and demand were growing, food shortages became acute, food prices skyrocketed, and the profitability of other economic activities such as mining and foreign trade declined.[9] All of these and other factors rendered hacienda agriculture more profitable. Thus, even this case would seem to confirm the hypothesis that the growth of the latifundium and its feudal-seeming conditions of servitude in Latin America has always been and still is the commercial response to increased demand and that it does not represent the transfer or survival of alien institutions that have remained beyond the reach of capitalist development. The emergence of latifundia, which today really are more or less (though not entirely) isolated, might then be attributed to the causes advanced in the fifth hypothesis—i.e., the decline of previously profitable agricultural enterprises whose capital was, and whose currently produced economic surplus still is, transferred elsewhere by owners and merchants who frequently are the same persons or families. Testing this hypothesis requires still more detailed analysis, some of which I have undertaken in a study on Brazilian agriculture.[10]

IX

All of these hypotheses and studies suggest that the global extension and unity of the capitalist system, its monopoly structure and uneven development throughout its history, and the resulting persistence of commercial rather than industrial capitalism in the underdeveloped world (including its most industrially advanced countries) deserve much more attention in the study of economic development and cultural change than they have hitherto received. Though science and truth know no national boundaries, it is probably new generations of scientists from the underdeveloped countries themselves who most need to, and best can, devote the necessary attention to these problems and clarify the process of underdevelopment and development. It is their people who in the last analysis face the task of changing this no longer acceptable process and eliminating this miserable reality.

They will not be able to accomplish these goals by importing sterile stereo-types from the metropolis which do not correspond to their satellite economic reality and do not respond to their liberating political needs. To change their reality they must understand it. For this reason, I hope that better confirmation of these hypotheses and further pursuit of the proposed historical, holistic, and structural approach may help the peoples of the underdeveloped countries to understand the causes and eliminate the reality of their development of underde-velopment and their underdevelopment of development.

Notes

1. *América Latina*, Año 6, No. 4, October-December 1963, p. 8.
2. Instituto Nacional Indigenista, *Los centros coordinadores indigenistas*, Mexico, 1962, p. 34.
3. *Ibid.*, pp. 33–34, 88.
4. "Capitalist Development and Underdevelopment in Chile" and "Capitalist Development and Underdevelopment in Brazil" in *Capitalism and Underdevelopment in Latin America*, to be published soon by Monthly Review Press.
5. Also see, "The Growth and Decline of Import Substitution," *Economic Bulletin for Latin America*, New York, IX, No. 1, March 1964; and Celso Furtado, *Dialectica do Desenvolvimiento*, Rio de Janeiro, Fundo de Cultura, 1964.
6. Others who use a similar approach, though their ideologies do not permit them to derive the logically following conclusions, are Aníbal Pinto S.C., *Chile: Un caso de desarrollo frustrado*, Santiago, Editorial Universitaria, 1957; Celso Furtado, *A formaçao económica do Brasil*, Rio de Janeiro, Fundo de Cultura, 1959 (recently translated into English and published under the title *The Economic Growth of Brazil* by the University of California Press); and Caio Prado Junior, *Historia Económica do Brasil*, São Paulo, Editora Brasiliense, 7th ed., 1962.
7. See for instance Ramón Guerra y Sánchez, *Azúcar y Población en las Antillas*, Havana 1942, 2nd ed., also published as *Sugar and Society in the Caribbean*, New Haven, Yale University Press, 1964.
8. Mario Góngora, *Origen de los "inquilinos" de Chile central*, Santiago, Editorial Universitaria, 1960; Jean Borde and Mario Góngora, *Evolución de la propiedad rural en el Valle del Puango*, Santiago, Instituto de Sociología de la Universidad de Chile; Sergio Sepúlveda, *El trigo chileno en el mercado mundial*, Santiago, Editorial Universitario, 1959.
9. Woodrow Borah makes depression the centerpiece of his explanation in "New Spain's Century of Depression," *Ibero-Americana*, Berkeley, No. 35, 1951. François Chevalier speaks of turning in upon itself in the most authoritative study of the subject, "La formación de los grandes latifundios en México," Mexico, *Problemas Agrícolas e Industriales de México*, VIII, No. 1, 1956 (translated from the French and recently pub-lished by the University of California Press). The data which provide the basis for my contrary interpretation are supplied by these authors themselves. This problem is dis-cussed in my "Con qué modo de producción convierte la gallina maíz en huevos de oro?" *El Gallo Ilustrado*, Suplemento de *El Día*, Mexico, Nos. 175 and 179, October 31 and November 28, 1965; and it is further analyzed in a study of Mexican agriculture under preparation by the author.
10. "Capitalism and the Myth of Feudalism in Brazilian Agriculture," in *Capitalism and Underdevelopment in Latin America*, cited in footnote 4 above.

8

S. Amin

The Origin and Development of Underdevelopment

1. A Theory of the Transition to Peripheral Capitalism

Marx's writings on non-European societies are not extensive: little more than four hundred pages, mostly consisting of articles for the *New York Daily Tribune*, focused on topical matters—the Sepoy mutiny in India and the Taiping rebellion in China, the opium trade, etc.—and often looked at merely from the standpoint of British domestic politics. Marx discusses only in a subordinate way the problems of Asiatic society and of the transformation of this society as a result of colonial subjection. Three types of problems are in fact touched on by him.

From time to time Marx discusses the nature of precolonial "Asiatic" society, notably in the passage in the *Grundrisse* where he formulates the concept of the Asiatic mode of production. He emphasizes the obstacle that the village community— in other words, the absence of private ownership of land—puts in the way of the development of capitalism. Here he reveals brilliant insight, when we recall the state of knowledge about non-European societies at that time.

Discussing the transformation that colonial rule was bringing to these societies, especially in India, Marx claimed that this would lead the East to full capitalist development. True, he noted that colonial policy was opposed to this, forbidding the establishment of modern industry in the colonies after having destroyed the crafts. But he considered that no power would be able to hinder for long the local development of capitalism on the European model. The article

---

EDITOR'S NOTE: *Amin, a highly original, but heterodox, Marxist of Egyptian origin, was the great synthesizer of Frank and Baran with his radical neo-Marxian analysis of the distinction between "disarticulation" and "autocentered" accumulation. The theses in this short work are classical, testable, and entirely convincing propositions about the nature of peripheral development. These ideas would ultimately point to the necessity for "delinking" (with the West) as a critical issue for peripheral economies.*

devoted to "The Future Results of British Rule in India" is explicit on this point: the plundering of India by the British aristocracy and merchant capital will be followed by industrialization carried out by the bourgeoisie of the metropolitan country; the railways will give rise to autocentric industries. Marx is so certain of this that he fears lest a developed bourgeois East may eventually prevent victory of the socialist revolution in Europe. He writes in a letter to Engels (in Avineri, p. 464): "On the Continent the revolution is imminent and will immediately assume a socialist character. Is it not bound to be crushed in this little corner, considering that in a far greater territory the movement of bourgeois society is still in the ascendant?"

In fact, the monopolies, the rise of which Marx could not imagine, were to prevent any local capitalism that might arise from competing. The development of capitalism in the periphery was to remain extraverted, based on the external market, and could therefore not lead to a full flowering of the capitalist mode of production in the periphery. Writing as he was in this early period of colonialism, Marx perceived only those mechanisms of primitive accumulation for the benefit of the center that belonged to the mercantilist phase and were coming to an end, and which he therefore regarded as belonging to the prehistory of capital.

Marx did, however, glimpse another possible outcome—Eastern society proletarianized for the benefit of the center, with the latter, proletariat included, becoming "bourgeoisified," and the periphery emerging as the main revolutionary force. In *The Poverty of Philosophy* (p. 35) he writes of "millions of workers who had to perish in the East Indies so as to procure for the million and a half workers employed in England in the same industry, three years' prosperity out of ten."

For my part, I put forward, as regards the theory of the transition to peripheral capitalist economy, the following nine theses:

1. Economic theory interests itself occasionally in the problems of "transition from a subsistence economy to a money economy." In reality, however, the pattern of transition to peripheral capitalism is fundamentally different from that of transition to central capitalism. The onslaught from without, by means of trade, carried out by the capitalist mode of production upon the precapitalist formations, causes certain crucial retrogressions to take place, such as the ruin of the crafts without their being replaced by local industrial production. The agrarian crisis of the Third World of today is largely the result of these setbacks. The subsequent investment of foreign capital does not have the effect of correcting these retrogressive changes, owing to the extravert orientation of the industries that this capital establishes in the periphery.

2. Unequal international specialization is manifested in three kinds of distortion in the direction taken by the development of the periphery. The distortion toward export activities (extraversion), which is the decisive one, does not result from "inadequacy of the home market" but from the superior productivity of the center in all fields, which compels the periphery to confine itself to the role of

complementary supplier of products for the production of which it possesses a natural advantage: exotic agricultural produce and minerals. When, as a result of this distortion, the level of wages in the periphery has become lower, for the same productivity, than at the center, a limited development of industries focused on the home market of the periphery will have become possible, while at the same time exchange will have become unequal. The subsequent pattern of industrialization through import-substitution, together with the (as yet embryonic) effects of the new international division of labor inside the transnational firm, do not alter the essential conditions of extraversion, even if they alter the forms that it takes.

3. This initial distortion brings another in its train: the hypertrophy of the tertiary sector in the periphery, which neither the evolution of the structure of demand nor that of productivities can explain. At the center, hypertrophy of the tertiary sector reflects the difficulties in realizing surplus value that are inherent in the advanced monopoly phase, whereas in the periphery it is from the beginning a result of the limitations and contradictions characteristic of peripheral development: inadequate industrialization and increasing unemployment, strengthening of the position of ground rent, etc. A fetter on accumulation, this hypertrophy of unproductive activities, expressed especially in the excessive growth of administrative expenditure, is manifested in the Third World of today by the quasi-permanent crisis of government finance.

4. Unequal international specialization also underlies the distortion in the periphery toward light branches of activity, together with the employment of modern production techniques in these branches. This distortion is the source of special problems that dictate development policies in the periphery that are different from those on which the development of the West was based.

5. The theory of the multiplier effects of investment cannot be extended in a mechanical way to the periphery. The significance of the Keynesian multiplier does indeed correspond to the situation at the center in the phase of advanced monopoly, characterized by difficulties in realizing the surplus. Neither hoarding nor imports constitute, in the periphery, "leaks" that reduce the multiplier effect. What annuls this effect is the exporting of the profits of foreign capital. Furthermore, unequal specialization, and the marked propensity to import that follows from this, have the effect of transferring the effects of the multiplier mechanisms connected with the phenomenon known as the "accelerator" from the periphery to the center.

6. Analysis of the strategies of foreign monopolies in the underdeveloped countries shows that, so long as the dogma of the periphery's integration in the world market is not challenged, the periphery is without economic means of action in relation to the monopolies.

7. Underdevelopment is manifested not in level of production per head, but in certain characteristic structural features that oblige us not to confuse the underdeveloped countries with the now-advanced countries as they were at an earlier

stage of their development. These features are: (1) the extreme unevenness that is typical of the distribution of productivities in the periphery, and in the system of prices transmitted to it from the center, which results from the distinctive nature of the peripheral formations and largely dictates the structure of the distribution of income in these formations; (2) the disarticulation due to the adjustment of the orientation of production in the periphery to the needs of the center, which prevents the transmission of the benefits of economic progress from the poles of development to the economy as a whole; and (3) economic domination by the center, which is expressed in the forms of international specialization (the structures of world trade in which the center shapes the periphery in accordance with its own needs) and in the dependence of the structures whereby growth in the periphery is financed (the dynamic of the accumulation of foreign capital).

8. The accentuation of the features of underdevelopment, in proportion as the economic growth of the periphery proceeds, necessarily results in the blocking of growth, in other words, the impossibility, whatever the level of production per head that may be obtained, of going over to autocentric and autodynamic growth.

9. While at the center the capitalist mode of production tends to become exclusive, the same is not true of the periphery. Consequently, the peripheral formations are fundamentally different from those of the center. The forms assumed by these peripheral formations depend, on the one hand, upon the nature of the precapitalist formations that were there previously, and, on the other, upon the forms and epochs in which they were integrated into the world system. This analysis enables us to grasp the essential difference that contrasts the peripheral formations to the "young central formations"—the latter, based on predominance of the simple commodity mode of production, possessing for this reason a capacity for independent evolution toward a fully developed capitalist mode of production. Whatever their differences of origin, the peripheral formations all tend to converge upon a typical model, characterized by the dominance of agrarian capital and ancillary (comprador) commercial capital. The domination by central capital over the system as a whole, and the vital mechanisms of primitive accumulation for its benefit which express this domination, subject the development of peripheral national capitalism to strict limitations, which are ultimately dependent upon political relations. The mutilated nature of the national community in the periphery confers an apparent relative weight and special functions upon the local bureaucracy that are not the same as those of the bureaucratic and technocratic social groups at the center. The contradictions typical of the development of underdevelopment, and the rise of petty-bourgeois strata reflecting these contradictions, explain the present tendency to state capitalism. This new path of development for capitalism in the periphery does not constitute a mode of transition to socialism but rather expresses the future form in which new relations will be organized between center and periphery.

9

RAÚL PREBISCH

The Latin American Periphery in the Global System of Capitalism

I. The Dynamics of the Centres

Peripheral development is an integral part of the world system of capitalism, but the conditions in which it takes place are different from those in the centres, whence the specificity of peripheral capitalism.

Technology plays a fundamental role in this: its development in the centres is accompanied by continuous changes in their social structure, and this is also true of the peripheral countries when the same technology penetrates them much later. The relations between the two correspondingly alter.

In the course of these continuous changes, some highly important constants are to be found. We shall mention the main ones.

While exerting considerable influence on peripheral development, the dynamics of the centres is limited in scope, on account of the centripetal nature of capitalism. Thus it fosters peripheral development only to the extent that concerns the interests of the dominant groups in the centres.

The centripetal nature of capitalism is constantly manifested in the relations between the centres and the periphery. It is in the former that technical progress originates and that the benefits of the concomitant rise in productivity tend to be concentrated. Thanks to the higher demand which accompanies the rise in productivity, industrialization is likewise concentrated there, spurred on by ceaseless

---

EDITOR'S NOTE: *A powerful figure in economic affairs as early as the interwar period in Latin America, Prebisch went on to become a towering influence in the United Nations–based Economic Commission for Latin America. Rejecting neoclassical trade theory, Prebisch argued in "structuralist" terms for policy-guided domestic industrialization avoiding primary exports and supporting import substitution. This is probably the best example of a non-Marxian, bourgeois "Third-Worldism" bent on fostering an industrial and "national" capitalism in the Third World through policy efforts.*

technological innovation which diversifies the production of goods and services to an ever greater extent.

Thus, in the spontaneous course of development the periphery tends to be left on the margin of this industrialization process in the historical evolution of capitalism.

Rather than deliberate, this exclusion is the consequence of the play of market laws at the international level.

At a later stage, when becoming industrialized as a result of international crises the periphery again tends to be shut off from the major trade flows in manufactures of the centres. The periphery has had to learn to export, and it is doing so primarily through its own efforts, as the transnationals have contributed far more to the internationalization of forms of consumption than to the internationalization of production through trade with the centres.

This largely explains the inherent tendency towards external disequilibrium in past and present peripheral development: an attempt has been made to correct this tendency first through import substitution and subsequently through the export of manufactures.

The centres have by no means encouraged this process through changes in their production structure; and by failing to open their doors to manufacturing imports from the periphery, they force the latter to continue with import substitution. Substitution is not the result of any doctrinaire preference, but rather something imposed by the centripetal nature of capitalism. However, it has been taking place within narrow national compartments, at the expense of economic efficiency and of vigorous development.

The economic interest of the dominant groups of the centres form a cluster with strategic, ideological and political interests in the centres, giving rise to stubborn forms of dependence in centre-periphery relations.

In those relations, the economic interests of the dominant groups of the centres are articulated with those of the peripheral countries, and in the play of these power relations the technical and economic superiority of the former weighs heavily. The structural changes which accompany the development and spread of technology are highly important. In the periphery, besides their significance for its development these changes eventually give rise to disruptive pressures when the internal conflictive tendencies characteristic of development spill over towards the centres, where they arouse an adverse reaction from the power cluster. This is a clear manifestation of the above-mentioned dependence.

The economic interest of the dominant groups continues to prevail in the centres as in the periphery. Its efficiency in the market, at the national and international level, cannot be denied. But the market, despite its enormous economic and political importance, neither is nor can be the supreme regulator of the development of the periphery and of its relations with the centres.

This is patently clear in the present crisis of those relations. The market has not been able to cope with the ambivalence of technology, which has had an incalculable effect on material wellbeing, but has also brought irresponsible exploitation of non-renewable natural resources and a striking deterioration of the biosphere, not to mention other serious consequences.

Nor have the laws of the market remedied the major flaws in centre-periphery relations, nor still less the exclusive and conflictive tendencies in peripheral development.

Individual decisions in the market-place must be combined with collective decisions outside it which override the interest of the dominant groups. All this, however, calls for a great vision, a vision of change, both in peripheral development and in relations with the centres; a vision based on far-reaching projects combining farsighted economic, social and political considerations.

II. The Internal Dynamics of Peripheral Capitalism

The dynamics of the centres does not tend to penetrate deeply the social structure of the periphery; it is essentially limited.

In contrast, the centres propagate and spread in the periphery their technology, forms of consumption and lifestyles, institutions, ideas and ideologies. Peripheral capitalism increasingly draws its inspiration from the centres and tends to develop in their image and likeness.

This imitative development takes place belatedly in a social structure which differs in major respects from the developed structures of the centres.

The penetration of technology takes place through capital accumulation, in terms both of physical means and of the training of human beings. As the process develops, changes continuously take place in the social structure, which embraces a series of partial structures linked together by close relations of interdependence; the technical, production and employment structures, the power structure and the distribution structure. These changes must be analysed to throw light on the complex internal dynamics of peripheral capitalism.

1. Structural Changes, Surplus and Accumulation

The penetration of technology gradually creates successive layers of rising productivity and efficiency which are superimposed upon less productive and efficient technical layers, while at the base of this technological structure precapitalist or semicapitalist layers usually persist. These changes in the technical structure are accompanied by changes in the employment structure, as labour is continuously shifting from the less to the more productive layers. However, the income structure does not develop in line with the changes in technology and occupation. Thus, the mass of the labour force does not increase its earnings correlatively with the growth of productivity in the play of market forces.

This is explained by the regressive competition of the new manpower in the technical layers of low productivity, or else unemployed, which is seeking to enter productive activity. Only a part of the fruits of technical progress are transferred to a limited fraction of the labour force which, above all through its social power, has been able to acquire the ever greater skills required by technology.

The part of the fruits of higher productivity which is not transferred constitutes the surplus, which is appropriated primarily by the upper social strata, where most physical capital as well as land ownership are concentrated.

The surplus does not tend to disappear through a fall in prices resulting from competition among enterprises—even if this were unrestricted—but rather is retained and circulates among them. This is a structural and dynamic phenomenon. The growth of the production of final goods, thanks to the continuous accumulation of capital, means that there must be a preceding growth of production in process which will later give rise to the final goods. For this purpose, enterprises pay higher incomes, giving rise to the greater demand which absorbs the final supply increased by the growth of productivity, without prices falling.

In fact, the incomes thus paid in the successive stages of the process (including the surplus) through the creation of money are much greater than would be necessary to prevent prices from falling. The reason for this is that only part of those incomes immediately becomes demand for final goods. Another part is diverted towards demand for services, in the market and the State spheres, where it circulates and gradually returns to demand for goods. In addition to the incomes paid to factors of production, enterprises purchase imported goods, and thus the exporting countries recover the incomes they paid in producing them as well as the corresponding surplus. The opposite occurs in the case of exports.

There is no strict correspondence between demand for goods and supply, but the necessary adjustments are made spontaneously or through the precautionary corrective intervention of the monetary authority when the capacity for sharing out the surplus has not yet developed.

The unequal distribution of income in favour of the upper strata encourages them to imitate the forms of consumption of the centres, an imitation which tends to spread to the middle strata. The privileged-consumer society which thus develops represents a considerable waste of capital accumulation potential.

This waste concerns not merely the amount but also the composition of capital. Closely linked with the technology which increases productivity and income, use is made of technology which constantly diversifies production of goods and services. As this change occurs in the production structure, together with other forms of investment, the proportion of non-reproductive capital increases without any growth of productivity or multiplication of employment, to the detriment of the reproductive capital necessary for fostering development.

These trends inherent in the internal logic of capitalism in the centres appear prematurely in the periphery on account of the great inequality in distribution.

In addition to all this, again at the expense of accumulation, there is the exorbitant siphoning-off of income by the centres, especially through the transnationals, as a result of their technical and economic superiority and hegemonic power.

This insufficient, stunted accumulation of reproductive capital, aggravated by the trend towards hypertrophy of the State and the extraordinary growth of the population, is the main reason why the system cannot intensively absorb the lower strata of the social structure and cope with other manifestations of redundancy of labour. This is the system's exclusive tendency.

These lower strata abound in agriculture, and as the demand for agricultural goods scarcely becomes diversified, labour tends to shift towards other activities. However, given the system's inadequate capacity to absorb labour, a serious redundancy arises which explains the relative deterioration of labour income in agriculture.

As long as this insufficient capacity to absorb labour lasts, technical progress in agriculture will not raise those incomes and correct their relative decline. Instead, it tends to harm relative prices when production outstrips demand. This is usually true of agricultural exports in particular, and has the effect of checking their growth to the detriment of development.

2. Changes in the Power Structure and Crisis of the System

As technology penetrates the social structure, changes take place which are reflected in the power structure. The middle strata expand, and as the process of democratization advances their trade-union and political power develops and increasingly forms a counterweight to the economic power of those, especially in the upper strata, in whose hands most of the means of production are concentrated. It is therefore in these strata that the labour force possessing social power is mainly found. These power relations between upper and middle strata exist both in the market and in the State spheres. In this way ever-increasing pressure develops for sharing out the fruits of the growth of productivity.

This twofold pressure is largely manifested through a rise in the remuneration of the labour force, either to increase its share in the fruits of productivity or to offset the unfavourable effects of certain factors, above all the tax burden which it bears directly or indirectly and through which the State copes with the trend towards its own hypertrophy.

Bureaucratic power and military power have their own dynamics in the State apparatus, supported by the political power of the middle strata in particular, as a result of which State activities develop beyond considerations of economic efficiency, both as concerns the amount and diversification of State services and in terms of the spurious absorption of labour.

In this way, through the growth of employment and social services the State seeks to correct the system's insufficient absorption of labour and its distributive unfairness; and this is a major factor in its hypertrophy.

To express the foregoing in a nutshell: the distribution of the fruits of the system's rising productivity is fundamentally the result of the changing play of power relations, in addition, of course, to individual differences in ability and dynamism.

As the labour force's sharing capacity increases and it acquires the ability to recoup its tax burden and compensate for the effects of other factors, the rise in remuneration tends to overtake the drop in the costs of enterprises resulting from successive rises in productivity. The excess then tends to be transferred to prices, and this is followed by fresh rises in remuneration in the familiar inflationary spiral.

In these circumstances, for it to be possible to absorb supply, increased by higher costs, it is essential that demand, and the incomes underpinning it, should increase in a correlative manner.

If the monetary authority resists the necessary creation of money in order to avoid or check the spiral, the growth of demand will be insufficient to meet the growth of final production, leading to economic recession which will continue until the authority changes its attitude and prices can rise in line with the higher costs. The rise in prices means that the surplus may once again increase through new rises in productivity, but only temporarily since it is once again compressed by the subsequent rise in remuneration. Thus accumulation declines with adverse consequences for development, besides the disturbances which accompany the heightening of the distributive quarrel.

It should be noted, however, that these phenomena occur when, thanks to the process of democratization, the labour force's trade-union and political power becomes ever greater in both the market and the State spheres, and the latter's expenditure steadily expands through its own dynamics.

In these circumstances, the spiral becomes inherent in peripheral development; and the conventional rules of the monetary game are powerless to avert or suppress it.

These rules are highly valid when distributive power (for sharing out and recouping) is non-existent or very incipient. This is the case when the democratization process is very weak or obstructed or manipulated by the dominant groups: democracy in appearance but not in substance.

Such, then, is the crisis of the system when the arbitrary play of power relations becomes very strong, which is what occurs in the advanced stage of peripheral development. The crisis of the system may be postponed for some time, particularly when plentiful resources are available from the exploitation of non-renewable natural wealth.

The political power of the upper strata, apparently on the wane with the advance of democracy, surges up again when the disturbances brought about by the inflationary crisis give rise to economic disorder and social disintegration. At that point the use of force is introduced, which makes it possible to break the trade-union and political power of the disadvantaged strata.

If the holders of the military power are not necessarily under the sway of the economic and political power of the upper strata, one is tempted to ask why they intervene to serve the privileged-consumer society. Here undoubtedly a complex set of factors comes into play. The fundamental explanation, however, is that since the upper strata hold the dynamic key of the system, i.e., the capacity for capital accumulation, they must be left to get on with it from a desire to restore smooth development; but the social cost is tremendous, not to mention the political cost.

What in fact happens is that democratic liberalism breaks down, while the ideas of economic liberalism flourish: a fake liberalism which, far from leading to the dissemination of the benefits of development, flagrantly consolidates social inequity.

Democratic liberalism has not yet managed to become firmly rooted in the Latin American periphery. We are all too familiar with its vicissitudes, its promising advances and painful setbacks. But the past cannot account for everything: new, complex elements spring up as changes occur in the social structure. And the significance of the use of force is not what it was in the past: the creation of that total split between democratic liberalism and economic liberalism, despite the fact that both sprang from the same philosophical source.

3. The Great Paradox of the Surplus

The foregoing considerations lead to very important conclusions, perhaps the most important in our interpretation of peripheral capitalism.

The surplus is subject to two contrary movements. On the one hand, it grows through successive increases in productivity. On the other, it shrinks through the pressure for sharing which stems from the market and from the State. The system functions smoothly as long as the surplus grows continuously as a result of those two movements.

Consequently, the upper strata, in whose hands most of the means of production are concentrated, can increase capital accumulation and at the same time their privileged consumption: they possess the dynamic key of the system.

This essential condition is satisfied so long as the sharing out of the surplus, both in the market and the State spheres through the play of power relations, occurs at the expense of successive rises in productivity. The surplus will continue to expand, although at a dwindling rate. However, the sharing out cannot go beyond the threshold at which the surplus would begin to shrink.

At that limit, however, the surplus will have become proportionately greatest in relation to the total product. Why is it impossible to continue improving the sharing, when there would be plenty of room for doing so by reducing the surplus? This is the weak point of the system of distribution and accumulation, because if the pressure for sharing outstrips the increase in productivity, the rise in the cost of goods will cause enterprises to raise prices.

The total surplus would undoubtedly allow much more sharing out at the expense of size, but there is nothing in the system to make this happen. It is conceivable that enterprises might take part of the surplus and transfer it to the labour force without raising costs; this would be direct participation in the surplus. But the system does not work like that. Any rise in remuneration over the increment in productivity raises costs, with the consequences described above.

Not all the pressure for sharing, however, takes the form of higher remuneration. As was pointed out earlier, in order to share out the surplus the State resorts to taxes falling on the labour force, which the latter seeks to recoup through higher remuneration; but the State also has the possibility of directly taxing the surplus or the incomes of the social groups in the upper strata who have no capacity for recouping such taxes. These taxes are not transferred to costs, but if their amount squeezes the surplus the rate of accumulation and of growth is weakened, thus accentuating the exclusive and conflictive tendencies.

Whatever the angle from which it is approached, there is no solution to the problem within the system, so long as the capacity for redistribution is strengthened in the advanced stage of the democratization process. Either the result is the inflationary spiral, if sharing leads to higher production costs—which, in addition to the upheaval caused by the spiral, undermines the dynamics of the surplus—or else some of the surplus is taken directly, again with adverse consequences for its dynamics, which sooner or later must be resolved using inflationary means.

However much thought one devotes to the question, it appears that the rules of the game of peripheral capitalism do not allow for an attack on its two major flaws: its exclusive tendency, which may only be remedied by a more intense accumulation of capital at the expense of the privileged strata and of the income transferred to the centres; and its conflictive tendency, unrelentingly heightened in the unrestricted play of power relations.

There is a great paradox in all this. When the surplus grows so far as to reach its ceiling and the pressure for sharing continues, the system reacts by seeking to achieve continued growth of the surplus. In order to attain this objective, it resorts to the use of force. However, the use of force is not a solution; the only solution is to change the system.

4. Crisis of the System and the Use of Force

Given the nature of the system, at the advanced stage of peripheral development and of the democratization process it is impossible to avert the tendency towards crisis. In the system's internal logic there is no lasting way of ensuring that the pressure for sharing does not jeopardize the dynamic role of the surplus and lead inevitably to the inflationary spiral.

The attempt to restore the dynamics of the system through the use of force entails the risk of serious disruption, usually involving a combination of theoretical inconsistency and practical incongruity.

If the system is handled skilfully, however, particularly in favourable external conditions, high rates of accumulation and of development may be achieved with striking prosperity for the privileged social strata, but at the cost of severe compression of the income of a considerable part of the labour force.

This solution, however, by no means strikes at the roots of the system's exclusive and conflictive nature. When the democratization process is resumed sooner or later, the pressure for sharing will tend to lead the system into a new political cycle, aggravated by the deformation which has taken place in the production structure to satisfy the exaltation of the privileged-consumer society.

III. Towards a Theory of Change

1. The Two Options for a Change

The system of accumulation and distribution of the benefits of technical progress is not subject to any regulating principle from the standpoint of the collective interest. If appropriation is arbitrary when market laws prevail, so is redistribution when political and trade-union power becomes a counterweight to those laws.

It is therefore essential for the State to regulate the social use of the surplus, in order to step up the rate of accumulation and progressively correct distributive disparities of a structural nature, which are quite distinct from functional disparities.

At bottom, there are only two ways in which the State can undertake this regulatory activity: by taking into its own hands the ownership and management of the means of production which give rise to the surplus; or by using the surplus in a spirit of collective rationality without concentrating ownership in its own hands.

The political and economic significance of these two options is essentially different. I lean towards the second on account of two fundamental considerations. In the first place, because the major flaws of the system do not lie in private property itself but rather in the private appropriation of the surplus and the harmful consequences of the concentration of the means of production. Secondly, because the first option is incompatible with the paramount concept of democracy and the human rights inherent in it, while in the second that concept becomes fully compatible, both in theory and in practice, with vigorous development and distributive equity.

2. The Dissemination of Capital and Self-Management

The transformation of the system necessarily calls for raising the rate of accumulation of reproductive capital, particularly at the expense of the consumption of the upper strata. The social use of the surplus enables this to be done by disseminating ownership of capital among the labour force thanks to the surplus of the large enterprises in whose hands most of the means of production are concentrated.

In the remaining enterprises, greater accumulation would be undertaken by the owners themselves, but as they rose in the capital scale an increasing proportion would have to go to the labour force in order to avoid concentration.

The change in the social composition of capital thus occurring in the large enterprises would have to be accompanied by gradual participation in capital until reaching self-management. Some principles of this type of management could also be followed in State enterprises, in special conditions which justified doing so.

These guidelines refer to countries which have attained advanced stages in their development; at less advanced stages, the social use of the surplus could take different forms. In any event, in either case it would be necessary to establish suitable incentives so that the transformations could take place without major upheavals.

This latter concern could lead to intermediate solutions, one of which might be to encourage greater accumulation, even in the large enterprises, in the same hands as at present, together with measures for the redistribution of some of the surplus.

3. The Market and Planning

In the new system all enterprises, whatever their nature, could develop freely in the market, in conformity with some basic, impersonal conditions established by the regulatory action of the State concerning both the social use of the surplus and other responsibilities pertaining to the State.

This regulatory activity has to fulfil objectives which the market itself cannot attain, but which would enable it to achieve great economic, social and ecological efficiency.

The criteria guiding the State's regulatory activity should be established through democratic planning. Planning means collective rationality, and that rationality requires that the surplus should be devoted to accumulation and redistribution, as well as to State expenditure and investment. Accumulation and redistribution are closely linked, since productivity and income should gradually rise as the labour force in the lower strata, as well as the labour employed spuriously by the system, are absorbed more and more productively. This is a dynamic redistribution, accompanied by other direct forms of social advancement responding to pressing needs.

Planning involves technical work of the utmost importance, which cannot be undertaken without a high degree of functional independence; it is, however, a technical and not a technocratic task, as it must be subordinated to democratically-adopted political decisions.

All this requires constitutional changes in the State machinery and new rules of the game ensuring both stability in the social use of the surplus and flexibility in responding to major changes in prevailing circumstances.

4. Synthesis of Socialism and Liberalism and Power Structure

The option for change outlined here represents a synthesis of socialism and liberalism. Socialism in that the State democratically regulates accumulation and distribution; liberalism in that it enshrines the essence of economic freedom, closely linked to political freedom in its original philosophical version.

This option calls for very important changes in the structure of political power, as does the option of concentrating ownership and regulatory activity in the hands of the State. In the course of the alterations of the social structure, the power of the upper strata is counterbalanced by the redistributive power of the middle and, possibly, lower strata. The latter, however, eventually shatters itself against the former in the dynamics of the system. Nevertheless, the crisis of the system opens the way for changing it, as it opens the possibility of reducing the power of the upper strata.

These changes in the power structure would perforce be confined to the periphery, as the power relations between the periphery and the centres, under the hegemony of the latter, especially the leading dynamic centre of capitalism, could not be radically changed by the action of the periphery alone. The power of the centres is considerable, and furthermore it lacks a sense of foresight, as is evidenced by its serious disruptions of the biosphere. The crisis may perhaps have the virtue—as has often been true of major crises in the past—of making the centres aware of the need of great foresight in their relations with the periphery and for containing their own power. I am inclined to think that if the main dynamic centre of capitalism had had this awareness, the breakdown of the international monetary system might have been avoided.

The myth of the worldwide expansion of capitalism has been exploded, as has that of the development of the periphery in the image and likeness of the centres. The myth of the regulatory virtue of market laws is also being dispelled.

Major changes are needed; but it is necessary to know why, how and for whom the changes are made. A theory of change is also needed; these pages, called forth by the pressing need for debate and enlightenment, seek to contribute to the formulation of such a theory.

10

Jairus Banaji

For a Theory of Colonial Modes of Production

The question of the characterisation of the Indian economy prior to Independence has not been posed in explicit terms or in a theoretically rigorous fashion. This article attempts to make a beginning in that direction.

The recent writings of Utsa Patnaik[1] on the current changes in Indian agriculture have raised a number of important theoretical issues. Central to these has been the question of the characterisation of the Indian economy prior to Independence. This question, however, has not been posed in explicit terms or in a theoretically rigorous fashion. The following article attempts to make a beginning in this direction. In general it supports the positions advanced by Patnaik in her brilliant polemics with A. Rudra, particularly concerning the identification of capitalist development, and with P. Chattopadhyay, concerning the "specificity" of the colonial economy.

The transposition of the model of the feudal mode of production as it prevailed historically in Europe and Japan to most, or parts, of the colonial world was based on one of two errors—by which we mean breaks with Marxist theory. It was based either on a circulationist definition of modes of production or on a confusion of relations of exploitation and relations of production. In the first case, the feudal mode of production was identified as a "system of production for use"; it was defined in terms of the prevalence of "natural economy," of relationships prevalent in the sphere of exchange. It would be beside the point to argue that the predominantly autarchic subsistence-oriented character of production in the colonial world is an illusion, that the colonial economies showed high de-

---

EDITOR'S NOTE: *A highly original contribution from India, this article continues the Baran-Frank idea emphasizing the retrograde nature of the so-called colonial mode of production, neither capitalist nor feudal in itself, but a mode of* superexploitation *corresponding to the primary accumulation needs of the European centers.*

grees of monetisation, penetration of commerce and so on. This is in fact the mode of argument characteristic of Gunder Frank. It fails to point to the theoretical error implicit in the circulationist position, namely, that modes of production are not defined, in the first instance, in terms of exchange relationships, that the two spheres are relatively autonomous, from which it follows that a "money-commodity" economy, for example, is compatible with different modes of production. It is true that shifts in the sphere of exchange, e.g., a sudden expansion of commerce, induce transformations in the sphere of production, e.g., substitution of more profitable forms of production or transition to money rent. However, modes of production are not reducible to the field of variations between a fully developed commodity economy and an economy of subsistence. A more common approach was the characterisation of the colonial economies as predominantly "feudal" due to the prevalence of relations of exploitation either akin to or identical with *serfdom*. Thus if the first error can be identified as the one committed by Sweezy in the famous debate on the transition from feudalism to capitalism, the second would be that committed by his opponent Dobb.[2] The conceptual sleight-of-hand behind this position has not been often understood, least of all by those who, like Gunder Frank, declare themselves firmly opposed to the characterisation of the colonial economies as feudal. The reason for this is that to most marxists relations of production and relations or forms of exploitation have been synonymous terms, conceptually identical or almost so.

Relations of Production and Forms of Exploitation

It is important to establish the conceptual distance between these terms in the clearest possible manner. (We do not, of course, claim that the distance was always marked in the work of Marx himself.) We may define relations of exploitation as the particular form in which surplus is appropriated from the direct producers, not the specific form, e.g., labour rent, rent in kind, but the general form, e.g., serfdom, where the direct producers are tied to the means of production through some form of extra-economic coercion. Relations of production, on the other hand, are the specific historically determined form which particular relations of exploitation assume due to a certain level of development of the productive forces, to the predominance of particular property forms (feudal landed property, etc.) and so on. Thus, in a strict, i.e., scientific or marxist sense, "feudalism" is not the "same as" serfdom, though the latter constitutes the dominant relation of exploitation in the feudal mode of production—not the only one, for slavery survived well into the feudal epoch. Similarly, wage labour and the capitalist mode of production are concepts based at different levels, even though the latter presupposes the former. Thus capitalism cannot be defined in terms of the existence or non-existence of wage labour, for the latter is only transformed into a capitalist relation of production under certain historical conditions, in the first place its insertion into a framework of extended reproduction where "unlimited expansion, perpetual progress, becomes the law of production" in contrast to all pre-capitalist modes of production where "production was every time resumed in the same form and on the same scale as previously."[3] Wage labour, as such, as a relation of exploitation, is possible and has occurred historically in a simple reproduction context, e.g., in Indian agriculture in the nineteenth century, or the potteries of southern Gaul in the first century of the Roman Empire. It would be rash to argue merely from the presence of this form of exploitation that we are dealing in such instances with a nascent capitalism. Thus the error which deduces feudalism from the prevalence of serfdom and the one which deduces capitalism from the existence of wage labour are symmetrical; they both confuse relations of production with relations of exploitation.

The point can be reinforced. Engels, it is well known, in one of his last letters to Marx stated, "it is certain that serfdom and bondage are not a peculiarly medieval-feudal form, we find them everywhere or nearly everywhere 'where conquerors have the land cultivated for them by the old inhabitants.' " This remarkable statement would be literally meaningless if we did not accept the theoretical validity of the distinction we have been trying to establish.

In reaction to the "feudal" thesis, once maintained by most of the Communist Parties of the colonial world who used the struggle against "feudalism" as a means of postponing the struggle for a socialist programme, a second position became current among marxists, due to the work of Gunder Frank. Due to their umbilical ties to a world market dominated by the capitalist mode of production the colonial economies were characterised as capitalist, distinguished from "metropolitan capitalism" by their subordinate and dependent status within the "system of world capitalism." Here too, as with some defenders of the feudal-thesis, the distance between exchange and production relationships was not clearly defined. The process of integration of particular areas of the globe into a world market dominated by the capitalist mode of production was confused with the process of installation of the capitalist mode within those areas. The critique of Gunder Frank (and by extension, of those who, like Jean-Loup Herbert or Kathleen Gough, argue an identical position for Guatemala, India and so [on][4]) has been made along these lines by a series of marxists, particularly from Latin America—Ernesto Laclau, Ciro Cardoso, Martinez-Alier[5]—and need not be elaborated.

The distance between these concepts—integration of a given area into a world market dominated by capitalism/local installation of the capitalist mode of production—can only be established in terms of a theory of colonialism. Paradoxically, it was the absence of such a theory in the work of marxists who appeared to be preoccupied with the problem of colonialism which accounts for their failure to establish the distance properly, to draw the line between the concepts. The beginnings of such a theory exist, however, in the work of those who reject both the feudal and the capitalist characterisation and argue that colonialism must be understood in terms of a specific mode of production, neither feudal nor capitalist though "resembling" both at different levels. This third position has been argued for Egypt by Mahmoud Hussein in an excellent analysis of Nasserism,[6] by Ciro Cardoso for Latin America,[7] by Utsa Patnaik and Bipan Chandra for India[8] and finally by Pierre Philippe Rey in a theoretical work on the articulation of modes of production.[9] Many of Chattopadhyay's criticisms of U. Patnaik[10] spring from a failure to understand this position or indeed its theoretical significance. This is due in part, however, to the fact that with the exception of Cardoso, none of the other writers have formulated the position in a theoretically rigorous or explicit manner. One symptom of this lack of theoretical rigour is a shifting terminology which comprises a series of images—the colonial mode of production appears as a "unique transitional structure" in Patnaik, or as a "system of abortive transition to capitalism" in Hussein or merely as a "distinct social formation" in B. Chandra.

One reason for this hesitation in explicitly characterising the colonial economy in terms of a single coherent mode of production may be the widespread tendency among marxists to think [of] the transition to the capitalist mode in terms of the model of the "coexistence of modes of production." Once this model, derived from the historical experience of Europe, is transposed to the colonial world, the task of rethinking the structure of the transition to capitalism within the colonies becomes superfluous. Colonial history then becomes the history of the slow disintegration of a pre-capitalist mode of production, however characterised ("feudal," "semi-feudal," etc.) and of the slow expansion of a nascent capitalist mode of production. The roots of the present backwardness of the former colonies are traced back to this mysterious condition of limbo, of stagnation in the empty spaces between two modes of production. Despite its predominantly metaphorical character this mode of thought can support itself with any number of pseudo-theories; thus the prolonged survival of "the pre-capitalist" mode of production which it posits can be attributed to the tenacious resistance which the rural communities of Asia put up to commercial penetration due to their internal structure, or the growing numbers of peasants divorced from the land and linked to the process of production in an inherently unstable fashion can be misrecognised as the "industrial reserve army" which any growth of capitalism generates.[11]

The model of co-existing modes of production is superficially attractive precisely because of the historical complexity of the colonial period—its endless variety of forms and relations of exploitation, ranging from chattel slavery and more mitigated forms of slave labour through a variety of forms of serfdom and bondage to exploitation based on wage labour, and comprising numerous transitional and intermediate forms where one relation of exploitation would merge with another (of semi-servile, semi-serf, semi-proletarian); the coexistence of money-commodity and subsistence economies, both in space, with some regions of a given country integrated into commercial circuits and others enclosed in natural economy, and in time, with the same regions experiencing the expansion and contraction of the market in successive stages (*cf* the crisis of the Brazilian sugar industry at the close of the 17th century).

But in theory there is no reason why a given mode of production should not combine a variety of relations of exploitation. Secondly, the penetration of money and commerce are not necessarily an index of the growth of capitalist production relations. In the colonial world it was not local industrial capital but money-lending capital which gained reinforcement, in many instances, from a quickening of the pace of circulation and commodity production. Commercial penetration in fact intensified serfdom, as it had in some instances during the feudal epoch in Europe. And finally, the expropriation of the peasantry which became a common phenomenon of the colonial world did not proceed along European and Russian lines. It did not, in other words, lead to the constitution of a proletariat concentrated in industry.

Marx was conscious of the specificity of the agrarian systems installed by colonialism in India. He described them in 1853 as the products of "agrarian revolutions," i.e., as systems founded on a break with the pre-colonial order. Moreover, Marx was aware that they were not reducible to a single model. "In Bengal we have a combination of English landlordism, of the Irish middlemen system, of the Austrian system transforming the landlord into the tax-gatherer and of the Asiatic system making the state the real landlord. In Madras and Bombay we have a French peasant proprietor who is at the same time a serf, and a *metayer* of the State ... The ryot is subject like the French peasant to the extortion of the private usurer; but he has no hereditary, no permanent titles in his land, like the French peasant. Like the serf he is forced to cultivation, but he is not secured against want like the serf. Like the *metayer* he has to divide his produce with the State, but the State is not obliged, with regard to him, to advance the fund and the stock, as it is obliged to do with regard to the *metayer*."[12] Marx did not go on, however, to posit a distinct colonial mode of production, perhaps because in this period, 1850s, he telescoped the process of capitalist expansion within India, even though the capitalist mode of production as such was almost totally absent.

The most striking fact about the colonial period was the absence of a process of capitalist expansion, for some six decades at least in manufacturing, and for about a century in agriculture. Lenin was quite wrong when he coupled India with Russia as one of the countries in the world where agricultural capitalism was "driving patriarchal agriculture out of its last refuges," for the *contrast* between the stagnation and backwardness of Indian agriculture in the final decades of the nineteenth century and the remarkable development of capitalism in Russian agriculture in the same period is difficult to ignore. One has only to read the sections in "Development of Capitalism in Russia" on the employment of agricultural machinery or the growth of commercial [relations] in agriculture[13] and compare the data assembled for Indian agriculture on capital formation[14] or trends in productivity[15] to be convinced of this fact. It is true that like the Russian peasantry of the late nineteenth century, the Indian peasantry of that period had lost its "patriarchal" character, that in both countrysides a large section of the peasantry was composed of agricultural workers and semi-proletarian dwarf-holders, but while in Russia this phenomenon reflected the rapid expansion of agricultural capitalism and was linked to an undermining of the stagnation of agriculture, a transformation of its technique and a development of the productive forces of social labour—as shown by Lenin in the work referred to—in India it reflected quite different tendencies.

If we accept the reality of colonial modes of production as specific entities with their own coherence and laws of development, then it must be said at the outset that unlike other modes of production this one could only have come into being within the sphere of capitalist production; to be more exact, within the sphere of the reproduction of the capitalist mode of production on an ever larger scale. It is worth quoting Lenin again—"unlimited expansion . . . becomes the law of production." To secure this unlimited expansion in its initial phases the bourgeoisie in Europe resorted to three specific mechanisms—colonial plunder, international lending and an intensified exploitation of the home peasantry. These were the basic mechanisms in the process of primary accumulation, or that phase of the capitalist reproduction process in which the main sector of capitalist production (industry) and the chief areas of capitalist production (Europe and the white colonies) were dependent on external sources of accumulation—in sectoral terms on agriculture, and in geographical terms on the predominantly agrarian nations. From the sixteenth to the nineteenth centuries, however, colonial plunder constituted the dominant mode or mechanism of primary accumulation, for the imports of British capital which were a key element in the industrialisation of the white colonies (USA, Canada, etc.) constituted a secondary mode of primary accumulation, given that a large proportion of the capital which flowed across the Atlantic derived, as Bagchi has argued in a recent paper, from Britain's exploitation of India. An analogous mediation had occurred several centuries earlier when the gold and silver extracted by Spain from the mines of Peru and Mexico flowed, for a number of reasons, into the English, French and Dutch economies. Hamilton estimates the value of this gold and silver extracted between 1503 and 1660, at over 500 million *pesos*. Dutch exploitation of the East Indies in the late seventeenth and in the eighteenth century yielded, according to another calculation, a total of 600 million florins.[16] In the eighteenth century growing British domination of the slave trade, expansion of the trade in colonial products, grown mostly in plantations abroad, and the early stages of the plunder of India continued the process of primary accumulation and resulted finally in the industrial dominance of Britain. In the following century, a series of further shifts—e.g., displacement of Spain from South America, British reinforcement of the colonial modes of production on that continent, and Britain's use of Indian export surpluses[17]—enabled the world's leading capitalist nation to help finance the industrialisation of the white colonies. We make no attempt to determine the

phases of the primary accumulation process according to rigorous criteria and
have merely indicated the main chronological stages.

Retrograde Logic

The colonial modes of production were precisely the circuits through which
capital was drained out of the colonies in the form of bullion, consumption
goods, raw materials and so on. The financing of primary accumulation outside
the colonial world was their chief historical function and it was this fact which
determined their peculiarly retrograde logic. We can describe this in the following terms: the colonial modes of production transmitted to the colonies the pressures of the accumulation process in the metropolis without unleashing any
corresponding expansion in the forces of production.

This "logic" in turn determined several long-term tendencies of *decisive* importance in the history of the colonial nations. Unlike its parent mode of production in the West, distinguished historically by its continuous expansion of the
productive forces, the mode of production installed in the colonies reduced the
entire process of production to an immense superexploitation of variable capital.
As is well known and as several writers have pointed out,[18] for whole periods of
its history the problem of labour supplies was the dominant preoccupation and
driving force of colonialism, and the short-term devices and long-term strategies
through which this problem was resolved in different conjunctures constitute the
essential point of departure for a closer understanding of specific colonial situations.[19] While forced labour was commonly used in the earlier stages of colonial
history to ensure the supply of labour, particularly in the plantation and mining
sector and under Spanish rule (the *polo* system in the Philippines, the *mita*
system in Peru), two other mechanisms dominated its later stages—firstly, the
attempt to lower the opportunity cost of the peasantry by a progressive reduction
of its overall productivity,[20] and secondly, the installation of semi-feudal landed
property and incorporation of the peasantry within its framework. Economic,
fiscal and legal modes of coercion were the decisive elements in both strategies.
While in some sectors of the colonial world the first strategy resulted in a rapid
proletarisation of the peasantry, in other sectors, particularly Latin America and
Asia, the expansion of semi-feudal landed properties (the *hacienda* in Mexico
and Peru, the *encomienda* in Guatemala and the Philippines, the *zamindari* estate
in parts of India) imparted to the colonial status of the peasantry more complex
and peculiar forms combining the characteristics of servile and proletarian exploitation and thus reminiscent of the transitional economy of post-Reform Russia described by Lenin.

Our characterisation of the dominant property forms in the colonial world as
"semi-feudal" does not in the least invalidate U. Patnaik's argument that in India
this form was based on ownership in a "quasi-bourgeois sense."[21] For, while the
agrarian regime installed by the colonial state was a direct transposition from the

feudal world of contemporary Europe—thus jurists of the 16th and 17th centuries like Matienzo (1570) and Solorzano Pereira (1647) argued that colonialism had created a new form of feudalism[22]—the process of its reproduction became increasingly dependent in the course of time on juridical mechanisms specific to the capitalist epoch. In Peru, Mexico, [and] Bolivia in the course of the nineteenth century these mechanisms provided the chief basis for a renewed expansion of the latifundia, a renewed assault on the surviving land communities of that zone and for their final reduction to colonial status. The drive was so successful that by the late nineteenth century some two-thirds of the Bolivian peasantry had been incorporated into the estates, while in Mexico in this period about 90 per cent of the peasantry were thought to be landless.

Due to the expansion of semi-feudal landed property in the colonial world capitalism in the West was assured of a mechanism through which it could reinforce backward relations of exploitation directly in the service of its own accumulation process, both where the peasantry was tied to the world market as a producer of primary goods and where the chief mode of exploitation consisted in a "tribute" to the colonial State. In these areas of semi-feudal predominance agrarian concentration was a natural feature of the colonial economy—at one pole of the countryside a mass of pauperised peasants attempting to force a subsistence from soil of poor quality and with primitive techniques of production; at the other big properties worked either by tenants tied to the soil through numerous forms of bondage or by rural wage workers as integrated units of production. The predominance of this structure in the specific conditions of technical backwardness imposed on the colonies by capitalism, tended to stifle the emergence of a vigorous middle peasantry from whose ranks a peasant capitalism might have emerged.

Already by the turn of the century the lower strata of the peasantry were numerically preponderant in countries like Egypt, India, Indonesia and so on, and a large segment of these strata was either completely landless or nearly so, as some of the more reliable statistical data we have show. Thus in Java in 1903 of all those holding land in individual hereditary possession or with fixed shares of communal land, 70.9 per cent cultivated less than 0.7 hectares. In Residencies of Java like Bantam, Semarang, Cheribun, [and] Kedoe this proportion was either close to or over 80 per cent. Pelzer states that "even in 1903 Java was a country of dwarf holdings. . . . A sizeable landless class already existed."[23] In Egypt in 1894 around 80 per cent of holdings were under 5 *feddans* or approximately 5 acres. By the closing stages of colonial rule the average size of small subsistence holdings and the rate of landlessness were generally much worse. In Vietnam in the 1940s 60 percent of the peasantry was landless;[24] in Burma around half the peasants were tenants or agricultural labourers in 1921, before the crisis of the ensuing decade added to this proportion; in the Philippines in 1939 over half the farms cultivated less than 2 hectares, while the Census classified 35 per cent of all farmers as tenants, the proportion varying from over 50 per cent in areas which suffered directly from the colonial impact, e.g., Central Luzon, to generally low levels in areas remote from it—Mindanao, Palawan, etc. Likewise North Africa after French rule, where agricultural workers and poor peasants composed the bulk of rural population, 75 per cent in Algeria, 58 per cent in Tunisia; significantly, the proportion was lowest in Morocco, 49 per cent, which was colonised only as late as 1911. The situation of the Andean peasantry was not dissimilar in the early decades of this century. The factors accelerating the expansion of these rural strata and leading to the general impoverishment of the colonial peasantries are not too difficult to surmise and may be mentioned briefly.

The prevalence of a generally high rate of exploitation, evident, for example, in the level of rents, wages and interest on capital, or in the periodic enhancement of fiscal pressure, coupled with the predominance of big property, rising demographic levels and atrophy of the manufacturing sector resulted in growing pressure on the land, symptomised by the progressive fragmentation of holdings, by the emergence of what Lenin called "dwarf, parcellised, proletarian farms." At the low level of technique which characterised colonial agriculture this meant declining per capita productivity, particularly in foodgrains where, in fact, acreage in many instances contracted due to the introduction of cropping patterns centred on high value cash crops.

Thwarted Industrialisation

A key element in this enhanced dependence on the land within the dual framework of rural concentration and low technique, was the atrophy of manufacturing—what A. K. Bagchi has called "thwarted industrialisation"—induced not only by the conscious discriminatory policies of the colonial State but also firstly, by the drain of capital from the colonies, the enormous capitalisation for which the colonial modes of production were brought into being; secondly, by the continued dominance of non-productive forms of investment, particularly trade and moneylending, due to the high rates of return which they promised;[25] thirdly, by the domination of the home market by imports and by its constricted character; and finally, by the precarious character of accumulation in sectors of primary commodities, where periods of accumulation were abruptly followed by crisis and phases of contracted reproduction in which sharecropping or communal agriculture would re-establish themselves.[26] It was not unnatural, therefore, that manufacturing within colonies developed most rapidly only in periods of world capitalist crisis, when the bonds tying the colonial nations to imperialism were temporarily relaxed. As long as these bonds remained firm, due partly to their reinforcement by the colonial modes of production, the accumulation process suffered a permanent blockage and the expansion of employment outlets outside the sector experiencing the intensity of colonial exploitation worst, *viz*, agriculture, remained closed. Thus the growing expropriation of the colonial peasantries did not lead to the constitution of a proletariat, but primarily to the constitution of a rural semi-proletariat, either totally landless or cultivating dwarf holdings, and, in the second place, to the emergence—particularly in N. Africa and S. America—of an urban or suburban lumpen-proletariat. The process of proletarisation followed irregular distorted lines in the colonies, and this fact reflected not the "slowness" of capitalist development but the peculiarly retrograde or backward character of colonial exploitation.

Marx was, later in his life, aware of this peculiarly retrograde character of the colonial mode of production. Far from applauding the "revolutionary" role of British imperialism in India—applause which only made sense and which was fully justified if he expected capitalism to "take root" within the colony more or less immediately—he remarked, in the third volume of "Capital," "[rent in kind] may assume dimensions which seriously imperil reproduction of the conditions of labour, the means of production themselves, rendering the expansion of production more or less impossible and reducing the direct producers to the physical minimum of means of subsistence. This is particularly the case when this form is met with and exploited by a conquering commercial nation, e.g., the English in India." To marxists the progressive role of capitalism has always been its relentless expansion of the productive forces, its continual raising of the productivity of labour, its transformation and improvement of technique. In all these respects the colonial modes of production, though born within the sphere of capitalist production, were at the opposite end to it—with the exception of investments in irrigation, concentrated in a few districts (Punjab, Godavari, Krishna . . .), technique remained on the whole backward, the rate of capital formation was low or even negative, productivity stagnated or declined. By the end of the colonial epoch the predominantly agrarian nations of Egypt, Indonesia, India and so on were net importers of foodgrains. A technically backward agriculture and a superexploited pauperised peasantry on dwarf holdings or without land—these are the dominant images of colonial agriculture. Both facts are consistent with the logic which regulated the colonial modes of production, determined, as we have said, by their specific function within the framework of capitalist reproduction, *viz*, to serve as circuits of accumulation for capitalist development outside the colonies, to be exploited without being developed.

For in its colonial phase, imperialism was not primarily interested in the reproduction of the capitalist mode within the colonies (we do not include the temperate white zones of colonial settlement in this term). The export of capital to the colonial world in the epoch of the colonial modes of production was thus of limited scope and purely secondary significance. In the interwar period, with the onset of crisis and relaxation or near collapse of the commercial links tying the colonies to imperialism, the expansion of manufacturing through import-substitution provided the economic basis for the bourgeois nationalist assault on colonialism—the main planks of which were firstly, rapid industrialisation, with or without state intervention, and secondly, agricultural capitalism, i.e., an under-mining of the secular stagnation of the agricultural sector.

As its growing dependence on foreign aid and on the technical collaboration of the imperialist bourgeoisie shows, the colonial bourgeoisie has come to imple-ment this programme of "independent" capitalist development under the aegis of imperialism. The colonial bourgeoisie is incapable of accomplishing the two major tasks facing it. It is caught up in a continual process of frustrated primary accumulation. For the transition from the pre-capitalist world to the capitalist mode of production *via* the colonial modes of production, i.e., in the specific historical conditions imposed on the colonies, results everywhere in a back-ward dependent capitalism whose own horizon of reproduction is infinitely more restricted than that which faced the nascent bourgeoisie of Europe. The neo-colonialist development for which the colonial bourgeoisie has opted in a number of important countries (Egypt, Indonesia, India, Pakistan . . .) offers no long-term solution, for its whole logic consists in reproducing the dilemma which confronted that bourgeoisie at its political birth. And it is in this dilemma that the history of the colonial modes of production is most clearly inscribed.

We have deliberately ignored the variations and discontinuities in colonial history—for example, many parts of the argument are not directly applicable to the countries of sub-Saharan Africa, or those sectors of South America which were settled through pioneer colonisation and whose agriculture was established on a capitalist footing from the start. We have also ignored the problem of the variations of the colonial mode of production itself, of its different forms and of their own specific contradictions. Finally, we may have given the impression that where it prevailed the colonial mode of production left no room for the develop-ment of the capitalist mode within the economy; this however, was not the case and the problem of how in such instances, e.g. Peru where coastal agriculture was organised on capitalist lines, the two modes of production articulated is further material for analysis. However, our aim has been the more modest one of stimulating discussion on the question of the marxist characterisation of the colonial economies prior to the growth of a local industrial bourgeoisie. It is time to break with metaphorical epithets and passive transpositions.

Notes

1. Particularly "Development of Capitalism in Agriculture—1," *Social Scientist*, September 1972, and the reply to Paresh Chattopadhyay in *Economic and Political Weekly*, September 30, 1972.
2. "The Transition from Feudalism to Capitalism: A Symposium," *Science and Soci-ety*, 1967.
3. Lenin, "A Characterisation of Economic Romanticism," *Collected Works*, Vol. 2 (Moscow 1963), p. 164.
4. J. L. Herbert, *Indianite et lutte des classes*, Paris 1972, K. Gough, *Monthly Re-view*, February 1969.

5. Ernesto Laclau, "Feudalism and Capitalism in L America," *New Left Review*, May/June 1971, C. F. S. Cardoso, "S. M. Pelaez y el Caracter del regimen colonial," *Estudios Sociales Centroamericanos*, 1972, J. Martinez-Alier, "El latifundio en Andalucia y en America Latina," *Cuadernos de Ruedo Iberico*, Oct./Nov. 1967 [my thanks to E. Laclau for the last two references].

6. M. Hussein, *La Lutte de classes en Egypte (1945–68)*, Paris 1971.

7. See 5.

8. B. Chandra, "Colonialism and Modernisation," Indian History Congress presidential address.

9. P. P. Rey, *Sur l' articulation des modes de production*, 2 volumes (Centre d'etude de planification socialiste; unpublished).

10. P. Chattopadhyay, *Economic and Political Weekly*, March 25,1972.

11. *Cf* U. Patnaik, *Economic and Political Weekly*, September 30, 1972.

12. *On Colonialism* (Moscow 1968), p. 79.

13. *The Development of Capitalism in Russia* (Moscow 1956), CW 3, p. 224 f., 263 f. Lenin's remark coupling India and Russia is on p. 353. In the passage he is quoting from an article by Engels.

14. *Cf* T. Shukla, *Capital Formation in Indian Agriculture*, Bombay 1965.

15. *Cf* G. Blyn, *Agricultural Trends in India: Output, Availability, and Productivity*, Philadelphia 1966.

16. Figures from Mandel, *Marxist Economic Theory*, Volume 2, p. 443.

17. A. K. Bagchi, "Foreign Capital and Economic Development in India—A Schematic View," *Frontier*, September 25, 1971; the other article of Bagchi's referred to is "Some International Foundations of Capitalist Growth and Underdevelopment," *Economic and Political Weekly*, Special Number, 1972. Our arguments lean heavily on Bagchi's work.

18. *Cf* R. Stavenhagen, "Seven Erroneous Theses about L America," in Petras and Zeitlin (eds.), *Reform or Revolution.*

19. *E.g.* G. Arrighi's analysis of the Rhodesian case in "Labour Supplies in Historical Perspective: A Study of the Proletarianisation of the African Peasantry in Rhodesia," *Journal of Development Studies*, 1970.

20. *Cf* G. Arrighi, article cited, and *The Political Economy of Rhodesia* (The Hague 1967) for an excellent analysis.

21. *Social Scientist*, September 1972.

22. *Cf* Lipschutz, *Annales* 1966.

23. K. Pelzer, *Pioneer Settlement in the Asiatic Tropics*, New York 1945.

24. *Cf* G. Chaliand, *The Peasants of N Vietnam* (Penguin 1969).

25. This point is stressed by U. Patnaik, *Economic and Political Weekly*, September 30, 1972.

26. J. Piel, *Past and Present*, No. 46, who calls this process "speculative latifundism."

Part III

Afterthoughts on Development

11

A. HIRSCHMAN

The Rise and Decline of Development Economics

Development economics is a comparatively young area of inquiry. It was born just about a generation ago, as a subdiscipline of economics, with a number of other social sciences looking on both skeptically and jealously from a distance. The forties and especially the fifties saw a remarkable outpouring of fundamental ideas and models which were to dominate the new field and to generate controversies that contributed much to its liveliness. In that eminently "exciting" era, development economics did much better than the object of its study, the economic development of the poorer regions of the world, located primarily in Asia, Latin America, and Africa. Lately it seems that at least this particular gap has been narrowing, not so much unfortunately because of a sudden spurt in economic development, but rather because the forward movement of our subdiscipline has notably slowed down. This is of course a subjective judgment. Articles and books are still being produced. But as an observer and long-time participant I cannot help feeling that the old liveliness is no longer there, that new ideas are ever harder to come by and that the field is not adequately reproducing itself.

When scientific activity is specifically directed at solving a pressing problem, one can immediately think of two reasons why, after a while, interest in this activity should flag. One is that the problem is in fact disappearing—either because of the scientific discoveries of the preceding phase or for other reasons. For example, the near demise of interest in business-cycle theory since the end of World War II was no doubt due to the remarkably shock-free growth experienced

EDITOR'S NOTE: *In the early 1980s the mainstream development paradigm, widely discredited, adopted a retrospective mood full of regret and apology for its previous stance of "unreasonable hopes and ambitions." Hirschman's treatise, echoing the "rise-and-decline" theme, captures this spirit of self-criticism and self-correction perfectly. From the point of view of the victims of the development crusade, of course, the apology was both too little and too late.*

during that period by the advanced industrial countries, at least up to the mid-seventies. But this reason cannot possibly be invoked in the present case: The problems of poverty in the Third World are still very much with us.

The other obvious reason for the decline of scientific interest in a problem is the opposite experience, that is, the disappointing realization that a "solution" is by no means at hand and that little if any progress is being made. Again, this explanation does not sound right in our case, for in the last thirty years considerable advances have taken place in many erstwhile "underdeveloped" countries—even a balance sheet for the Third World as a whole is by no means discouraging.[1]

In sum, the conditions for healthy growth of development economics would seem to be remarkably favorable: the problem of world poverty is far from solved, but encouraging inroads on the problem have been and are being made. It is therefore something of a puzzle why development economics flourished so briefly.

In looking for an explanation, I find it helpful to take a look at the conditions under which our subdiscipline came into being. It can be shown, I believe, that this happened as a result of an a priori unlikely conjunction of distinct ideological currents. The conjunction proved to be extraordinarily productive, but also created problems for the future. First of all, because of its heterogeneous ideological makeup, the new science was shot through with tensions that would prove disruptive at the first opportunity. Secondly, because of the circumstances under which it arose, development economics became overloaded with unreasonable hopes and ambitions that soon had to be clipped back. Put very briefly and schematically, this is that tale I shall tell—plus a few stories and reflections on the side.

I. A Simple Classification of Development Theories

The development ideas that were put forward in the forties and fifties shared two basic ingredients in the area of economics. They also were based on one unspoken political assumption with which I will deal in the last section of this paper.

The two basic economic ingredients were what I shall call the rejection of the *monoeconomics claim* and the assertion of the *mutual-benefit claim.* By rejection of the monoeconomics claim I mean the view that underdeveloped countries as a group are set apart, through a number of specific economic characteristics common to them, from the advanced industrial countries and that traditional economic analysis, which has concentrated on the industrial countries, must therefore be recast in significant respects when dealing with underdeveloped countries. The mutual-benefit claim is the assertion that economic relations between these two groups of countries could be shaped in such a way as to yield gains for both. The two claims can be either asserted or rejected, and, as a result, four basic positions exist, as shown in the following table.

Types of Development Theories

| | Monoeconomics claim: | |
	asserted	*rejected*
Mutual-benefit claim: *asserted*	Orthodox economics	Development economics
rejected	Marx?	Neo-Marxist theories

Even though there are of course positions that do not fit neatly just one of its cells, this simple table yields a surprisingly comprehensive topology for the major theories on development of the periphery. In the process, it makes us realize that there are two unified systems of thought, orthodox economics and neo-Marxism, and two other less consistent positions that are therefore likely to be unstable: Marx's scattered thoughts on development of "backward" and colonial areas, on the one hand, and modern development economics, on the other. I shall take up these four positions in turn, but shall give major attention to development economics and to its evolving relations with—and harassment by—the two adjoining positions.

The orthodox position holds to the following two propositions: (a) economics consists of a number of simple, yet "powerful" theorems of universal validity: there is only one economics ("just as there is only one physics"); (b) one of these theorems is that, in a market economy, benefits flow to all participants, be they individuals or countries, from all voluntary acts of economic intercourse ("or else they would not engage in those acts"). In this manner, both the monoeconomics and the mutual-benefit claims are asserted.

The opposite position is that of the major neo-Marxist theories of development which hold: (a) exploitation or "unequal exchange" is the essential, permanent feature of the relations between the underdeveloped "periphery" and the capitalist "center"; (b) as a result of this long process of exploitation, the political-economic structure of the peripheral countries is very different from anything ever experienced by the center, and their development cannot possibly follow the same path—for example, it has been argued that they cannot have a successful industrialization experience under capitalist auspices. Here, both the mutual-benefit claim and the monoeconomics claim are rejected.

A cozy internal consistency, bent on simplifying (and oversimplifying) reality and therefore favorable to ideology formation, is immediately apparent in both the orthodox and the neo-Marxist positions. This is in contrast with the remaining two positions. It should be clear why I have placed Marx into the southwesterly cell (mutual-benefit claim rejected, monoeconomics claim asserted). Writing in *Capital* on primitive accumulation on the one hand, Marx describes the spoliation to which the periphery has been subject in the course of the early development of capitalism in the center. Thus he denies any claim of mutual benefit from trade between capitalist and "backward" countries. On the other hand, his well-known statement, "The industrially most developed country does nothing but hold up to those who follow it on the industrial ladder, the image of its own future," coupled with the way in which he viewed England's role in India as "objectively" progressive in opening the way to industrialization by railroad construction, suggests that he did not perceive the "laws of motion" of countries such as India as being substantially different from those of the industrially advanced ones. Marx's opinions on this latter topic are notoriously complex and subject to a range of interpretations, as is indicated by the question mark in the table. But to root *neo*-Marxist thought firmly in the southeasterly cell took considerable labors (which involved, among other things, *uprooting* an important component of the thought of Marx). The story of these labors and revisions has been told elsewhere,[2] and my task here is to deal with the origin and dynamics of the other "hybrid" position: development economics.

It is easy to see that the conjunction of the two propositions—(a) certain special features of the economic structure of the underdeveloped countries make an important portion of orthodox analysis inapplicable and misleading, and (b) there is a possibility for relations between the developed and underdeveloped countries to be mutually beneficial and for the former to contribute to the development of the latter—was essential for our subdiscipline to arise where and when it did: namely, in the advanced industrial countries of the West, primarily in England and the United States, at the end of World War II. The first proposition is required for the creation of a separate theoretical structure, and the second was needed if Western economists were to take a strong interest in the matter—if the likelihood or at least the hope could be held out that their own countries could play a positive role in the development process, perhaps after certain achievable reforms in international economic relations. In the absence of this perception it would simply not have been possible to mobilize a large group of activist "problem solvers."

II. The Inapplicability of Orthodox Monoeconomics to Underdeveloped Areas

Once a genuinely new current of ideas is firmly established and is being busily developed by a large group of scholars and researchers, it becomes almost impossible to appreciate how difficult it was for the new to be born and to assert itself. Such difficulties are particularly formidable in economics with its dominant paradigm and analytical tradition—a well-known source of both strength and weakness for that social science. Accordingly, there is need for an explanation of the rise and at least temporary success of the heretical, though today familiar, claim that large portions of the conventional body of economic thought and policy advice are not applicable to the poorer countries—the more so as much of this intellectual movement arose in the very "Anglo-Saxon" environment which had long served as home for the orthodox tradition.

Elements of such an explanation are actually not far to seek. Development economics took advantage of the unprecedented discredit orthodox economics had fallen into as a result of the depression of the thirties and of the equally unprecedented success of an attack on orthodoxy from within the economics "establishment." I am talking of course about the Keynesian Revolution of the thirties, which became the "new economics" and almost a new orthodoxy in the forties and fifties. Keynes had firmly established the view that there were *two* kinds of economics: one—the orthodox or classical tradition—which applied, as he was wont to put it, to the "special case" in which the economy was fully employed; and a very different system of analytical propositions and of policy prescriptions (newly worked out by Keynes) that took over when there was substantial unemployment of human and material resources.[3] The Keynesian step from one to two economics was crucial: the ice of monoeconomics had been broken and the idea that there might be yet another economics had instant credibility—particularly among the then highly influential group of Keynesian economists, of course.

Among the various observations that were central to the new development economics and implicitly or explicitly made the case for treating the underdeveloped countries as a sui generis group of economies, two major ones stand out, that relating to rural underemployment and that stressing the late-coming syndrome in relation to industrialization.

1. Rural Underemployment

The early writers on our subject may have looked for an even closer and more specific connection with the Keynesian system than was provided by the general proposition that different kinds of economies require different kinds of economics. Such a connection was achieved by the unanimous stress of the pioneering contributions—by Kurt Mandelbaum, Paul Rosenstein-Rodan and Ragnar Nurkse—on *underemployment* as a crucial characteristic of underdevelopment. The focus on rural *under*employment was sufficiently similar to the Keynesian concern with *un*employment to give the pioneers a highly prized sensation of affinity with the Keynesian system, yet it was also different enough to generate expectations of eventual independent development of our fledgling branch of economic knowledge.

The affinities were actually quite impressive. As is well known, the Keynesian system took unemployment far more seriously than had been done by traditional economics and had elaborated a theory of macroeconomic equilibrium with unemployment. Similarly, the early development economists wrote at length about the "vicious circle of poverty"—a state of low-level equilibrium—which can prevail under conditions of widespread rural underemployment. Moreover, the equilibrium characteristics of an advanced economy with urban unemployment and those of an underdeveloped economy with rural underemployment were both held to justify interventionist public policies hitherto strictly proscribed by orthodox economics. The Keynesians stressed the task of expansionary fiscal policy in combating unemployment. The early development economists went farther and advocated some form of public investment planning that would mobilize the underemployed for the purpose of industrialization, in accordance with a pattern of "balanced growth."

In these various ways, then, the claim of development economics to stand as a separate body of economic analysis and policy derived intellectual legitimacy and nurture from the prior success and parallel features of the Keynesian Revolution.

The focus on rural underemployment as the principal characteristic of underdevelopment found its fullest expression in the work of Arthur Lewis. In his powerful article "Economic Development with Unlimited Supplies of Labour" he managed—almost miraculously—to squeeze out of the simple proposition about underemployment a full set of "laws of motion" for the typical underdeveloped country, as well as a wide range of recommendations for domestic and international economic policy.

With the concept of rural underemployment serving as the crucial theoretical underpinning of the separateness of development economics, it is not surprising that it should have been chosen as a privileged target by the defenders of orthodoxy and monoeconomics.[4] For example, Theodore W. Schultz devoted a full chapter of his well-known book *Transforming Traditional Agriculture* (Yale, 1964) to an attempt at refuting what he called "The Doctrine of Agricultural Labor of Zero Value."[5] This suggests an interesting point about the scientific status of economics, and of social science in general. Whereas in the natural or medical sciences Nobel prizes are often shared by two persons who have collaborated in, or deserve joint credit for, a given scientific advance, in economics the prize is often split between one person who has developed a certain thesis and another who has labored mightily to prove it wrong.

At the outset of his celebrated article, Lewis had differentiated the underdeveloped economy from Keynesian economics by pointing out that in the Keynesian system there is underemployment of labor as well as of other factors of production, whereas in an underdevelopment situation only labor is redundant. In this respect, my own work can be viewed as an attempt to generalize the diagnosis of underemployment as the characteristic feature of underdevelopment. Underdeveloped countries did have hidden reserves, so I asserted, not only of labor, but of savings, entrepreneurship, and other resources. But to activate them,

Keynesian remedies would be inadequate. What was needed were "pacing devices" and "pressure mechanisms"; whence my strategy of unbalanced growth.

My generalization of the underemployment argument may have somewhat undermined the claim of development economics to autonomy and separateness. As the work of Herbert Simon on "satisficing" and that of Harvey Leibenstein on "X-efficiency" were to show, the performance of the advanced economies also "depends not so much on finding optimal combinations for given resources as on calling forth and enlisting . . . resources and abilities that are hidden, scattered, or badly utilized"—that was the way I had put it in *The Strategy of Economic Development* for the less developed countries.[6] A feature I had presented as being specific to the situation of one group of economies was later found to prevail in others as well. Whereas such a finding makes for reunification of our science, what we have here is not a return of the prodigal son to an unchanging, ever-right and -righteous father. Rather, our understanding of the economic structures of the West will have been modified and enriched by the foray into other economies.

This kind of dialectical movement—first comes, upon looking at outside groups, the astonished finding of Otherness, and then follows the even more startling discovery that our own group is not all that different—has of course been characteristic of anthropological studies of "primitive" societies from their beginning and has in fact been one of their main attractions. In the field of development economics, something of this sort has also happened to the ideas put forward by Arthur Lewis. The dynamics of development with "unlimited" supplies of labor, which was supposed to be typical of less developed countries, have in fact prevailed in many "Northern" economies during the postwar period of rapid growth, owing in large part to massive immigration, temporary or permanent, spontaneous or organized, from the "South."[7] One of the more interesting analytical responses to this situation has been the dual labor market theory of Michael Piore and others. This theory is easily linked up with the Lewis model, even though that connection has not been made explicit as far as I know.

2. Late Industrialization

I have suggested in the preceding pages that the concept of underemployment achieved its position as foundation stone for development economics because of its affinity to the Keynesian system and because of the desire of the early writers on our subject to place themselves, as it were, under the protection of a heterodoxy that had just recently achieved success. There was, moreover, something arcane about the concept, often also referred to as "disguised unemployment," that served to enhance the scientific aura and status of the new field.

Along with the mysteries, however, the common sense of development also suggested that some rethinking of traditional notions was required. It became clear during the depression of the thirties and even more during World War II that industrialization was going to hold an important place in any active development policy of many underdeveloped countries. These countries had long specialized—or had been made to specialize—in the production of staples for export to the advanced industrial countries which had supplied them in return with modern manufactures. To build up an industrial structure under these "late-coming" conditions was obviously a formidable task that led to the questioning of received doctrine according to which the industrial ventures appropriate to any country would be promptly acted upon by perceptive entrepreneurs and would attract the required finance as a result of the smooth working of capital markets. The long delay in industrialization, the lack of entrepreneurship for larger ventures, and the real or alleged presence of a host of other inhibiting factors made for the conviction that, in underdeveloped areas, industrialization required a deliberate, intensive, guided effort. Naming and characterizing this effort led to a competition of metaphors: big push (Paul Rosenstein-Rodan), takeoff (Walt W. Rostow), great spurt (Alexander Gerschenkron), minimum critical effort (Harvey Leibenstein), backward and forward linkages (Albert O. Hirschman). The discussion around these concepts drew on both theoretical arguments—new rationales were developed for protection, planning, and industrialization itself—and on the experience of European industrialization in the nineteenth century.

In the latter respect, the struggle between advocates and adversaries of monoeconomics was echoed in the debate between Rostow and Gerschenkron. Even though Rostow had coined what became the most popular metaphor (the "takeoff"), he had really taken a monoeconomics position. For he divided the development process into his famous five "stages" with identical content for all countries, no matter when they started out on the road to industrialization. Gerschenkron derided the notion "that the process of industrialization repeated itself from country to country lumbering through [Rostow's] pentametric rhythm"[8] and showed, to the contrary, how the industrialization of the late-coming European countries such as Germany and Russia differed in fundamental respects from the English industrial revolution, largely because of the intensity of the "catching-up" effort on the part of the latecomers. Even though it was limited to nineteenth-century Europe, Gerschenkron's work was of great importance for development economics by providing *historical* support for the case against monoeconomics. As industrialization actually proceeded in the periphery, it appeared that Third World industrialization around mid-twentieth century exhibited features rather different from those Gerschenkron had identified as characteristic for the European latecomers.[9] But for the historically oriented, Gerschenkron's work supplied the same kind of reassurance Keynesianism had given to the analytically minded: he showed once and for all that there can be more than one path to development, that countries setting out to become industrialized are likely to forge their own policies, sequences, and ideologies to that end.

Subsequent observations strengthened the conviction that industrialization in the less developed areas required novel approaches. For example, modern, capital-intensive industry was found to be less effective in absorbing the "unlimited supplies of labor" available in agriculture than had been the case in the course of earlier experiences of industrialization. Advances in industrialization were frequently accompanied by persistent inflationary and balance-of-payment pressures which raised questions about the adequacy of traditional remedies and led, in Latin America, to the "sociological" and "structuralist" theses on inflation, which, interestingly, have now gained some currency in the advanced countries, usually without due credit being given. Also, the vigorous development of the transnational corporation in the postwar period raised entirely new "political economy" questions about the extent to which a country should attract, restrict, or control these purveyors of modern technology and products.

III. The Mutual-Benefit Assumption

The new (far from unified) body of doctrine and policy advice that was built up in this manner was closely connected, as noted earlier, with the proposition that the core industrial countries could make an important, even an essential, contribution to the development effort of the periphery through expanded trade, financial transfers, and technical assistance.

The need for large injections of financial aid fitted particularly well into those theories advocating a "big push." It was argued that such an effort could only be mounted with substantial help from the advanced countries, as the poor countries were unable to generate the needed savings from within. Here the underlying model was the new growth economics, which, in its simplest (Harrod-Domar) version, showed a country's growth rate to be determined by the propensity to save and the capital-output ratio. Growth economics had evolved independently from development economics, as a direct offshoot of the Keynesian system and its macroeconomic concepts. While devised primarily with the advanced industrial countries in mind, it found an early practical application in the planning exercises for developing countries that became common in the fifties. These exercises invariably contained projections for an expansion of trade and aid. Their underlying assumption was necessarily that such enlarged economic relations between rich and poor countries would be beneficial for both. Now this proposition fits nicely into orthodox monoeconomics, but it might have been expected to arouse some suspicion among development economists and to mix rather poorly with some of the other elements and assertions of the new subdiscipline. For example, so it could have been asked, why are the countries of the South in a state where, according to some, it takes a huge push to get them onto some growth path? Why are they so impoverished in spite of having long been drawn into the famous "network of world trade"[10] which was supposed to yield mutual benefits for all participants? Is it perhaps because, in the process, some countries have been caught in the net to be victimized by some imperialist spider? But such indelicate questions were hardly put in the halcyon days of the immediate postwar years, except perhaps in muted tones by a few faraway voices, such as Raúl Prebisch's. Of that more later.

Action-oriented thought seldom excels in consistency. Development economics is no exception to this rule; it was born from the marriage between the new insights about the sui generis economic problems of the underdeveloped countries and the overwhelming desire to achieve rapid progress in solving these problems with the instruments at hand, or thought to be within reach, such as large-scale foreign aid. A factor in "arranging" this marriage, in spite of the incompatibilities involved, was the success of the Marshall Plan in Western Europe. Here the task of postwar reconstruction was mastered with remarkable speed, thanks, so it appeared at least, to a combination of foreign aid with some economic planning and cooperation on the part of the aid recipients. It has often been pointed out that this European success story led to numerous failures in the Third World, that it lamentably blocked a realistic assessment of the task of development, in comparison with that of reconstruction.

But the matter can be seen in a different light. True, the success of the Marshall Plan deceived economists, policymakers, and enlightened opinion in the West into believing that infusion of capital helped along by the right kind of investment planning might be able to grind out growth and welfare all over the globe. But—and here is an application of what I have called the "Principle of the Hiding Hand"—on balance it may have been a good thing that we let ourselves be so deceived. Had the toughness of the development problem and the difficulties in the North-South relationship been correctly sized up from the outset, the considerable intellectual and political mobilization for the enterprise would surely not have occurred. In that case, and in spite of the various "development disasters" which we have experienced (and which will be discussed later in this essay), would we not be even farther away from an acceptable world than we are today?

In sum, one historical function of the rise of development economics was to inspire confidence in the manageability of the development enterprise and thereby to help place it on the agenda of policymakers the world over. The assertion of the mutual-benefit claim served this purpose.

IV. The Strange Alliance of Neo-Marxism and Monoeonomics Against Development Economics

Predictably, when the path to development turned out to be far less smooth than had been thought, the hybrid nature of the new subdiscipline resulted in its being subjected to two kinds of attacks. The neoclassical Right faulted it for having forsaken the true principles of monoeconomics and for having compounded,through its newfangled policy recommendations, the problem it set out to solve. For the neo-Marxists, on the other hand, development economics had not gone far enough in its analysis of the predicament of the poor countries: so serious was their problem pronounced to be that nothing but total change in their socioeconomic structure and in their relations to the rich countries could make a difference; pending such change, so-called development policies only created new forms of exploitation and "dependency." The two fundamentalist critiques attacked development economics from opposite directions and in totally different terms: but they could converge in their specific indictments—as they indeed did, particularly in the important arena of industrialization. Because the adherents of neoclassical economics and those of various neo-Marxist schools of thought live in quite separate worlds, they were not even aware of acting in unison. In general, that strange de facto alliance has hardly been noted; but it plays an important role in the evolution of thinking on development and its story must be briefly told.

Doubts about the harmony of interests between the developed and underdeveloped countries arose at an early stage among some of the major contributors to the new subdiscipline. There was widespread acceptance of the view that the advanced industrial countries could henceforth contribute to the development of the less advanced, particularly through financial assistance, but questions were raised in various quarters about the equitable distribution of the gains from trade, both in the past and currently. In 1949, Raúl Prebisch and Hans Singer formulated (simultaneously and independently) their famous "thesis" on the secular tendency of the terms of trade to turn against countries exporting primary products and importing manufactures.[11] They attributed this alleged tendency to the power of trade unions in the advanced countries and to conditions of underemployment in the periphery. The argument was put forward to justify a sustained policy of industrialization. Arthur Lewis was led by his model in a rather similar direction: as long as "unlimited supplies of labor" in the subsistence sector depress the real wage throughout the economy, any gains from productivity increases in the export sector are likely to accrue to the importing countries; moreover, in a situation in which there is surplus labor at the ruling wage, prices give the wrong signals for resource allocation in general and for the international division of labor in particular; the result was a further argument for protection and industrialization.

Both the Prebisch-Singer and the Lewis arguments showed that without a judiciously interventionist state in the periphery, the cards were inevitably stacked in favor of the center. On the whole, it looked as though this was the result of some unkind fate rather than of deliberate maneuvers on the center's part. Critics from the Left later took Arthur Lewis to task for viewing unlimited supplies of labor as a datum, rather than as something that is systematically *produced* by the colonizers and capitalists.[12] Lewis was of course fully aware of such situations and specifically notes at one point that in Africa the imperial powers impoverished the subsistence economy "by taking away the people's land, or by demanding forced labour in the capitalist sector, or by imposing taxes to drive people to work for capitalist employers."[13] For Lewis these practices were simply not a crucial characteristic of the model—after all, a decline in infant mortality could have the same effect in augmenting labor supply as a head tax.

It appears nevertheless that the debate among development economists in the fifties included the canvassing of some antagonistic aspects of the center-periphery relation. The theories just noted attempted to show that the gain from trade might be unequally distributed (perhaps even to the point where one group of countries would not gain at all) but did not go so far as to claim that the relationship between two groups of countries could actually be exploitative in the sense that trade and other forms of economic intercourse would enrich one group *at the expense* of another—an assertion that would be unthinkable within the assumptions of the classical theory of international trade. Yet, even this kind of assertion was made at a relatively early stage of the debate. Gunnar Myrdal invoked the principle of cumulative causation (which he had first developed in his *American Dilemma*) in seeking to understand the reason for persistent and increasing income disparities *within* countries; but the notion was easily extended to contacts between countries. Myrdal's argument on the possibility of further impoverishment of the poor region (or country) was largely based on the likelihood of its losing skilled people and other scarce factors, and also on the possible destruction of its handicrafts and industries. Independently of Myrdal, I had developed similar ideas: Myrdal's "backwash effect"—the factors making for increasing disparity—became "polarization effect" under my pen, whereas his "spread effect"—the factors making for the spread of prosperity from the rich to the poor regions—was named by me "trickling down effect." (Optimal terminology is probably achieved by combining Myrdal's "spread" with my "polarization" effects.) We both argued, though with different emphases, that the possibility of the polarization effect being stronger than the spread effect must be taken seriously, and thus went counter not only to the theory of international trade, but to the broader traditional belief, so eloquently expressed by John Stuart Mill,[14] that contact between dissimilar groups is always a source of all-around progress. Anyone who had observed the development scene with some care could not but have serious doubts about this view: in Latin America, for example, industrial progress was particularly vigorous during the World Wars and the Great Depression when contacts with the industrial countries were at a low ebb. To me, this meant no more than that *periods* of isolation may be beneficial and I saw some alternation of contact and isolation as creating optimal conditions for industrial development.[15] In any event, both Myrdal and I looked at the polarization effects as forces that can be opposed and neutralized by public policies; and I tried to show that instead of invoking such policies as a deus ex machina (as I thought Myrdal did), it is possible to see them as arising out of, and in reaction to, the experience of polarization.

A strange thing happened once it had been pointed out that interaction between the rich and poor countries could in certain circumstances be in the nature of an antagonistic, zero-sum game: very soon it proved intellectually and politically attractive to assert that such was the essence of the relationship and that it held as an iron law through all phases of contacts between the capitalist center and the periphery. Just as earlier those brought up in the classical tradition of Smith and Ricardo were unable to conceive of a gain from trade that is not mutual, so did it become impossible for the new polarization enthusiasts to perceive anything but pauperization and degradation in each of the successive phases of the periphery's history.[16] This is the "development of underdevelopment" thesis, put forward by André Gunder Frank, and also espoused by some of the more extreme holders of the "dependency" doctrine. Given the historical moment at which these views arose, their first and primary assignment was to mercilessly castigate what had up to then been widely believed to hold the promise of economic emancipation for the underdeveloped countries: industrialization. We are now in the mid-sixties, at which time real difficulties and growing pains were experienced by industry in some leading Third World countries after a prolonged period of vigorous expansion. This situation was taken advantage of in order to characterize all of industrialization as a total failure on a number of (not always consistent) counts: it was "exhausted," "distorted," lacked integration, led to domination and exploitation by multinationals in alliance with a domestic "lumpen bourgeoisie," was excessively capital-intensive and therefore sabotaged employment, and fostered a more unequal distribution of income along with a new, more insidious, kind of dependency than ever before.

At just about the same time, the neoclassical economists or monoeconomists—as they should be called in accordance with the terminology of this essay—were sharpening their own knives for an assault on development policies that had pushed industrialization for the domestic market. In contrast to the multiple indictment from the Left, the monoeconomists concentrated on a single, simple, but to them capital, flaw of these policies: misallocation of resources. By itself this critique was highly predictable and might not have carried more weight than warnings against industrialization emanating from essentially the same camp ten, or twenty, or fifty years earlier. But the effectiveness of the critique was now greater for various reasons. First of all, as a result of the neo-Marxist writings just noted, some of the early advocates of industrialization had now themselves become its sharpest critics. Second, specific policies which in the early stage had been useful in promoting industrialization, though at the cost of inflationary and balance-of-payments pressures, did run into decreasing returns in the sixties: they achieved less industrialization at the cost of greater inflation and balance-of payments problems than before. Third, the practice of deliberate industrialization had given rise to exaggeration and abuse in a number of countries, and it became easy to draw up a list of horrible examples that served to incriminate the whole effort. Fourth, a new set of policies emphasizing exports of manufactures from developing countries became attractive, because of the then rapid expansion of world trade, and the possibilities of success of such policies was demonstrated by countries like Taiwan and South Korea. Under these conditions, the neoclassical strictures became more persuasive than they had been for a long time.

The target of the complementary neo-Marxist and neoclassical writings was not just the new industrial establishment, which in fact survived the onslaught rather well; on the ideological plane, the intended victim was the new development economics, which had strongly advocated industrial development and was now charged with intellectual responsibility for whatever had gone wrong. The blows from Left and Right that fell upon the fledgling and far from unified subdiscipline left it, indeed, rather stunned: so much so that the most intrepid defense of what had been accomplished by the postwar industrialization efforts in the Third World came not from the old stalwarts, but from an English socialist in the tradition of Marx's original position on the problem of backward areas, the late Bill Warren.[17]

V. The Real Wounding of Development Economics

It would of course be silly— as silly as the German proverb *Viel Feind, viel Ehr* (many enemies, much honor)—to hold that any doctrine or policy that is attacked simultaneously from both Left and Right is, for that very reason, supremely invested with truth and wisdom. I have already noted that the neoclassical critics made some valid points, just as the neo-Marxists raised a number of serious issues, particularly in the areas of excessive foreign control and of unequal income distribution. But normally such criticisms should have led to some reformulations and eventually to a strengthening of the structure of development economics. In fact, however, this was not to be the case. No new synthesis appeared. Several explanations can be offered. For one thing, development economics had been built up on the basis of a construct, the "typical underdeveloped country," which became increasingly unreal as development proceeded at very different rates and took very different shapes in the various countries of Latin America, Asia, and Africa. Lenin's law of uneven development, originally formulated with the major imperialist powers in mind, caught up with the Third World! It became clear, for example, that, for the purpose of the most elementary propositions of development strategy, countries with large populations differ substantially from the ever more numerous ministates of the Third World,[18] just as there turned out to be few problems in common between petroleum exporters and petroleum-importing developing countries. The concept of a unified body of analysis and policy recommendations for all underdeveloped countries, which contributed a great deal to the rise of the subdiscipline, became in a sense a victim of the very success of development and of its unevenness.

But there was a more weighty reason for the failure of development economics to recover decisively from the attacks it had been subjected to by its critics. It lies in the series of political disasters that struck a number of Third World countries from the sixties on, disasters that were clearly *somehow* connected with the stresses and strains accompanying development and "modernization." These development disasters, ranging from civil wars to the establishment of murderous authoritarian regimes, could not but give pause to a group of social scientists, who, after all, had taken up the cultivation of development economics in the wake of World War II not as narrow specialists, but impelled by the vision of a better world. As liberals, most of them presumed that "all good things go together"[19] and took it for granted that if only a good job could be done in raising the national income of the countries concerned, a number of beneficial effects would follow in the social, political, and cultural realms.

When it turned out instead that the promotion of economic growth entailed not infrequently a sequence of events involving serious retrogression in those other areas, including the wholesale loss of civil and human rights, the easy self-confidence that our subdiscipline exuded in its early stages was impaired. What looked like a failure to mount a vigorous counterattack against the unholy alliance of neo-Marxists and neoclassicists may well have been rooted in increasing self-doubt, based on mishaps far more serious than either the "misallocation of resources" of the neoclassicists or the "new dependency" of the neo-Marxists.

Not that all the large and gifted group of development economists which had in the meantime been recruited into the new branch of knowledge turned suddenly silent. Some retreated from the position "all good things go together" to "good economics is good for people."[20] In other words, rather than assuming that economic development would bring progress in other fields, they thought it legitimate to operate on the basis of an implicit Pareto-optimality assumption: like plumbing repairs or improvements in traffic control, the technical efforts of economists would improve matters in one area while at worst leaving others unchanged, thus making society as a whole better off. Economic development policy was here in effect downgraded to a technical task exclusively involved with efficiency improvements. An illusion was created and sought that, by confining itself to smaller-scale, highly technical problems, development economics could carry on regardless of political cataclysms.

There was, however, another reaction that was to have a considerable impact. Experiencing a double frustration, one over the appalling political events as such, and the other over their inability to comprehend them, a number of analysts and practitioners of economic development were moved to look at the economic performance itself with a more critical eye than before. In a Freudian act of displacement, they "took out" their distress over the political side on the weaker aspects of the economic record. Within countries with authoritarian regimes, the displacement was often reinforced, unintentionally of course, by the official censorship that was much more rigorous with regard to political dissent than in matters of economic performance.

It was, in a sense, an application of the maxim "all good things go together" *in reverse*. Now that political developments had taken a resoundingly wrong turn,

one had to prove that the economic story was similarly unattractive. Some economists were satisfied once the balance between political and economic performance had been restored in this fashion, be it at a wretchedly low level. But others
were in a more activist mood. Impotent in the face of political injustice and
tyranny, yet feeling a faint sense of responsibility, they were attempting to make
amends by exposing *economic* injustice. In doing so, they paid little attention to
John Rawls who argued, at just about that time, in *A Theory of Justice* that "a
departure from the institutions of equal liberty . . . cannot be justified by or
compensated for by greater social or economic advantage."[21] But perhaps it was
fortunate—and a measure of the vitality of the development movement—that the
disappointment over politics led to an attempt at righting at least those wrongs
economists could denounce in their professional capacity.

Here then is one important origin of the concern with income distribution
which became a dominant theme in the development literature in the early seventies. Albert Fishlow's finding, on the basis of the 1970 census, that income
distribution in Brazil had become more unequal and that some low-income
groups may even have come to be worse off in absolute terms, in spite of
(because of?) impressive growth, was particularly influential.[22] An alarm based
on this and similar data from other countries was sounded by Robert McNamara,
the President of the World Bank, in his annual address to the Board of Governors
meeting in 1972. A large number of studies followed, and an attempt was made
to understand how development could be shaped in accordance with distributional goals, or to formulate policies that would combine the objectives of growth
and distribution.

Before long, attention was directed not only to the relative aspects of income
distribution, but to the absolute level of need satisfaction among the poorer
groups of a country's population. Thus was born the concern with *basic needs*—
of food, health, education, etc.—that is currently a principal preoccupation of
development economics. Just as the construct of the "typical underdeveloped
country" gave way to diverse categories of countries, each with characteristics of
its own, so did the heretofore unique maximand of development economics
(income per capita) dissolve into a variety of partial objectives, each requiring
consultation with different experts—on nutrition, public health, housing, and
education, among others.

There is of course much to be said for this new concreteness in development
studies, and particularly for the concern with the poorer sections. Nevertheless,
development economics started out as the spearhead of an effort that was to bring
all-around emancipation from backwardness. If that effort is to fulfill its promise,
the challenge posed by dismal politics must be met rather than avoided or
evaded. By now it has become quite clear that this cannot be done by economics
alone. It is for this reason that the decline of development economics cannot be
fully reversed: our subdiscipline had achieved its considerable luster and excitement through the implicit idea that it could slay the dragon of backwardness

virtually by itself or, at least, that its contribution to this task was central. We now know that this is not so; a consoling thought is that we may have gained in maturity what we have lost in excitement.

Looking backward, the whole episode seems curious. How could a group of social scientists that had just lived through the most calamitous "derailments of history" *in various major economically advanced countries* entertain such great hopes for economic development per se? Here I can perhaps offer some enlightenment by drawing on my recent work in the history of ideas. In *The Passions and the Interests* I showed that the rise of commerce and money-making activities in the seventeenth and eighteenth centuries was then looked upon as promising for political stability and progress; and I stressed that such optimistic expectations were not based on a new respect for these activities, but rather on *continuing contempt* for them: unlike the passionate, aristocratic pursuit of glory and power with its then well-recognized potential for disaster, the love of money was believed to be "incapable of causing either good *or evil* on a grand scale."[23] A similar perception may have been at work in relation to the less developed countries of Asia, Africa, and Latin America of the twentieth century. The Western economists who looked at them at the end of World War II were convinced that these countries were not all that complicated: their major problems would be solved if only their national income per capita could be raised adequately. At an earlier time, contempt for the countries designated as "rude and barbarous" in the eighteenth century, as "backward" in the nineteenth and as "underdeveloped" in the twentieth had taken the form of relegating them to permanent lowly status, in terms of economic and other prospects, on account of unchangeable factors such as hostile climate, poor resources, or inferior race. With the new doctrine of economic growth, contempt took a more sophisticated form: suddenly it was taken for granted that progress of these countries would be smoothly linear if only they adopted the right kind of integrated development program! Given what was seen as their overwhelming problem of poverty, the underdeveloped countries were expected to perform like wind-up toys and to "lumber through" the various stages of development singlemindedly; their reactions to change were not to be nearly as traumatic or aberrant as those of the Europeans, with their feudal residues, psychological complexes and exquisite high culture. In sum, like the "innocent" and *doux* trader of the eighteenth century, these countries were perceived to have only *interests* and *no passions.*

Once again, we have learned otherwise.

Notes

1. See, for example, David Morawetz, *Twenty-Five Years of Economic Development: 1950 to 1975* (Washington, D.C.: World Bank, 1977).

2. B. Sutcliffe, "Imperialism and Industrialization in the Third World," in R. Owen and B. Sutcliffe, eds., *Studies in the Theory of Imperialism* (London: Longman, 1972), pp.

180–86, and P. Singer, "Multinacionais: internacionalização e crise," Caderno CEBRAP No. 28 (São Paulo: Editora Brasiliense,1977), pp. 50–56. On the complexity of Marx's views, even in the preface of *Capital* where the cited phrase appears, see Chapter 4, this volume, pp. 89–90. [Not in this volume. See A. Hirschman, *Essays in Trespassing: Economics to Politics and Beyond* (Cambridge, England: Cambridge University Press, 1981).]

3. Dudley Seers leaned on this established terminological usage with his article "The Limitations of the Special Case," *Bulletin of the Oxford University Institute of Economics and Statistics*, 25 (May 1963): 77–98, in which he pleaded for recasting the teaching of economics so as to make it more useful in dealing with the problems of the less-developed countries. The "special case" that had falsely claimed generality was, for Keynes, the fully employed economy; for Seers, it was the economy of the advanced capitalist countries, in contrast to conditions of underdevelopment.

4. See, for example, Jacob Viner, "Some Reflections on the Concept of 'Disguised Unemployment,' " in *Contribuições à Análise do Desenvolvimiento Econômico* (Essays in honor of Eugênio Gudin), (Rio de Janeiro: Agir, 1957), pp. 345–54.

5. His principal empirical argument was the actual decline in agricultural output suffered when the labor force suddenly diminished in a country with an allegedly redundant labor force in agriculture, as happened during the 1918–19 influenza epidemic in India. Arthur Lewis pointed out later that the consequences he had drawn from the assumption of zero marginal productivity in agriculture would remain fully in force provided only the supply of labor at the given wage in industry exceeds the demand, a condition that is much weaker than that of zero marginal productivity. See W. Arthur Lewis, "Reflections on Unlimited Labor," in *International Economics and Development: Essays in Honor of Raúl Prebisch* (New York and London: Academic Press, 1972), pp. 75–96.

6. New Haven: Yale University Press, 1958, p. 5.

7. C. P. Kindleberger, *Europe's Postwar Growth: The Role of Labor Supply* (Cambridge, Mass.: Harvard University Press, 1967).

8. *Economic Backwardness in Historical Perspective* (Cambridge, Mass.: Harvard University Press, 1962), p. 355.

9. A. O. Hirschman, "The Political Economy of Import-Substituting Industrialization in Latin America," published in 1968 and reprinted in Hirschman, *A Bias for Hope: Essays on Development and Latin America* (New Haven: Yale University Press, 1971), Chapter 3.

10. This was the title of a well-known League of Nations study stressing the benefits of multilateral trade which were being threatened in the thirties by the spread of bilateralism and exchange controls. Its principal author was Folke Hilgerdt, a Swedish economist. In the immediate postwar period, Hilgerdt, then with the United Nations, noted that trade, however beneficial, had not adequately contributed to a narrowing of income differentials between countries. With Hilgerdt coming from the Heckscher-Ohlin tradition and having celebrated the contributions of world trade to welfare, this paper, which was published only in processed form in the proceedings of a congress(I have not been able to locate it), was influential in raising questions about the benign effects of international economic relations on the poorer countries.

11. An account of the emergence of the thesis is now available in Joseph Love, "Raúl Prebisch and the Origins of the Doctrine of Unequal Exchange," *Latin American Research Review* 15 (November 1980): 45–72. See also my earlier essay "Ideologies of Economic Development in Latin America" (1961), reprinted in *A Bias for Hope*, Chapter 13. The latest review of the ensuing controversy and related evidence is in two articles by John Spraos: "The Theory of Deteriorating Terms of Trade Revisited," *Greek Economic*

Review 1 (December 1979): 15–42, and "The Statistical Debate on the Net Barter Terms of Trade between Primary Commodities and Manufactures," *Economic Journal* 90 (March 1980): 107–28.

12. G. Arrighi, "Labour Supplies in Historical Perspective: A Study of the Proletarianization of the African Peasantry in Rhodesia," *Journal of Development Studies* 6 (April 1970): 197–234.

13. W. Arthur Lewis, "Economic Development with Unlimited Supplies of Labour," published in 1954 and reprinted in A. N. Agarwala and S. P. Singh, eds., *The Economics of Underdevelopment* (London: Oxford University Press, 1958), p. 410.

14. "It is hardly possible to overrate the value, in the present low state of human improvement, of placing human beings in contact with persons dissimilar to themselves, and with modes of thought and action unlike those with which they are familiar. . . . Such communication has always been, and is peculiarly in the present age, one of the primary sources of progress." J. S. Mill, *Principles of Political Economy*, Book III, Chapter 17, para. 5.

15. *Strategy*, pp. 173–5, 199–201.

16. This view has been aptly labeled "catastrofismo" by Aníbal Pinto.

17. B. Warren, "Imperialism and Capitalist Accumulation," *New Left Review*, no. 81 (Sept.–Oct. 1973): 3–45, and "The postwar economic experience of the Third World," in *Toward a New Strategy for Development*, pp. 144–68.

18. This is stressed, for example, by Clive Y. Thomas, *Dependence and Transformation: The Economics of the Transition to Socialism* (New York: Monthly Review Press, 1974), passim.

19. See Robert Packenham, *Liberal America and the Third World* (Princeton: Princeton University Press, 1973), pp. 123–9.

20. An expression attributed to Arnold Harberger, in an article in the *New York Times* of February 7, 1980.

21. Cambridge, Mass.: Harvard University Press, 1971, p. 61.

22. "Brazilian Size Distribution of Income," *American Economic Review* 62 (May 1972): 391–402.

23. Princeton: Princeton University Press, 1977, p. 58.

12

AMARTYA SEN

Development: Which Way Now?*

I. The Promise and the Default

"Development economics is a comparatively young area of inquiry. It was born just about a generation ago, as a subdiscipline of economics, with a number of other social sciences looking on both skeptically and jealously from a distance."[1] So writes Albert Hirschman, but the essay that begins so cheerfully turns out to be really an obituary of development economics—no longer the envy of the other social sciences. In this illuminating essay, aptly called "The Rise and Decline of Development Economics," Hirschman puts his main thesis thus:

> our subdiscipline had achieved its considerable lustre and excitement through the implicit idea that it could slay the dragon of backwardness virtually by itself or, at least, that its contribution to this task was central. We now know that this is not so.[2]

The would-be dragon-slayer seems to have stumbled on his sword.

There is some plausibility in this diagnosis, but is it really true that development economics has no central role to play in the conquest of underdevelopment

---

*Presidential Address of the Development Studies Association given in Dublin on 23 September 1982. In preparing the final version of the paper, I have benefited from the comments of Carl Riskin, Louis Emmerij, Albert Hirschman, Seth Masters, Hans Singer, and the editorial referees of this journal, and from the discussions following my DSA address, and also that following a talk I gave on a related theme at the Institute of Social Studies in the Hague on 11 October 1982.

EDITOR'S NOTE: *As the reigning dean of development economics, Sen offers a subtle combination of repudiation and apology for the sins of the profession, the real object being to quietly direct attention away from simple quantitative indicators to the more sophisticated social and political analyses presumed by his notions of "entitlements" and "capabilities." Politically, the paper represents the (successful) effort to poach the agenda of the left, effectively co-opting it into mainstream ideology.*

and economic backwardness? More specifically, were the original themes in terms of which the subject was launched really so far from being true or useful? I shall argue that the obituary may be premature, the original themes—while severely incomplete in coverage—did not point entirely in the wrong direction, and the discipline of development economics does have a central role to play in the field of economic growth in developing countries. But I shall also argue that the problematique underlying the approach of traditional development economics is, in some important ways, quite limited, and has not—and could not have— brought us to an adequate understanding of economic development. Later on, I shall take up the question as to the direction in which we may try to go instead.

There is a methodological problem in identifying a subject—or a subdiscipline as Hirschman calls it—with a given body of beliefs and themes rather than with a collection of subject matters and problems to be tackled. But Hirschman is certainly right in pointing towards the thematic similarities of the overwhelming majority of contributions in development economics. While some development economists such as Peter Bauer and Theodore Schultz have not been party to this thematic congruence, they have also stood outside the mainstream of what may be called standard development economics, as indeed the title of Peter Bauer's justly famous book, *Dissent on Development*,[3] indicates. The subdiscipline began with a set of favourite themes and the main approaches to the subject have been much moulded by these motifs. Clearly, the subject cannot live or die depending just on the success or failure of these themes, but the main approaches would need radical reformulation if these themes were shown to be fundamentally erroneous or misguided.

Hirschman identifies two major ideas with which development economics came into being, namely "rural underemployment" (including so-called "disguised unemployment") and "late industrialisation." The former idea led naturally to a focus on utilisation of underemployed manpower and to acceleration of capital accumulation. The latter called for an activist state and for planning to overcome the disadvantages of lateness through what Hirschman calls "a deliberate, intensive, guided effort." The subject expended a lot of time in developing "new rationales . . . for protection, planning, and industrialisation itself."[4]

While there have been differences in assertion and emphasis *within* the mainstream of the subdiscipline, it is fair to say that in terms of policy the following have been among the major strategic themes pursued ever since the beginning of the subject: (1) industrialisation, (2) rapid capital accumulation, (3) mobilisation of underemployed manpower, and (4) planning and an economically active state.[5] There are, of course, many other common themes, e.g. emphasis on skill formation, but they have not typically been as much subjected to criticism as these other themes, and there is thus much to be said for concentrating on these four.

These themes (especially the need for planning, but also the deliberate fostering of industrialisation and capital accumulation and the acceptance of the possibility of surplus labour) are closely linked to criticisms of the traditional neoclassical models as applied to developing countries. Hirschman calls this eschewal of "universal" use of neoclassical economics the rejection of "monoeconomics." Monoeconomics sounds perhaps a little like a disease that one could catch if not careful. I shall avoid the term, though some would no doubt have thought it quite appropriate to characterise universal neoclassical economics as a contagious affliction.

It was argued by development economists that neoclassical economics did not apply terribly well to underdeveloped countries. This need not have caused great astonishment, since neoclassical economics did not apply terribly well anywhere else. However, the role of the state and the need for planning and deliberate public action seemed stronger in underdeveloped countries, and the departure from traditional neoclassical models was, in many ways, more radical.

The discrediting of traditional development economics that has lately taken place, and to which Hirschman made reference, is undoubtedly partly due to the resurgence of neoclassical economics in recent years. As Hirschman (1981) rightly notes, "the claim of development economics to stand as a separate body of economic analysis and policy derived intellectual legitimacy and nurture from the prior success and parallel features of the Keynesian Revolution" (p. 7). The neoclassical resurgence against Keynesian economics was to some extent paralleled by the neoclassical recovery in the field of economic development. The market, it was argued, has the many virtues that standard neoclassical analysis has done so much to analyse, and state intervention could be harmful in just the way suggested by that perspective.

The neoclassical resurgence has drawn much sustenance from the success of some countries and the failure of others. The high performance of economies like South Korea, Taiwan, Hong Kong and Singapore—based on markets and profits and trade—has been seen as bringing Adam Smith back to life. On the other hand, the low performance of a great many countries in Asia, Africa and Latin America has been cited as proof that it does not pay the government to mess about much with the market mechanism. Recently, doubts raised about the record of China, and the vocal desire of the Chinese leadership to make greater use of material incentives, have been interpreted as proof that even a powerful socialist regime cannot break the basic principles on which the market mechanism is founded.

The attack on state activism and planning has been combined with criticism of some of the other features of traditional development economics. It has been argued that enterprise is the real bottleneck, not capital, so that to emphasise capital accumulation and the creation of surplus—as was done for example by Maurice Dobb (1951; 1960) and Paul Baran (1957)—was to climb the wrong tree. The charge of misallocation of resources has been levelled also against industrialisation, especially for the domestic market. Hirschman (1981) notes: "By itself this critique was highly predictable and might not have carried more weight than warnings against industrialisation emanating from essentially the same camp ten, or twenty, or fifty years earlier." But—as he goes on to say—the effectiveness of this critique was now greater for various reasons, including the fact that "some of the early advocates of industrialisation had now themselves become its sharpest critics" (p. 18). Hirschman refers in this context to some "neo-Marxist" writings and the views of some members of the so-called "dependency" school. Certainly, the particular pattern of industrial expansion in Latin America provides many examples of exploitative relations with the metropolitan countries, particularly the United States of America, and the internal effects were often quite terrible in terms of fostering economic inequality and social distortion. But to move from there to a rejection of industrialisation as such is indeed a long jump.

I should explain that Hirschman, from whom I have been quoting extensively, does not in many cases endorse these attacks on the policy strategies of traditional development economics. But he provides excellent analyses of the arguments figuring in the attacks. I believe Hirschman is more hesitant in his defence of traditional development economics than he need have been, but his own reasons for rejecting that tradition—to which he himself has of course contributed much[6]—rests primarily on the argument that development economics has tended to be contemptuous of underdeveloped countries, albeit this contempt has taken a "sophisticated form." These countries have been "expected to perform like wind-up toys and 'lumber through' the various stages of development singlemindedly." As Hirschman (1981) puts it, "these countries were perceived to have only *interests* and *no passions*" (p. 24).[7]

I believe this diagnosis has much truth in it. But I also believe that, contemptuous and simplistic though development economics might have been in this respect, the main themes that were associated with the origin of development economics, and have given it its distinctive character, are not rejectable for that reason. I shall argue that they address common problems, which survive despite the particular passions.

II. Traditional Themes in the Light of Recent Experiences

Growth is not the same thing as development and the difference between the two has been brought out by a number of recent contributions to development economics.[8] I shall take up the complex question of the content of economic development presently (in Sections III–V below). But it can scarcely be denied that economic growth is one aspect of the process of economic development. And it happens to be the aspect on which traditional development economics—rightly or wrongly—has concentrated. In this section I do not assess the merits of that concentration (on which more later), but examine the appropriateness of the traditional themes, given that concentration. Dealing specifically with economic growth as it is commonly defined, the strategic relevance of these themes is examined in the light of recent experiences. How do these theories—formulated and presented mainly in the 'forties and 'fifties—fare in the light of the experiences of the 'sixties and the 'seventies?

The *World Development Report 1982* (henceforth *WDR*) presents comparative growth data for the period 1960–80 for "low-income economies" and "middle-income economies," with a dividing line at US \$410 in 1980. Leaving out small countries (using a cut-off line of 10 million people) and excluding the OPEC countries which have had rather special economic circumstances during the 'seventies, we have 14 countries in the low-income category for which data on economic growth (GNP or GDP) are given in *WDR*. Correspondingly, there are 18 such countries in the middle-income category. Table 1 presents these data. For three of the low-income countries, namely China, Bangladesh and Afghanistan, the GNP growth figures are not given in *WDR* and they have been approximately identified with GDP growth. In interpreting the results, this has to be borne in mind, and only those conclusions can be safely drawn which would be unaffected by variations of these estimates within a wide range.

The fourteen low-income economies vary in terms of growth rate of GNP *per capita* during 1960–80 from *minus* 0.7 per cent in Uganda to 3.7 per cent in China. The top three countries in terms of economic growth are China (3.7 per cent), Pakistan (2.8 per cent) and Sri Lanka (2.4 per cent). (Note that China's pre-eminent position would be unaffected even if the approximated growth figure is substantially cut.) In the middle-income group, the growth performance again varies a great deal, ranging from *minus* 1.0 per cent for Ghana to 8.6 per cent for Romania. The top three countries in terms of economic growth are Romania (8.6 per cent), South Korea (7.0 per cent) and Yugoslavia (5.4 per cent).

How do these high-performance countries compare with others in the respective groups in terms of the parameters associated with the main theses of traditional development economics? Take capital accumulation first. Of the three top growth-performers, two also have the highest share of gross domestic investment in GDP, namely Sri Lanka with 36 per cent and China with 31 per cent. Pakistan comes lower, though it does fall in the top half of the class of fourteen countries.

Turning now to the middle-income countries, the top three countries in terms of growth are also the top three countries in terms of capital accumulation, namely Yugoslavia with 35 per cent, Romania with 34 per cent, and South Korea with 31 per cent. Thus, if there is anything to be learned from the experience of these successful growers regarding the importance of capital accumulation, it is certainly not a lesson that runs counter to the traditional wisdom of development economics.

It might, however, be argued that to get a more convincing picture one should look also at failures and not merely at successes. I don't think the cases are quite symmetrical, since a failure can be due to some special "bottleneck" even when all other factors are favourable. Nevertheless, it is not useless to examine the

Table 1

	GNP per head		1980 gross domestic investment (% of GDP)	1980 share of industry in GDP (%)
	1980 Value ($)	1960–80 Growth (%)		
Low-income				
Bangladesh	130	1.3*	17	13
Ethiopia	140	1.4	10	16
Nepal	140	0.2	14	13
Burma	170	1.2	24	13
Afghanistan	—	0.9*	14	—
Zaire	220	0.2	11	23
Mozambique	230	−0.1	10	16
India	240	1.4	23	26
Sri Lanka	270	2.4	36	30
Tanzania	280	1.9	22	13
China	290	3.7*	31	47
Pakistan	300	2.8	18	25
Uganda	300	−0.7	3	6
Sudan	410	−0.2	12	14
Middle-income				
Ghana	420	−1.0	5	21
Kenya	420	2.7	22	21
Egypt	580	3.4	31	35
Thailand	670	4.7	27	29
Philippines	690	2.8	30	37
Morocco	900	2.5	21	32
Peru	930	1.1	16	45
Colombia	1,180	3.0	25	30
Turkey	1,470	3.6	27	30
S. Korea	1,520	7.0	31	41
Malaysia	1,620	4.3	29	37
Brazil	2,050	5.1	22	37
Mexico	2,090	2.6	28	38
Chile	2,150	1.6	18	37
South Africa	2,300	2.3	29	53
Romania	2,340	8.6	34	64
Argentina	2,390	2.2	—	—
Yugoslavia	2,620	5.4	35	43

Source: World Development Report 1982, tables 1–5. The countries included are all the ones within the "Low-income" and "Middle-income" categories, other than those with less than 10 million population, members of OPEC, and countries without GNP or GDP growth figures. Asterisked growth rates are based on GDP growth figures per head (tables 2 and 17).

cases of failure as well, especially with respect to capital accumulation, since it has been seen in traditional development economics to be such a *general* force towards economic growth.

The three worst performers in the low-income category in terms of growth rate are, respectively, Uganda with *minus* 0.7 per cent, Sudan with *minus* 0.2 per cent, and Mozambique with *minus* 0.1 per cent. In terms of capital accumulation, Uganda's rank is also the worst there, with only 3 per cent of GDP invested. Mozambique is the second lowest investor, and Sudan the fifth lowest.

What about growth failures in the middle-income countries? The worst performers in terms of growth rate are Ghana with *minus* 1 per cent, Peru with 1.1 per cent, and Chile with 1.6 per cent. As it happens these countries are also respectively the lowest, the second lowest and the third lowest accumulators of capital in the category of the middle-income countries.

So both in terms of cases of success and those of failure, the traditional wisdom of development economics is scarcely contradicted by these international comparisons. Quite the contrary.

Hans Singer (1952) in his paper entitled "The Mechanics of Economic Development," published thirty years ago, seems to be almost talking about today's worst case of growth failure in the combined category of low-income and middle-income countries, namely Ghana. Using the Harrod–Domar model with an assumed capital–output ratio, Singer argues that a country with 6 per cent savings and a population growth rate of 1.25 per cent will be a "stationary economy." While Ghana has managed an investment and savings ratio of just below 6 per cent (5 per cent to be exact) it has had a population growth between 2.4 and 3.0 per cent during these decades as opposed to Singer's assumption of 1.25 per cent. Rather than being stationary, Ghana has accordingly slipped back, going down at about 1 per cent a year. The Harrod–Domar model is an over-simplification, of course, but the insight obtained from such reasoning is not altogether without merit.

I turn now to the theme of industrialisation. In the category of low-income countries, the top performers—China, Pakistan and Sri Lanka—happen to be among the four countries with the highest share of industries in GDP. In the middle-income group, the top growers—Romania, South Korea and Yugoslavia—are among the top five countries in terms of the share of industries in GDP.[9]

The picture at the other end, i.e. for countries with growth failures, is certainly less neat than at the top end in this case, or at either end in the case of capital accumulation. It is, however, certainly true that Uganda, which occupies the bottom position in the low-income category in terms of growth rate, also has the bottom position in terms of the share of industries, and similarly Ghana, with the lowest record of growth in the middle-income group, also has the lowest share of industries in that group. But the positions of second and third lowest are not quite so telling. In the low-income category, low-performing Sudan and

Mozambique have middling industrial ratios. In the middle-income group, the second-lowest growth performer, Peru, has the third *highest* ratio of industries in that group, though the third-lowest growth performer, Chile, has a middling industrial ratio. The picture is, thus, a bit more muddled at the lower end of growth performance.[10]

Altogether, so far as growth is concerned, it is not easy to deny the importance of capital accumulation or of industrialisation in a poor pre-industrial country. Turning to the thesis of underemployment and the role of labour mobilisation, there have been several powerful attempts at disestablishing the thesis of "disguised unemployment," e.g. by Theodore Schultz (1964), but they have not been altogether successful.[11] Furthermore, what is really at issue is the crucial role of labour mobilisation and use, and not whether the opportunity cost of labour is exactly zero.[12] It is worth noting, in this context, that the high growth performers in both groups have distinguished records of labour-using economic growth, and some (e.g. China and South Korea) have quite outstanding achievements in this area. While they have very different political systems, their respective successes in labour mobilisation have been specially studied and praised.[13]

The question of planning and state activism is a field in which comparative quantitative data is particularly difficult to find. But some qualitative information is of relevance. Of the three top growing economies in the low-income group, one—China—is obviously not without an active state. While Pakistan is in no way a paradigmatic example of determined state planning, it has been frequently cited as a good example of what harm government meddling can do.[14] The third—Sri Lanka—has been recently studied a great deal precisely because of its active government intervention in a number of different fields, including health, education and food consumption.

In the middle-income group, of the three top performers, Romania and Yugoslavia clearly do have a good deal of planning. The third—South Korea—has had an economic system in which the market mechanism has been driven hard by an active government in a planned way. Trying to interpret the South Korean economic experience as a triumph of unguided market mechanism, as is sometimes done, is not easy to sustain. I have discussed this question elsewhere,[15] and I shall not spend any time on it here. I should only add that, aside from having a powerful influence over the direction of investment through control of financial institutions (including nationalised banks), the government of South Korea fostered an export-oriented growth on the secure foundations of more than a decade of intensive import substitution, based on trade restrictions, to build up an industrial base. Imports of a great many items are still prohibited or restricted. The pattern of South Korean economic expansion has been carefully planned by a powerful government. If this is a free market, then Walras's auctioneer can surely be seen as going around with a government white paper in one hand and a whip in the other.

The point is not so much that the government is powerful in the high-growth developing countries. It is powerful in nearly *every* developing country. The issue concerns the systematic involvement of the state in the *economic* sphere, and the pursuit of *planned* economic development. The carefully planned government action in, say, China or Sri Lanka or South Korea or Romania, contrasts—on the whole strongly—with the economic role of the government in such countries as Uganda or Sudan or Chile or Argentina or Ghana.

This examination of the main theses of traditional development economics has been too brief and tentative, and certainly there is no question of claiming anything like definitiveness in the findings. But, in so far as anything has emerged, it has not gone in the direction of debunking traditional development economics; just the contrary.

Before I move on to develop some criticisms of my own, I should make one last defensive remark about traditional development economics. The general policy prescriptions and strategies in this tradition have to be judged in terms of the climate of opinion and the over-all factual situation prevailing at the time these theories were formulated. Development economics was born at a time when government involvement in deliberately fostering economic growth in general, and industrialisation in particular, was very rare, and when the typical rates of capital accumulation were quite low. That situation has changed in many respects, and, while that may suggest the need to emphasise different issues, it does not in any way invalidate the wisdom of the strategies then suggested.

The point can be brought out with an example. In the 1952 paper of Hans Singer from which I have already quoted, one of the conclusions that Singer emphasised is the need to raise the then existing rate of saving. He argued, with some assumptions about production conditions, that to achieve even a 2 per cent rate of *per capita* growth, with a population growing at 1.25 per cent per year, "a rate of net savings of $16\frac{1}{4}$ per cent is necessary," and that "this rate of saving is about three times the rate actually observed in underdeveloped countries" (Singer, 1952, pp. 397–8). The current average rate of saving is no longer a third of that figure, but substantially *higher* than the figure. The weighted average ratio of gross domestic saving for low-income developing countries is estimated to be about 22 per cent, and that for middle-income developing countries about 25 per cent; and, even after deducting for depreciation, Singer's target has certainly been exceeded. And, even with a faster growth of population than Singer anticipated, the weighted average of GDP growth rates *per capita* has been about $2\frac{1}{2}$ per cent per year for low income countries and more than 3 per cent per year for middle-income countries over the 'seventies.[16]

The point of policy interest now is that, despite these *average* achievements, the performances of different countries are highly divergent. There is still much relevance in the broad policy themes which traditional development economics has emphasised. The strategies have to be adapted to the particular conditions and to national and international circumstances, but the time to bury traditional development economics has not yet arrived.

III. Fast Growth and Slow Social Change

I believe the real limitations of traditional development economics arose not from the choice of means to the end of economic growth, but in the insufficient recognition that economic growth was no more than a means to some other objectives. The point is not the same as saying that growth does not matter. It may matter a great deal, but, if it does, this is because of some associated benefits that are realised in the process of economic growth.

It is important to note in this context that the same level of achievement in life expectancy, literacy, health, higher education, etc., can be seen in countries with widely varying income per capita. To take just one example, consider Brazil, Mexico, South Korea, China and Sri Lanka.[17]

China and Sri Lanka, with less than a seventh of GNP per head in Brazil or Mexico, have similar life expectancy figures to the two richer countries. South Korea, with its magnificent and much-eulogised growth record, has not yet overtaken China or Sri Lanka in the field of longevity, despite being now more than five times richer in terms of *per capita* GNP. If the government of a poor developing country is keen to raise the level of health and the expectation of life, then it would be pretty daft to try to achieve this through raising its income per head, rather than going directly for these objectives through public policy and social change, as China and Sri Lanka have both done.

Not merely is it the case that economic growth is a means rather than an end, it is also the case that for some important ends it is not a very efficient means either. In an earlier paper (Sen, 1981b) it was shown that had Sri Lanka been a typical developing country, trying to achieve its high level of life expectancy not through direct public action, but primarily through growth (in the same way as typical developing countries do), then it would have taken Sri Lanka—depending on assumptions—here between 58 years and 152 years to get where it already now happens to be.[18] It might well be the case that "money answereth all things," but the answer certainly comes slowly.

IV. Entitlements and Capabilities

Perhaps the most important thematic deficiency of traditional development economics is its concentration on national product, aggregate income and total supply of particular goods rather than on "entitlements" of people and the "capabilities" these entitlements generate. Ultimately, the process of economic development has to be concerned with what people can or cannot do, e.g. whether they can live long, escape avoidable morbidity, be well nourished, be

Table 2

Country	Life expectancy at birth 1980 (years)	GNP per head, 1980 (U.S. dollars)
Brazil	63	2,050
China	64	290
Mexico	65	2,090
South Korea	65	1,520
Sri Lanka	66	270

able to read and write and communicate, take part in literary and scientific pursuits, and so forth. It has to do, in Marx's words, with "replacing the domination of circumstances and chance over individuals by the domination of individuals over chance and circumstances."[19]

Entitlement refers to the set of alternative commodity bundles that a person can command in a society using the totality of rights and opportunities that he or she faces. Entitlements are relatively simple to characterise in a purely market economy. If a person can, say, earn $200 by selling his labour power and other saleable objects he has or can produce, then his entitlements refer to the set of all commodity bundles costing no more than $200. He can buy any such bundle, but no more than that, and the limit is set by his ownership ("endowment") and his exchange possibilities ("exchange entitlement"), the two together determining his over-all entitlement.[20] On the basis of this entitlement, a person can acquire some capabilities, i.e. the ability to do this or that (e.g. be well nourished), and fail to acquire some other capabilities. The process of economic development can be seen as a process of expanding the capabilities of people. Given the functional relation between entitlements of persons over goods and their capabilities, a useful—though derivative—characterisation of economic development is in terms of expansion of entitlements.[21]

For most of humanity, about the only commodity a person has to sell is labour power, so that the person's entitlements depend crucially on his or her ability to find a job, the wage rate for that job, and the prices of commodities that he or she wishes to buy. The problems of starvation, hunger and famines in the world could be better analysed through the concept of entitlement than through the use of the traditional variables of food supply and population size. The intention here is not, of course, to argue that the supply of goods—food in this case—is irrelevant to hunger and starvation, which would be absurd, but that the supply is just one influence among many; and, in so far as supply is important, it is so precisely because it affects the entitlements of the people involved, typically through prices. Ultimately, we are concerned with what people can or cannot do, and this links directly with their "entitlements" rather than with over-all supplies and outputs in the economy.[22]

The failure to see the importance of entitlements has been responsible for millions of people dying in famines. Famines may not be at all anticipated in situations of good or moderate over-all levels of supply, but, notwithstanding that supply situation, acute starvation can hit suddenly and widely because of failures of the entitlement systems, operating through ownership and exchange. For example, in the Bangladesh famine of 1974, a very large number died in a year when food availability per head was at a peak—higher than in any other year between 1971 and 1975. The floods that affected agriculture did ultimately—much later than the famine—reduce the food output, but its first and immediate impact was on the rural labourers who lost jobs in planting and transplanting rice, and started starving long before the main crop that was affected was to be harvested. The problem was made worse by forces of inflation in the economy, reducing the purchasing power especially of rural labourers, who did not have the economic muscle to raise their money wages correspondingly.[23]

Entitlements may not operate only through market processes. In a socialist economy entitlements will depend on what the families can get from the state through the established system of command. Even in a non-socialist economy, the existence of social security—when present—makes the entitlements go substantially beyond the operation of market forces.

A major failing of traditional development economics has been its tendency to concentrate on supply of goods rather than on ownership and entitlement. The focus on growth is only one reflection of this. Extreme concentration on the ratio of food supply to population is another example of the same defective vision.[24] Recently the focus has shifted somewhat from growth of *total incomes* to the *distribution of incomes*. This may look like a move in the right direction, and indeed it is. But I would argue that "income" itself provides an inadequate basis for analysing a person's entitlements. Income gives the means of buying things. It expresses buying power in terms of some scalar magnitude—given by one real number. Even if there are no schools in the village and no hospitals nearby, the income of the villager can still be increased by adding to his purchasing power over the goods that are available in the market. But this rise in income may not be able to deal at all adequately with his entitlement to education or medical treatment, since the rise in income as such guarantees no such thing.

In general, one real number reflecting some aggregate measure of market power can scarcely represent so complex a notion as entitlement. The power of the market force depends on relative prices and, as the price of some good rises, the hold of income on the corresponding entitlement weakens. With non-marketability, it slips altogether. In the extreme case, the entitlement to live, say, in a malaria-free environment is not a matter of purchase with income in any significant way.

In dealing with starvation and hunger, the focus on incomes—though defective—is not entirely disastrous. And of course it is a good deal better than the focus on total food output and population size. The weighting system of real income and cost-of-living pays sufficient attention to food in a poor community to make real income a moderately good "proxy" for entitlement to food in most cases.[25] But when it comes to health, or education, or social equality, or self-respect, or freedom from social harassment, income is miles off the target.

V. Political Complexities

To move from concentrating on growth to supplementing that with an account of income distribution is basically an inadequate response to what is at issue. It is also, in effect, an attempt to refuse to come to terms with the complexity of entitlement relations. The metric of income, as already discussed, is much too crude. Indeed, entitlements related even to purely economic matters, e.g. that to food, may actually require us to go beyond the narrow limits of economics altogether.

Take the case of famine relief. A hungry, destitute person will be *entitled* to some free food *if* there is a relief system offering that. Whether, in fact, a starving person will have such an entitlement will depend on whether such a public relief operation will actually be launched. The provision of public relief is partly a matter of political and social pressure. Food is, as it were, "purchased" in this context not with income but with political pressure. The Irish in the 1840s did not have the necessary political power. Nor did the Bengalis in the Great Bengal Famine of 1943. Nor the Ethiopians in Wollo in the famine of 1973. On the other hand, there are plenty of examples in the world in which timely public policy has averted an oncoming famine completely.

The operation of political forces affecting entitlements is far from simple. For example, with the present political system in India, it is almost impossible for a famine to take place. The pressure of newspapers and diverse political parties make it imperative for the government in power to organise swift relief. It has to act to retain credibility. No matter how and where famine threatens—whether with a flood or a drought, whether in Bihar in 1967–8, Maharashtra in 1971–3, or in West Bengal in 1978—an obligatory policy response prevents the famine actually occurring.

On the other hand, there is no such relief for the third of the Indian rural population who go to bed hungry every night and who lead a life ravaged by regular deprivation. The quiet presence of non-acute, endemic hunger leads to no newspaper turmoil, no political agitation, no riots in the Indian parliament. The system takes it in its stride.[26]

The position in China is almost exactly the opposite of this. On the one hand, the political commitment of the system ensures a general concern with eradicating regular malnutrition and hunger through more equal access to means of livelihood, and through entitlements *vis-à-vis* the state; and China's achievements in this respect have been quite remarkable. In a normal year, the Chinese poor are much better fed than the Indian poor. The expectation of life in China is between 66 and 69 years in comparison with India's miserable 52 years. On the other hand, if there is a political and economic crisis that confuses the regime and makes it pursue disastrous policies with confident dogmatism, then it cannot be forced to change its policies by crusading newspapers or by effective pressure from opposing political groups.

It is, in fact, now quite clear that in China during 1959–61 there were deaths on a very large scale due to famine conditions. The extent of the disaster has only recently become evident, even though there are still many uncertainties regarding the exact estimation of extra mortality.[27] Important mortality data were released in 1980 by Professor Zhu Zhengzhi of Beijing University,[28] indicating that the death rate rose from about 10.8 per thousand in 1957 to an average of 16.58 per thousand per year during 1958–61. This yields a figure of extra mortality of 14–16 million in China in the famine-affected years—a very large figure indeed. It is, in fact, very much larger than the extra mortality (calculated in the same way) even in the Great Bengal Famine of 1943 (namely about 3 million[29]), the largest famine in India in this century.

In 1981 the noted economist Sun Yefang released some further mortality data,[30] referring to "the high price in blood" of the economic policy pursued at that time. He reported that the death rate per thousand had risen to as high as 25.4 in 1960, indicating an extra mortality of 9 million in that year alone. His figures for the four years also yields a total of around 15 million extra deaths during the Chinese famine of 1959–61.[31] Others have suggested even higher mortality.[32]

These are truly staggering figures. Even if we take a level quite a bit below the lower limit of the estimates, the sudden extra mortality caused by the famine[33] would still be on a scale that is difficult to match even in pre-independent India (and there has of course been no famine in India since independence).

Is it purely accidental that a famine—indeed one on an enormous scale—could take place in China while none has occurred in post-independent India? The contrast is particularly odd when viewed in the context of the undoubted fact that China has been very much more successful than India in eliminating regular malnutrition. There may well be an accidental element in the comparative records on famines, but as already noted (on page 223), on a number of occasions potentially large famines have been prevented in India through quick, extensive and decisive government intervention. Reports on deaths from hunger reach the government and the public quickly and dramatically through active newspapers, and are taken up vigorously by parties not in power. Faced with a threatening famine, any government wishing to stay in office in India is forced to abandon or modify its on-going economic policy, and meet the situation with swift public action, e.g. redistribution of food within the country, imports from abroad, and widespread relief arrangements (including food for work programmes).

Policy failures in China during the famine years (and the Great Leap Forward period), which have been much discussed in China only recently, relate not merely to factors that dramatically reduced output, but also to distributional issues, e.g. inter-regional balances, and the draconian procurement policy that was apparently pursued relentlessly despite lower agricultural output.[34] Whatever the particular policy errors, the government in power was not forced to re-examine them, nor required to face harrowing newspaper reports and troublesome opposition parties. The contrast may not, therefore, be purely accidental.

In an interesting and important speech given in 1962—just after the famine—Chairman Mao made the following remarks to a conference of 7,000 cadres from different levels: "If there is no democracy, if ideas are not coming from the masses, it is impossible to establish a good line, good general and specific policies and methods. . . . Without democracy, you have no understanding of what is happening down below; the situation will be unclear; you will be unable to collect sufficient opinions from all sides; there can be no communication between top and bottom; top-level organs of leadership will depend on one-sided and incorrect material to decide issues, thus you will find it difficult to avoid being subjectivist; it will be impossible to achieve unity of understanding and unity of action, and impossible to achieve true centralism."[35] Ralph Miliband (1977), who has provided an illuminating and far-reaching analysis of the issue of democracy in capitalist and socialist societies from a Marxist perspective, points out that Mao's "argument for 'democracy' is primarily a 'functional' one" (pp. 149–50), and argues that this is an inadequate basis for understanding the need for "socialist democracy."[36] That more general question certainly does remain, but it is worth emphasising that even the purely "functional" role of democracy can be very crucial to matters of life and death, as the Chinese experiences of the famine of 1959–61 bring out.[37]

Finally, it is important to note that the protection that the Indian poor get from the active news distribution system and powerful opposition parties has very severe limits. The deprivation has to be dramatic to be "newsworthy" and politically exploitable (see Sen, 1982c). The Indian political system may prevent famines but, unlike the Chinese system, it seems unable to deal effectively with endemic malnutrition. In a normal year when things are running smoothly both in India and China, the Indian poor is in a much more deprived general state than his or her Chinese counterpart.[38]

VI. Concluding Remarks

I shall not try to summarise the main points of the paper, but I will make a few concluding remarks to put the discussion in perspective.

First, traditional development economics has not been particularly unsuccessful in identifying the factors that lead to economic growth in developing countries. In the field of causation of growth, there is much life left in traditional analyses (Section II).

Secondly, traditional development economics has been less successful in characterising economic development, which involves expansion of people's capabilities. For this, economic growth is only a means and often not a very efficient means either (Section III).

Thirdly, because of close links between entitlements and capabilities, focusing on entitlements—what commodity bundles a person can command—provides a helpful format for characterising economic development. Supplementing data on GNP *per capita* by income distributional information is quite inadequate to meet the challenge of development analysis (Section IV).

Fourthly, famines and starvation can be more sensibly analysed in terms of entitlement failures than in terms of the usual approach focusing on food output per unit of population. A famine can easily occur even in a good food supply situation, through the collapse of entitlements of particular classes or occupation groups (Section IV).

Fifthly, a study of entitlements has to go beyond purely economic factors and take into account political arrangements (including pressure groups and news distribution systems) that affect people's actual ability to command commodities, including food. These influences may be very complex and may also involve apparently perplexing contrasts, e.g. between (1) India's better record than China's in avoiding famines, and (2) India's total failure to deal with endemic malnutrition and morbidity in the way China has been able to do (Section V). Whether the disparate advantages of the contrasting systems can be effectively combined is a challenging issue of political economy that requires attention. Much is at stake.

Notes

1. Essay 1 in Hirschman (1981). [See chapter 11 of this volume, p. 191.]
2. Hirschman (1981), p. 23. [See chapter 11 of this volume, pp. 206–207.]
3. Bauer (1971). See also Schultz (1964) and Bauer (1981). For a forceful critical account without breaking from traditional development economics, see Little (1982).
4. Hirschman (1981), pp. 10–11.
5. See Rosenstein-Rodan (1943), Mandelbaum (1945), Dobb (1951), Datta (1952), Singer (1952), Nurkse (1953) and Lewis (1954, 1955).
6. See particularly Hirschman (1958, 1970).
7. For the conceptual framework underlying the distinction, see Hirschman (1977).
8. See, for example, Streeten (1981). See also Grant (1978), Morris (1979) and Streeten *et al.* (1981).
9. An additional one in this case is South Africa, and its industrial share is high mainly because mining is included in that figure. In fact, if we look only at manufacturing, South Africa falls below the others.
10. The rank correlation coefficient between *per capita* growth and the share of gross domestic investment in GDP is 0.72 for middle-income countries, 0.75 for low-income

countries and 0.82 for the two groups put together. On the other hand, the rank correlation coefficient between *per capita* growth and the share of industries is only 0.22 for middle-income countries, even though it is 60.59 for the low-income countries and 0.68 for the two groups put together.

11. My own views on this are presented in Sen (1975). See also Sen (1967), and the exchange with Schultz following that in the same number of this journal.

12. See Marglin (1976), chapter 2. Also Sen (1975), chapters 4 and 6. See also Fei and Ranis (1964).

13. See Little (1982). See also the important study of Ishikawa (1981), which discusses the empirical role of labour absorption in different Asian economies.

14. For example, Little *et al.* (1971).

15. Sen (1981b), and the literature cited there, especially Datta-Chaudhuri (1979).

16. See tables 2, 5, and 17 of the *World Development Report 1982*.

17. Taken from *World Development Report 1982*, table 1. The 1982 Chinese census indicates a higher expectation of life—around 69 years. The Sri Lankan figure of 66 years relates to 1971, and the current life expectancy is probably significantly higher.

18. See Sen (1981b), pp. 303–6. See also Jayawardena (1974), Marga Institute (1974), Isenman (1978), Alailima (1982), Gwatkin (1979).

19. Marx and Engels (1846); English translation taken from McLellan (1977), p. 190.

20. The notion of "entitlements" is explored in Sen (1981a). It is worth emphasising here, to avoid misunderstandings that seem to have occurred in some discussions of the concept, that (1) "exchange entitlement" is only a *part* of the entitlement picture and is incomplete without an account of ownership or endowment, and (2) "exchange entitlement" includes not merely trade and market exchange but also the use of production possibilities (i.e. "exchange with nature").

21. Capabilities, entitlements and utilities differ from each other. I have tried to argue elsewhere that "capabilities" provide the right basis for judging the advantages of a person in many problems of evaluation—a role that cannot be taken over either by utility or by an index of commodities (Sen, 1982a, pp. 29–38, 353–69). When we are concerned with such notions as the well-being of a person, or standard of living, or freedom in the positive sense, we need the concept of capabilities. We have to be concerned with what a person can do, and this is not the same thing as how much pleasure or desire fulfilment he gets from these activities ("utility"), nor what commodity bundles he can command ("entitlements"). Ultimately, therefore, we have to go not merely beyond the calculus of national product and aggregate real income, but also that of entitlements over commodity bundles viewed on their own. The focus on capabilities differs also from concentration on the mental metric of utilities, and this contrast is similar to the general one between pleasure, on the one hand, and positive freedom, on the other. The particular role of entitlements is *through* its effects on capabilities. It is a role that has substantial and far-reaching importance, but it remains derivative on capabilities. On these general issues, see Sen (1982a, d, 1983) and Kynch and Sen (1983).

22. See Sen (1981a, b), Arrow (1982), Desai (1983).

23. See Sen (1981a), chapter 9. Other examples of famines due to entitlement failure without a significant—indeed any—reduction of overall food availability can be found in chapter 6 (the Great Bengal Famine of 1943) and chapter 7 (the Ethiopian famine of 1973–4); see also chapter 7 (the Sahelian famines of the 1970s). On related matters, see also Sen (1976, 1977), Ghose (1979), Alamgir (1978, 1980), Chattopadhyay (1981), Oughton (1982), Ravallion (1983). See also Parikh and Rabar (1981) and Srinivasan (1982). Also the special number of *Development*, Aziz (1982).

24. On this and related issues, see Aziz (1975), Taylor (1975), Griffin (1978), Sinha and Drabek (1978), Spitz (1978), Lappé and Collins (1979), George and Paige (1982), Rao (1982).

25. However, the index of real income will continue to differ from the index of food entitlement since the price deflators will not be the same, though the two will often move together. A problem of a different sort arises from *intra*-family differences in food consumption (e.g. through "sex bias"), as a result of which both the real income and the food entitlement of the family may be rather deceptive indicators of nutritional situations of particular members of the family. On this issue, see Bardhan (1974), Sen (1983c), Kynch and Sen (1983) and Sen and Sengupta (1983).

26. See Sen (1982b, c).

27. See Aird (1982), pp. 277–8.

28. Zhu Zhengzhi (1980), pp. 54–5. These data have been analysed by Coale (1981). See also Bernstein (1983b).

29. See Sen (1981a), Appendix D. In both cases the death rate immediately preceding the famine-affected year is taken as the bench mark in comparison with which the "extra" mortality in famine-affected years are calculated.

30. Sun Yefang (1981) and People's Republic of China (1981).

31. See Bernstein (1983a, b).

32. See Bernstein's (1983b) account of the literature. See also Aird (1980). For a description of the intensity of the famine in a particular commune (the Liyuan Commune in Anhui province), see Research Group of the Fen Yang County Communist Party Committee (1983). "The commune's population of 5,730 people in 1957 had dropped to 2,870 people in 1961. More than half died of starvation [*e si*] or fled the area. . . . In 1955, the Houwang production team was a model elementary cooperative. The village had twenty-eight families, a total of 154 people. . . . fifty-nine people starved to death [*e si*], and the survivors fled the area" (p. 36).

33. The number of deaths due to a famine must not be confused with the number actually dying of starvation, since most people who die in a famine tend to die from other causes (particularly from diseases endemic in the region) to which they become more susceptible due to undernutrition, and also due to breakdown of sanitary arrangements, exposure due to wandering, eating non-eatables, and other developments associated with famines. See Sen (1981a), pp. 203–16.

34. See Bernstein (1983b), who also argues that the harsh procurement policies in China did not have the ideologically "anti-peasant" character that similar policies in the USSR did during 1932–3, but reflected "erroneous" reading of the level of output and of the economic situation.

35. Mao Zedong (1974), p. 164.

36. Miliband goes on to argue: "Much may be claimed for the Chinese experience. But what cannot be claimed for it, on the evidence, is that it has really begun to create the institutional basis for the kind of socialist democracy that would effectively reduce the distance between those who determine policy and those on whose behalf it is determined" (p. 151).

37. The Soviet famines of the 1930s and the Kampuchean famine of more recent years provide further evidence of penalties of this lacuna.

38. The crude death rate in China in 1980 was reported to be 8 per thousand in contrast with India's 14 (*World Development Report 1982*, table 18, p. 144). Only in famine situations did the reported death rate in China (e.g. 25.4 reported in 1960) exceed that in India.

References

Aird, J. (1980). "Reconstruction of an official data model of the population of China." U.S. Department of Commerce, Bureau of Census, 15 May.

—— (1982). "Population studies and population policy in China." *Population and Development Review*, vol. 8, pp. 267–97.

Alailima, P. J. (1982). "National policies and programmes of social development in Sri Lanka." Mimeographed, Colombo.

Alamgir, M. (1978). *Bangladesh: A Case of Below Poverty Level Equilibrium Trap.* Dhaka: Bangladesh Institute of Development Studies.

—— (1980). *Famine in South Asia—Political Economy of Mass Starvation in Bangladesh.* Cambridge, Mass.: Oelgeschlager, Gunn and Hain.

Arrow, K. J. (1982). "Why people go hungry." *New York Review of Books*, vol. 29, July 15, pp. 24–6.

Aziz, S. (1975) (ed.). *Hunger, Politics and Markets: The Real Issues in the Food Crisis.* New York: NYU Press.

—— (1982) (ed.). "The fight against world hunger." Special number of *Development*, 1982: 4.

Baran, P. A. (1957). *Political Economy of Growth.* New York: Monthly Review Press.

Bardhan, P. (1974). "On life and death questions." *Economic and Political Weekly*, vol. 9, pp. 1293–304.

Bauer, P. (1971). *Dissent on Development.* London: Weidenfeld and Nicolson.

—— (1981). *Equality, the Third World, and Economic Delusion.* Cambridge, Mass.: Harvard University Press.

Bernstein, T. P. (1983a). "Starving to death in China." *New York Review of Books*, vol. 30, 6 June, pp. 36–8.

—— (1983b). "Hunger and the state: grain procurements during the Great Leap Forward; with a Soviet perspective." Mimeographed, East Asia Center, Columbia University.

Chattopadhyay, B. (1981). "Notes towards an understanding of the Bengal famine of 1943," *Cressida*, vol. 1.

Coale, A. J. (1981). "Population trends, population policy, and population studies in China." *Population and Development Review*, vol. 7, pp. 85–97.

Datta, B. (1952). *Economics of Industrialization.* Calcutta: World Press.

Datta-Chaudhuri, M. K. (1979). "Industrialization and foreign trade: an analysis based on the development experience of the Republic of Korea and the Philippines." ILO Working Paper WP II–4, ARTEP, ILO, Bangkok.

Desai, M. J. (1983). "A general theory of poverty." Mimeographed, London School of Economics, To be published in *Indian Economic Review*.

Dobb, M. H. (1951). *Some Aspects of Economic Development.* Delhi: Delhi School of Economics.

—— (1960). *An Essay on Economic Growth and Planning.* London: Routledge.

Fei, J. C. H., and Ranis, G. (1964). *Development of the Labour Surplus Economy: Theory and Practice.* Homewood, Ill.: Irwin.

George, S. and Paige, N. (1982). *Food for Beginners.* London: Writers and Readers Publishing Cooperative.

Ghose, A. (1979). "Short term changes in income distribution in poor agrarian economies." ILO Working Paper WEP 10–6/WP 28, Geneva.

Grant, J. (1978). *Disparity Reduction Rates in Social Indicators.* Washington, D.C.: Overseas Development Council.

Griffin, K. (1978). *International Inequality and National Poverty.* London: Macmillan.

Gwatkin, D. R. (1979). "Food policy, nutrition planning and survival: the cases of Kerala and Sri Lanka." *Food Policy,* November.

Hirschman, A. O. (1958). The Strategy of Economic Development. New Haven, Conn.: Yale University Press.

—— (1970). *Exit, Voice, and Loyalty.* Cambridge, Mass.: Harvard University Press.

—— (1977). *The Passions and the Interests.* Princeton: Princeton University Press.

—— (1981). *Essays in Trespassing: Economics to Politics and Beyond.* Cambridge University Press.

Isenman, P. (1978). "The relationship of basic needs to growth, income distribution and employment—the case of Sri Lanka." Mimeographed, World Bank.

Ishikawa, T. (1981). *Essays on Technology, Employment and Institutions in Economic Development.* Tokyo: Kinokuniya.

Jayawardena, L. (1974). "Sri Lanka." In *Redistribution with Growth* (ed. H. Chenery et al.). London: Oxford University Press.

Kynch, J. and Sen, A. K. (1983). "Indian women: survival and well-being." Mimeographed; to be published in *Cambridge Journal of Economics.*

Lappé, F. M. and Collins, J. (1979). *Food First: Beyond the Myth of Security.* New York: Ballantine Books.

Lewis, W. A. (1954). "Economic development with unlimited supplies of labour." *Manchester School,* vol. 22, pp. 139–91.

—— (1955). *The Theory of Economic Growth.* Homewood, Ill.: Irwin.

Little, I. M. D. (1982). *Economic Development: Theory, Policy and International Relations.* New York: Basic Books.

—— Scitovsky, T. and Scott, M. (1971). *Industry and Trade in Some Developing Countries.* London: Oxford University Press.

McLellan, D. (1977) (ed.). *Karl Marx: Selected Writings.* Oxford: Oxford University Press.

Mandelbaum (Martin), K. (1945). *The Industrialization of Backward Areas.* Oxford: Blackwell.

Mao Tse-tung (Zedong) (1974). *Mao Tse-tung Unrehearsed, Talks and Letters: 1956–71* (ed. Schram). London: Penguin Books.

Marga Institute (1974). *Welfare and Growth in Sri Lanka.* Colombo: Marga Institute.

Marglin, S. A. (1976). *Value and Price in the Labour Surplus Economy.* Oxford: Clarendon Press.

Marx, K. and Engels, F. (1846). *The German Ideology.*

Miliband, R. (1977). *Marxism and Politics.* London: Oxford University Press.

Morris, M. D. (1979). *Measuring the Condition of the World's Poor: The Physical Quality of Life Index.* Oxford: Pergamon Press.

Nurkse, R. (1953). *Problems of Capital Formation in Underdeveloped Countries.* Oxford: Blackwell.

Oughton, E. (1982). "The Maharashtra drought of 1970–73: an analysis of scarcity." *Oxford Bulletin of Economics and Statistics,* vol. 44, pp. 169–97.

Parikh, K. and Rabar, F. (1981) (eds.). *Food for All in a Sustainable World.* Laxenburg: IIASA.

People's Republic of China (1981). *Foreign Broadcast Information Service,* no. 58, 26 March.

Rao, V. K. R. V. (1982). *Food, Nutrition and Poverty in India.* Brighton: Wheatsheaf Books.

Ravallion, M. (1983). *The Performance of Rice Markets in Bangladesh during the 1974 Famine.* Mimeographed, University of Oxford.

Research Group of the Feng Yang County Communist Party Committee (1982). "An investigation into the household production contract system in Liyuan Commune." *New York Review of Books*, vol. 30, 16 June, pp. 36–8; translated from *Nongye Jingji Congkan* (Collected Material on Agricultural Economics), 25 November 1980.

Rosenstein-Rodan, P. (1943). "Problems of industrialization in Eastern and South-Eastern Europe." *Economic Journal*, vol. 53, pp. 202–11.

Schultz, T. W. (1964). *Transforming Traditional Agriculture.* New Haven, Conn.: Yale University Press.

Sen, A. K. (1967). "Surplus labour in India: a critique of Schultz's statistical test." *Economic Journal*, vol. 77, pp. 154–61.

——— (1975). *Employment, Technology and Development.* Oxford: Clarendon Press.

——— (1976). "Famines as failures of exchange entitlement." *Economic and Political Weekly*, vol. 11, pp. 1273–80.

——— (1977). "Starvation and exchange entitlement: a general approach and its application to the Great Bengal Famine." *Cambridge Journal of Economics*, vol. 1, pp. 33–59.

——— (1981a). *Poverty and Famines: An Essay on Entitlement and Deprivation.* Oxford: Clarendon Press.

——— (1981b). "Public action and the quality of life in developing countries." *Oxford Bulletin of Economics and Statistics*, vol. 43, pp. 287–319.

——— (1981c). "Family and food: sex bias in poverty." Mimeographed, Oxford Institute of Economics and Statistics. To be published in *Rural Poverty in South Asia* (ed. P. Bardhan and T. N. Srinivasan).

——— (1982a). *Choice, Welfare and Measurement.* Oxford: Blackwell, and Cambridge, Mass.: MIT Press.

——— (1982b). "Food battles: conflict in the access to food." Coromandel Lecture, 13 December 1982. Reprinted in *Mainstream*, 8 January 1983.

——— (1982c). "How is India doing?" *New York Review of Books*, vol. 29, Christmas Number, pp. 41–5.

——— (1982d). *Commodities and Capabilities.* Hennipman Lecture, April 1982. To be published by North-Holland, Amsterdam.

——— (1983). "Poor, relatively speaking." *Oxford Economic Papers*, vol. 35.

——— and Sengupta, S. (1983). "Malnutrition of rural children and the sex-bias." *Economic and Political Weekly*, vol. 18.

Singer, H. W. (1952). "The mechanics of economic development." *Indian Economic Review*; reprinted in *The Economics of Underdevelopment* (ed. A. N. Agarwala and A. P. Singh). London: Oxford University Press, 1958.

Sinha, R. and Drabek, A. G. (1978) (eds.). *The World Food Problem: Consensus and Conflict.* Oxford: Pergamon Press.

Spitz, P. (1978). "Silent violence: famine and inequality." *International Social Science Journal*, vol. 30.

Srinivasan, T. N. (1982). "Hunger: defining it, estimating its global incidence and alleviating it." Mimeographed. To be published in *The Role of Markets in The World Food Economy* (ed. D. Gale Johnson and E. Schuh).

Streeten, P. (1981). *Development Perspectives.* London: Macmillan.

——— with S. J. Burki, Mahbub ul Haq, N. Hicks and F. Stewart (1981). *First Things First: Meeting Basic Needs in Developing Countries.* New York: Oxford University Press.

Sun Yefang (1981). Article in *Jingji Guanli* (Economic Management), no. 2, 15 February; English translation in People's Republic of China (1981).

Taylor, L. (1975). "The misconstrued crisis: Lester Brown and world food." *World Development*, vol. 3, pp. 827–37.

Zhu Zhengzhi (1980). Article in *Jingji Kexue*, no. 3.

13

DEEPAK LAL

The Misconceptions of "Development Economics"

Ideas have consequences. The body of thought that has evolved since World War II and is called "development economics" (to be distinguished from the orthodox "economics of developing countries")[1] has, for good or ill, shaped policies for, as well as beliefs about, economic development in the Third World. Viewing the interwar experience of the world economy as evidence of the intellectual deficiencies of conventional economics (embodied, for instance, in the tradition of Marshall, Pigou, and Robertson) and seeking to emulate Keynes' iconoclasm (and hopefully renown), numerous economists set to work in the 1950s to devise a new unorthodox economics particularly suited to developing countries (most prominently, Nurkse, Myrdal, Rosenstein-Rodan, Balogh, Prebisch, and Singer). In the subsequent decades numerous specific theories and panaceas for solving the economic problems of the Third World have come to form the corpus of a "development economics." These include: the dual economy, labor surplus, low level equilibrium trap, unbalanced growth, vicious circles of poverty, big push industrialization, foreign exchange bottlenecks, unequal exchange, "dependencia," redistribution with growth, and a basic needs strategy—to name just the most influential in various times and climes.

Those who sought a new economics claimed that orthodox economics was (1) unrealistic because of its behavioral, technological, and institutional assumptions and (2) irrelevant because it was concerned primarily with the efficient allocation of given resources, and hence could deal neither with the so-called dynamic

EDITOR'S NOTE: *As the 1980s progressed, the Reagan-Thatcher counterrevolution in ideology grew apace, and the dusty, hoary models of laissez-faire were retrieved from the archives to be pressed into service. The World Bank and its affiliates took a radical turn to the right, and Lal's paper articulates the smugly self-assured propaganda of trickle-down economics which they sponsored worldwide. Of course, at the moment of writing, this remains the dominant ideology of official policy, east, west, north or south.*

aspects of growth nor with various ethical aspects of the alleviation of poverty or the distribution of income. The twists and turns that the unorthodox theories have subsequently taken may be traced in four major areas: (1) the role of foreign trade and official or private capital flows in promoting economic development, (2) the role and appropriate form of industrialization in developing countries, (3) the relationship between the reduction of inequality, the alleviation of poverty, and the so-called different "strategies of development," and (4) the role of the price mechanism in promoting development.

The last is, in fact, the major debate that in a sense subsumes most of the rest, and it is the main concern of this article; for the major thrust of much of "development economics" has been to justify massive government intervention through forms of direct control usually intended to supplant rather than to improve the functioning of, or supplement, the price mechanism. This is what I label the *dirigiste dogma*, which supports forms and areas of *dirigisme* well beyond those justifiable on orthodox economic grounds.

The empirical assumptions on which this unwarranted *dirigisme* was based have been repudiated by the experience of numerous countries in the postwar period. This article briefly reviews these central misconceptions of "development economics." References to the evidence as well as an elucidation of the arguments underlying the analysis (together with various qualifications) can be found in the author's work cited in the accompanying box.*

Denial of "Economic Principle"

The most basic misconception underlying much of development economics has been a rejection (to varying extents) of the behavioral assumption that, either as producers or consumers, people, as Hicks said, "would act *economically*; when the opportunity of an advantage was presented to them, they would take it." Against these supposedly myopic and ignorant private agents (that is, individuals or groups of people), development economists have set some official entity (such as government, planners, or policymakers) which is both knowledgeable and compassionate. It can overcome the defects of private agents and compel them to raise their living standards through various *dirigiste* means.

Numerous empirical studies from different cultures and climates, however, show that uneducated private agents—be they peasants, rural-urban workers, private entrepreneurs, or housewives—act economically as producers and consumers. They respond to changes in relative prices much as neoclassical theory would predict. The "economic principle" is not unrealistic in the Third World; poor people may, in fact, be pushed even harder to seek their advantage than rich people.

---

*Not in this volume. See D. Lal, "Misconceptions of Development Economics," *Finance and Development* 22 (June 1985): 10–13.

Nor are the preferences of Third World workers peculiar in that for them too (no matter how poor), the cost of "sweat" rises the harder and longer they work. They do not have such peculiar preferences that when they become richer they will not also seek to increase their "leisure"—an assumption that underlies the view that there are large pools of surplus labor in developing countries that can be employed at a low or zero social opportunity cost. They are unlikely to be in "surplus" in any meaningful sense any more than their Western counterparts.

Nor are the institutional features of the Third World, such as their strange social and agrarian structures or their seemingly usurious informal credit systems, necessarily a handicap to growth. Recent applications of neoclassical theory show how, instead of inhibiting efficiency, these institutions—being second-best adaptations to the risks and uncertainties inherent in the relevant economic environment—are likely to enhance efficiency.

Finally, the neoclassical assumption about the possibilities of substituting different inputs in production has not been found unrealistic. The degree to which inputs of different factors and commodities can be substituted in the national product is not much different in developed or developing countries. Changes in relative factor prices do influence the choice of technology at the micro level and the overall labor intensity of production in Third World economies.

Market vs. Bureaucratic Failure

A second and major strand of the unwarranted *dirigisme* of much of development economics has been based on *laissez-faire*. As is well known, *laissez-faire* will only provide optimal outcomes if perfect competition prevails; if there are universal markets for trading all commodities (including future "contingent" commodities, that is, commodities defined by future conditions, such as the impact of weather on energy prices); and if the distribution of income generated by the *laissez-faire* economy is considered equitable or, if not, could be made so through lump-sum taxes and subsidies. As elementary economics shows, the existence of externalities in production and consumption and increasing returns to scale in production, or either of them, will rule out the existence of a perfectly competitive utopia. While, clearly, universal markets for *all* (including contingent) commodities do not exist in the real world, to that extent market failure must be ubiquitous in the real world. This, even ignoring distributional considerations, provides a *prima facie* case for government intervention. But this in itself does not imply that any or most forms of government intervention will improve the outcomes of a necessarily imperfect market economy.

For the basic cause of market failure is the difficulty in establishing markets in commodities because of the costs of making transactions. These transaction costs are present in any market, or indeed any mode of resource allocation, and include the costs of excluding nonbuyers as well as those acquiring and transmitting the relevant information about the demand and supply of a particular commodity to market participants. They drive a wedge, in effect, between the buyer's and the seller's price. The market for a particular good will cease to exist if the wedge is so large as to push the lowest price at which anyone is willing to sell above the highest price anyone is willing to pay. These transaction costs, however, are also involved in acquiring, processing, and transmitting the relevant information to design public policies, as well as in enforcing compliance. There may, consequently, be as many instances of bureaucratic as of market failure, making it impossible to attain a full welfare optimum. Hence, the best that can be expected in the real world of imperfect markets and imperfect bureaucrats is a second best. But judging between alternative second best outcomes involves a subtle application of second-best welfare economics, which provides no general rule to permit the deduction that, in a necessarily imperfect market economy, particular *dirigiste* policies will increase economic welfare. They may not; and they may even be worse than *laissez-faire*.

Foretelling the Future

Behind most arguments for *dirigisme*, particularly those based on directly controlling quantities of goods demanded and supplied, is the implicit premise of an omniscient central authority. The authority must also be omnipotent (to prevent people from taking actions that controvert its diktat) and benevolent (to ensure it serves the common weal rather than its own), if it is to necessarily improve on the working of an imperfect market economy. While most people are willing to question the omnipotence or benevolence of governments, there is a considerable temptation to believe the latter have an omniscience that private agents know they themselves lack. This temptation is particularly large when it comes to foretelling the future.

Productive investment is the mainspring of growth. Nearly all investment involves giving hostages to fortune. Most investments yield their fruits over time and the expectations of investors at the time of investment may not be fulfilled. Planners attempting to direct investments and outputs have to take a view about future changes in prices, tastes, resources, and technology, much like private individuals. Even if the planners can acquire the necessary information about current tastes, technology, and resources in designing an investment program, they must also take a view about likely changes in the future demand and supply of myriad goods. Because in an uncertain world there can be no agreed or objective way of deciding whether a particular investment gamble is sounder than another, the planned outcomes will be better than those of a market system (in the sense of lower excess demand for or supply of different goods and services) only if the planners' forecasts are more accurate than the decentralized forecasts made by individual decision makers in a market economy. There is no reason to believe that planners, lacking perfect foresight, will be more successful at foretelling the future than individual investors.

Outcomes based on centralized forecasts may, indeed, turn out to be worse than those based on the decentralized forecasts of a large number of participants in a market economy, because imposing a single centralized forecast on the economy in an uncertain world is like putting all eggs in one basket. By contrast, the multitude of small bets, based on different forecasts, placed by a large number of decision makers in a market economy *may be* a sounder strategy. Also, bureaucrats, as opposed to private agents, are likely to take less care in placing their bets, as they do not stand to lose financially when they are wrong. This assumes, of course, that the government does not have better information about the future than private agents. If it does, it should obviously disseminate it, together with any of its own forecasts. On the whole, however, it may be best to leave private decision makers to take risks according to their own judgments.

This conclusion is strengthened by the fact, emphasized by Hayek, that most relevant information is likely to be held at the level of the individual firm and the household. A major role of the price mechanism in a market economy is to transmit this information to all interested parties. The "planning without prices" favored in practice by some planners attempts to supersede and suppress the price mechanism. It thereby throws sand into one of the most useful and relatively low-cost social mechanisms for transmitting information, as well as for coordinating the actions of large numbers of interdependent market participants. The strongest argument against centralized planning, therefore, is that, even though omniscient planners might forecast the future more accurately than myopic private agents, there is no reason to believe that ordinary government officials can do any better—and some reason to believe they may do much worse.

It has nevertheless been maintained that planners in the Third World can and should directly control the pattern of industrialization. Some have put their faith in mathematical programming models based on the use of input-output tables developed by Leontief. But, partly for the reasons just discussed, little reliance can be placed upon either the realism or the usefulness of these models for deciding which industries will be losers and which will be winners in the future. There are many important and essential tasks for governments to perform (see below), and this irrational *dirigisme* detracts from their main effort.

Redressing Inequality and Poverty

Finally, egalitarianism is never far from the surface in most arguments supporting the *dirigiste dogma*. This is not surprising since there may be good theoretical reasons for government intervention, even in a perfectly functioning market economy, in order to promote a distribution of income desired on ethical grounds. Since the distribution resulting from market processes will depend upon the initial distribution of assets (land, capital, skills, and labor) of individuals and households, the desired distribution could, in principle, be attained either by redistributing the assets or by introducing lump-sum taxes and subsidies to achieve the desired result. If, however, lump-sum taxes and subsidies cannot be used in practice, the costs of distortion from using other fiscal devices (such as the income tax, which distorts the individual's choice between income and leisure) will have to be set against the benefits from any gain in equity. This is as much as theory can tell us, and it is fairly uncontroversial.

Problems arise because we lack a consensus about the ethical system for judging the desirability of a particular distribution of income. Even within Western ethical beliefs, the shallow utilitarianism that underlies many economists' views about the"just" distribution of income and assets is not universally accepted. The possibility that all the variegated peoples of the world are utilitarians is fairly remote. Yet the moral fervor underlying many economic prescriptions assumes there is already a world society with a common set of ethical beliefs that technical economists can take for granted and use to make judgments encompassing both the efficiency and equity components of economic welfare. But casual empiricism is enough to show that there is no such world society; nor is there a common view, shared by mankind, about the content of social justice.

There is, therefore, likely to be little agreement about either the content of distributive justice or whether we should seek to achieve it through some form of coercive redistribution of incomes and assets when this would infringe other moral ends, which are equally valued. By contrast, most moral codes accept the view that, to the extent feasible, it is desirable to alleviate abject, absolute poverty or destitution. That alleviating poverty is not synonymous with reducing the inequality of income, as some seem still to believe, can be seen by considering a country with the following two options. The first option leads to a rise in the incomes of all groups, including the poor, but to larger relative increases for the rich, and hence a worsening of the distribution of income. The second leads to no income growth for the poor but to a reduction in the income of the rich; thus the distribution of income improves but the extent of poverty remains unchanged. Those concerned with inequality would favor the second option; those with poverty the first. Thus, while the pursuit of efficient growth may worsen some inequality index, there is no evidence that it will increase poverty.

Surplus Labor and "Trickle Down"

As the major asset of the poor in most developing (as well as developed) countries is their labor time, increasing the demand for unskilled labor relative to its supply could be expected to be the major means of reducing poverty in the Third World. However, the shadows of Malthus and Marx have haunted development economics, particularly in its discussion of equity and the alleviation of poverty. One of the major assertions of development economics, preoccupied with "vicious circles" of poverty, was that the fruits of capitalist growth, with its reliance on the price mechanism, would not trickle down or spread to the poor. Various *dirigiste* arguments were then advocated to bring the poor into a growth process that would otherwise bypass them. The most influential, as well as the most famous, of the models of development advanced in the 1950s to chart the likely course of outputs and incomes in an overpopulated country or region was that of Sir Arthur Lewis. It made an assumption of surplus labor that, in a capitalist growth process, entailed no increase in the income of laborers until the surplus had been absorbed.

It has been shown that the assumptions required for even under-employed rural laborers to be "surplus" in Lewis' sense of their being available to industry at a constant wage, are very stringent, and implausible. It was necessary to assume that, with the departure to the towns of their relatives, those rural workers who remained would work harder for an unchanged wage. This implied that the preferences of rural workers between leisure and income are perverse, for workers will not usually work harder without being offered a higher wage. Recent empirical research into the shape of the supply curve of rural labor at different wages has found that—at least for India, the country supposedly containing vast pools of surplus labor—the curve is upward-sloping (and not flat, as the surplus labor theory presupposes). Thus, for a given labor supply, increases in the demand for labor time, in both the industrial and the rural sectors, can be satisfied only by paying higher wages.

The fruits of growth, even in India, will therefore trickle down, in the sense either of raising labor incomes, whenever the demand for labor time increases by more than its supply, or of preventing the fall in real wages and thus labor incomes, which would otherwise occur if the supply of labor time outstripped the increase in demand for it. More direct evidence about movements in the rural and industrial real wages of unskilled labor in developing countries for which data are available has shown that the standard economic presumption that real wages will rise as the demand for labor grows, relative to its supply, is as valid for the Third World as for the First.

Administrative Capacities

It is in the political and administrative aspects of *dirigisme* that powerful practical arguments can be advanced against the *dirigiste dogma*. The political and administrative assumptions underlying the feasibility of various forms of *dirigisme* derive from those of modern welfare states in the West. These, in turn, reflect the values of the eighteenth-century Enlightenment. It has taken nearly two centuries of political evolution for those values to be internalized and reflected (however imperfectly) in the political and administrative institutions of Western societies. In the Third World, an acceptance of the same values is at best confined to a small class of Westernized intellectuals. Despite their trappings of modernity, many developing countries are closer in their official workings to the inefficient nation states of seventeenth- or eighteenth-century Europe. It is instructive to recall that Keynes, whom so many *dirigiste*s invoke as a founding father of their faith, noted in *The End of Laissez-Faire*:

> But above all, the ineptitude of public administrators strongly prejudiced the practical man in favor of *laissez-faire*—a sentiment which has by no means disappeared. Almost everything which the State did in the 18th century in excess of its minimum functions was, or seemed, injurious or unsuccessful.

It is in this context that anyone familiar with the actual administration and implementation of policies in many Third World countries, and not blinkered by the *dirigiste dogma*, should find that oft-neglected work, *The Wealth of Nations*, both so relevant and so modern.

For in most of our modern-day equivalents of the inefficient eighteenth-century state, not even the minimum governmental functions required for economic progress are always fulfilled. These include above all providing public goods of which law and order and a sound money remain paramount, and an economic environment where individual thrift, productivity, and enterprise is cherished and not thwarted. There are numerous essential tasks for *all* governments to perform. One of the most important is to establish and maintain the country's infrastructure, much of which requires large, indivisible lumps of capital before any output can be produced. Since the services provided also frequently have the characteristics of public goods, natural monopolies would emerge if they were privately produced. Some form of government regulation would be required to ensure that services were provided in adequate quantities at prices that reflected their real resource costs. Government intervention is therefore necessary. And, given the costs of regulation in terms of acquiring the relevant information, it may be second best to supply the infrastructure services publicly.

These factors justify one of the most important roles for government in the development process. It can be argued that the very large increase in infrastructure investment, coupled with higher savings rates, provides the major explanation of the marked expansion in the economic growth rates of most Third World countries during the postwar period, compared with both their own previous performance and that of today's developed countries during their emergence from underdevelopment.

Yet the *dirigiste*s have been urging many additional tasks on Third World governments that go well beyond what Keynes, in the work quoted above, considered to be a sensible agenda for *mid-twentieth-century* Western polities:

> the most important *Agenda* of the State relate not to those activities which private individuals are already fulfilling, but to those functions which fall outside the sphere of the individual, to those decisions which are made by no one if the State does not make them. The important thing for governments is not to do things which

individuals are doing already, and to do them a little better or a little worse; but to do those things which at present are not done at all.

From the experience of a large number of developing countries in the postwar period, it would be a fair professional judgment that most of the more serious distortions are due not to the inherent imperfections of the market mechanism but to irrational government interventions, of which foreign trade controls, industrial licensing, various forms of price controls, and means of inflationary financing of fiscal deficits are the most important. In seeking to improve upon the outcomes of an imperfect market economy, the *dirigisme* to which numerous development economists have lent intellectual support has led to policy-induced distortions that are more serious than, and indeed compound, the supposed distortions of the market economy they were designed to cure. It is these lessons from accumulated experience over the last three decades that have undermined development economics, so that its demise may now be conducive to the health of both the economics and economies of developing countries.

Note

1. Development economics is used to denote economics with a particular view of developing countries and the development process, in contrast to the mere application of orthodox economics to the study of developing countries. For a discussion of this topic, see A.O. Hirschman's *Essays in Trespassing*, (Cambridge, 1981).

14

V. Shiva

Development, Ecology and Women

Development as a New Project of Western Patriarchy

"Development" was to have been a post-colonial project, a choice for accepting a model of progress in which the entire world remade itself on the model of the colonising modern west, without having to undergo the subjugation and exploitation that colonialism entailed. The assumption was that western style progress was possible for all. Development, as the improved well-being of all, was thus equated with the westernisation of economic categories—of needs, of productivity, of growth. Concepts and categories about economic development and natural resource utilisation that had emerged in the specific context of industrialisation and capitalist growth in a centre of colonial power, were raised to the level of universal assumptions and applicability in the entirely different context of basic needs satisfaction for the people of the newly independent Third World countries. Yet, as Rosa Luxemberg has pointed out, early industrial development in western Europe necessitated the permanent occupation of the colonies by the colonial powers and the destruction of the local "natural economy."[1] According to her, colonialism is a constant necessary condition for capitalist growth: without colonies, capital accumulation would grind to a halt. "Development" as capital accumulation and the commercialisation of the economy for the generation of "surplus" and profits thus involved the reproduction not merely of a particular form of creation of wealth, but also of the associated creation of poverty and dispossession. A replication of economic development based on commercialization of resource use for commodity production in the newly independent countries

EDITOR'S NOTE: *A new radical mood has emerged in the early 1990s, linking traditional leftist struggles to feminist and ecological crusades, forging a new, compelling critique of both capitalist and socialist "modernizers." Shiva is an international star of this movement, and her work poses a powerful challenge to almost all forms of traditional development economics.*

created the internal colonies.[2] Development was thus reduced to a continuation of the process of colonisation; it became an extension of the project of wealth creation in modern western patriarchy's economic vision, which was based on the exploitation or exclusion of women (of the west and non-west), on the exploitation and degradation of nature, and on the exploitation and erosion of other cultures. "Development" could not but entail destruction for women, nature and subjugated cultures, which is why, throughout the Third World, women, peasants and tribals are struggling for liberation from "development" just as they earlier struggled for liberation from colonialism.

The UN Decade for Women was based on the assumption that the improvement of women's economic position would automatically flow from an expansion and diffusion of the development process. Yet, by the end of the Decade, it was becoming clear that development itself was the problem. Insufficient and inadequate "participation" in "development" was not the cause for women's increasing under-development; it was rather, their enforced but asymmetric participation in it, by which they bore the costs but were excluded from the benefits, that was responsible. Development exclusivity and dispossession aggravated and deepened the colonial processes of ecological degradation and the loss of political control over nature's sustenance base. Economic growth was a new colonialism, draining resources away from those who needed them most. The discontinuity lay in the fact that it was now new national elites, not colonial powers, that masterminded the exploitation on grounds of "national interest" and growing GNPs, and it was accomplished with more powerful technologies of appropriation and destruction.

Ester Boserup[3] has documented how women's impoverishment increased during colonial rule; those rulers who had spent a few centuries in subjugating and crippling their own women into de-skilled, de-intellectualised appendages, disfavoured the women of the colonies on matters of access to land, technology and employment. The economic and political processes of colonial under-development bore the clear mark of modern western patriarchy, and while large numbers of women and men were impoverished by these processes, women tended to lose more. The privatisation of land for revenue generation displaced women more critically, eroding their traditional land use rights. The expansion of cash crops undermined food production, and women were often left with meagre resources to feed and care for children, the aged and the infirm, when men migrated or were conscripted into forced labour by the colonisers. As a collective document by women activists, organisers and researchers stated at the end of the UN Decade for Women, "The almost uniform conclusion of the Decade's research is that with a few exceptions, women's relative access to economic resources, incomes and employment has worsened, their burden of work has increased, and their relative and even absolute health, nutritional and educational status has declined."[4]

The displacement of women from productive activity by the expansion of development was rooted largely in the manner in which development projects appropriated or destroyed the natural resource base for the production of sustenance and survival. It destroyed women's productivity both by removing land, water and forests from their management and control, as well as through the ecological destruction of soil, water and vegetation systems so that nature's productivity and renewability were impaired. While gender subordination and patriarchy are the oldest of oppressions, they have taken on new and more violent forms through the project of development. Patriarchal categories which understand destruction as "production" and regeneration of life as "passivity" have generated a crisis of survival. Passivity, as an assumed category of the "nature" of nature and of women, denies the activity of nature and life. Fragmentation and uniformity as assumed categories of progress and development destroy the living forces which arise from relationships within the "web of life" and the diversity in the elements and patterns of these relationships.

The economic biases and values against nature, women and indigenous peoples are captured in this typical analysis of the "unproductiveness" of traditional natural societies:

> Production is achieved through human and animal, rather than mechanical, power. Most agriculture is unproductive; human or animal manure may be used but chemical fertilisers and pesticides are unknown. . . . For the masses, these conditions mean poverty.[5]

The assumptions are evident: nature is unproductive; organic agriculture based on nature's cycles of renewability spells poverty; women and tribal and peasant societies embedded in nature are similarly unproductive, not because it has been demonstrated that in cooperation they produce *less* goods and services for needs, but because it is assumed that "production" takes place only when mediated by technologies for commodity production, even when such technologies destroy life. A stable and clean river is not a productive resource in this view: it needs to be "developed" with dams in order to become so. Women, sharing the river as a commons to satisfy the water needs of their families and society are not involved in productive labour: when substituted by the engineering man, water management and water use become productive activities. Natural forests remain unproductive till they are developed into monoculture plantations of commercial species. Development thus, is equivalent to maldevelopment, a development bereft of the feminine, the conservation, the ecological principle. The neglect of nature's work in renewing herself, and women's work in producing sustenance in the form of basic, vital needs is an essential part of the paradigm of maldevelopment, which sees all work that does not produce profits and capital as non or unproductive work. As Maria Mies[6] has pointed out, this concept of surplus has a patriarchal bias because, from the point of view of nature and women, it is not based on material surplus produced *over and above* the requirements of the community: it is stolen and appropriated through violent modes from nature (who needs a share of her produce to reproduce herself) and from women (who need a share of nature's produce to produce sustenance and ensure survival).

From the perspective of Third World women, productivity is a measure of producing life and sustenance; that this kind of productivity has been rendered invisible does not reduce its centrality to survival—it merely reflects the domination of modern patriarchal economic categories which see only profits, not life.

Maldevelopment as the Death of the Feminine Principle

In this analysis, maldevelopment becomes a new source of male-female inequality. "Modernisation" has been associated with the introduction of new forms of dominance. Alice Schlegel[7] has shown that under conditions of subsistence, the interdependence and complementarity of the separate male and female domains of work is the characteristic mode, based on diversity, not inequality. Maldevelopment militates against this equality in diversity, and superimposes the ideologically constructed category of western technological man as a uniform measure of the worth of classes, cultures and genders. Dominant modes of perception based on reductionism, duality and linearity are unable to cope with equality in diversity, with forms and activities that are significant and valid, even though different. The reductionist mind superimposes the roles and forms of power of western male-oriented concepts on women, all non-western peoples and even on nature, rendering all three "deficient," and in need of "development." Diversity, and unity and harmony in diversity, become epistemologically unattainable in the context of maldevelopment, which then becomes synonymous with women's underdevelopment (increasing sexist domination), and nature's depletion (deepening ecological crises). Commodities have grown, but nature has shrunk. The poverty crisis of the South arises from the growing scarcity of water, food, fodder and fuel, associated with increasing maldevelopment and ecological destruction. This poverty crisis touches women most severely, first because they are the poorest among the poor, and then because, with nature, they are the primary sustainers of society.

Maldevelopment is the violation of the integrity of organic, interconnected and interdependent systems, that sets in motion a process of exploitation, inequality, injustice and violence. It is blind to the fact that a recognition of nature's harmony and action to maintain it are preconditions for distributive justice. This is why Mahatma Gandhi said, "There is enough in the world for everyone's need, but not for some people's greed."

Maldevelopment is maldevelopment in thought and action. In practice, this fragmented, reductionist, dualist perspective violates the integrity and harmony of man in nature, and the harmony between men and women. It ruptures the co-operative unity of masculine and feminine, and places man, shorn of the feminine principle, above nature and women, and separated from both. The violence to nature as symptomatised by the ecological crisis, and the violence to women, as symptomatised by their subjugation and exploitation arise from this subjugation of the feminine principle. I want to argue that what is currently called development is essentially maldevelopment, based on the introduction or accentuation of the domination of man over nature and women. In it, both are viewed as the "other," the passive non-self. Activity, productivity, creativity which were associated with the feminine principle are expropriated as qualities of nature and women, and transformed into the exclusive qualities of man. Nature and women are turned into passive objects, to be used and exploited for the uncontrolled and uncontrollable desires of alienated man. From being the creators and sustainers of life, nature and women are reduced to being "resources" in the fragmented, anti-life model of maldevelopment.

Two Kinds of Growth, Two Kinds of Productivity

Maldevelopment is usually called "economic growth," measured by the Gross National Product. Porritt, a leading ecologist has this to say of GNP:

> *Gross* National Product—for once a word is being used correctly. Even conventional economists admit that the hey-day of GNP is over, for the simple reason that as a measure of progress, it's more or less useless. GNP measures the lot, all the goods and services produced in the money economy. Many of these goods and services are not beneficial to people, but rather a measure of just how much is going wrong; increased spending on crime, on pollution, on the many human casualties of our society, increased spending because of waste or planned obsolescence, increased spending because of growing bureaucracies: it's all counted.[8]

The problem with GNP is that it measures some costs as benefits (e.g. pollution control) and fails to measure other costs completely. Among these hidden costs are the new burdens created by ecological devastation, costs that are invariably heavier for women, both in the North and South. It is hardly surprising, therefore, that as GNP rises, it does not necessarily mean that either wealth or welfare increase proportionately. I would argue that GNP is becoming, increasingly, a measure of how real wealth—the wealth of nature and that produced by women for sustaining life—is rapidly decreasing. When commodity production as the prime economic activity is introduced as development, it destroys the potential of nature and women to produce life and goods and services for basic needs. More commodities and more cash mean less life—in nature (through ecological destruction) and in society (through denial of basic needs). Women are devalued first, because their work cooperates with nature's processes, and second, because work which satisfies needs and ensures sustenance is devalued in general. Precisely because more growth in maldevelopment has meant less sustenance of life and life-support systems, it is now imperative to recover the feminine principle as the basis for development which conserves and is ecological. Feminism as ecology, and ecology as the revival of Prakriti, the source of all life, become the decentred powers of political and economic transformation and restructuring.

This involves, first, a recognition that categories of "productivity" and growth which have been taken to be positive, progressive and universal are, in reality, restricted patriarchal categories. When viewed from the point of view of nature's productivity and growth, and women's production of sustenance, they are found to be ecologically destructive and a source of gender inequality. It is no accident that the modern, efficient and productive technologies created within the context of growth in market economic terms are associated with heavy ecological costs, borne largely by women. The resource and energy intensive production processes they give rise to demand ever increasing resource withdrawals from the ecosystem. These withdrawals disrupt essential ecological processes and convert renewable resources into non-renewable ones. A forest for example, provides inexhaustible supplies of diverse biomass over time if its capital stock is maintained and it is harvested on a sustained yield basis. The heavy and uncontrolled demand for industrial and commercial wood, however, requires the continuous overfelling of trees which exceeds the regenerative capacity of the forest ecosystem, and eventually converts the forests into non-renewable resources. Women's work in the collection of water, fodder and fuel is thus rendered more energy and time-consuming. (In Garhwal, for example, I have seen women who originally collected fodder and fuel in a few hours, now travelling long distances by truck to collect grass and leaves in a task that might take up to two days.) Sometimes the damage to nature's intrinsic regenerative capacity is impaired not by over-exploitation of a particular resource but, indirectly, by damage caused to other related natural resources through ecological processes. Thus the excessive overfelling of trees in the catchment areas of streams and rivers destroys not only forest resources, but also renewable supplies of water, through hydrological destabilisation. Resource intensive industries disrupt essential ecological processes not only by their excessive demands for raw material, but by their pollution of air and water and soil. Often such destruction is caused by the resource demands of non-vital industrial products. In spite of severe ecological crises, this paradigm continues to operate because for the North and for the elites of the South, resources continue to be available, even now. The lack of recognition of nature's processes for survival *as factors in the process of economic development* shrouds the political issues arising from resource transfer and resource destruction, and creates an ideological weapon for increased control over natural resources in the conventionally employed notion of productivity. All other costs of the economic process consequently become invisible. The forces which contribute to the increased "productivity" of a modern farmer or factory worker for instance, come from the increased use of natural resources. Lovins has described this as the amount of "slave" labour presently at work in the world.[9] According to him, each person on earth, on an average, possesses the equivalent of about 50 slaves, each working a 40 hour week. Man's global energy conversion from all sources (wood, fossil fuel, hydroelectric power, nuclear) is currently approximately 8×10^{12} watts. This is more than 20 times the energy content of the food necessary to feed the present world population at the FAO standard diet of 3,600 cal/day. The "productivity" of the western male compared to women or Third World peasants is not intrinsically superior; it is based on inequalities in the distribution of this "slave" labour. The average inhabitant of the USA for example has 250 times more "slaves" than the average Nigerian. "If Americans were short of 249 of those 250 "slaves," one wonders how efficient they would prove themselves to be?"

It is these resource and energy intensive processes of production which divert resources away from survival, and hence from women. What patriarchy sees as productive work, is, in ecological terms highly destructive production. The second law of thermodynamics predicts that resource intensive and resource wasteful economic development must become a threat to the survival of the human species in the long run. Political struggles based on ecology in industrially advanced countries are rooted in this conflict between *long term survival options* and *short term over-production and over-consumption*. Political struggles of women, peasants and tribals based on ecology in countries like India are far more acute and urgent since they are rooted in the *immediate threat to the options for survival* for the vast majority of the people, *posed by resource intensive and resource wasteful economic growth* for the benefit of a minority.

In the market economy, the organising principle for natural resource use is the maximisation of profits and capital accumulation. Nature and human needs are managed through market mechanisms. Demands for natural resources are restricted to those demands registering on the market; the ideology of development is in large part based on a vision of bringing all natural resources into the market economy for commodity production. When these resources are already being used by nature to maintain her production of renewable resources and by women for sustenance and livelihood, their diversion to the market economy generates a scarcity condition for ecological stability and creates new forms of poverty for women.

Two Kinds of Poverty

In a book entitled *Poverty: the Wealth of the People*[10] an African writer draws a distinction between poverty as subsistence, and misery as deprivation. It is useful to separate a cultural conception of subsistence living as poverty from the material experience of poverty that is a result of dispossession and deprivation. Culturally perceived poverty need not be real material poverty: subsistence economies which satisfy basic needs through self-provisioning are not poor in the sense of being deprived. Yet the ideology of development declares them so because they do not participate overwhelmingly in the market economy, and do not consume commodities produced for and distributed through the market *even though they might be satisfying those needs through self-provisioning mechanisms*. People are perceived as poor if they eat millets (grown by women) rather than commercially produced and distributed processed foods sold by global agribusiness. They are seen as poor if they live in self-built housing made from natural material like bamboo and mud rather than in cement houses. They are seen as poor if they wear handmade garments of natural fibre rather than synthetics. Subsistence, as culturally perceived poverty, does not necessarily imply a low physical quality of life. On the contrary, millets are nutritionally far superior to processed foods, houses built with local materials are far superior, being better adapted to the local climate and ecology, natural fibres are preferable to man-made fibres in most cases, and certainly more affordable. This cultural perception of prudent subsistence living as poverty has provided the legitimisation for the development process as a poverty removal project. As a culturally biased project it destroys wholesome and sustainable lifestyles and creates real material poverty, or misery, by the denial of survival needs themselves, through the diversion of resources to resource intensive commodity production. Cash crop production and food processing take land and water resources away from sustenance needs, and exclude increasingly large numbers of people from their entitlements to food. "The inexorable processes of agriculture-industrialisation and internationalisation are probably responsible for more hungry people than either cruel or unusual whims of nature. There are several reasons why the high-technology-export-crop model increases hunger. Scarce land, credit, water and technology are pre-empted for the export market. Most hungry people are not affected by the market at all. . . . The profits flow to corporations that have no interest in feeding hungry people without money."[11]

The Ethiopian famine is in part an example of the creation of real poverty by development aimed at removing culturally perceived poverty. The displacement of nomadic Afars from their traditional pastureland in Awash Valley by commercial agriculture (financed by foreign companies) led to their struggle for survival in the fragile uplands which degraded the ecosystem and led to the starvation of cattle and the nomads.[12] The market economy conflicted with the survival economy in the Valley, thus creating a conflict between the survival economy and nature's economy in the uplands. At no point has the global marketing of agricultural commodities been assessed against the background of the new conditions of scarcity and poverty that it has induced. This new poverty moreover, is no longer cultural and relative: it is absolute, threatening the very survival of millions on this planet.

The economic system based on the patriarchal concept of productivity was created for the very specific historical and political phenomenon of colonialism. In it, the input for which efficiency of use had to be maximised in the production centres of Europe, was industrial labour. For colonial interest therefore, it was rational to improve the labour resource *even at the cost of wasteful use of na-*

ture's wealth. This rationalisation has, however, been illegitimately universalised to all contexts and interest groups and, on the plea of increasing productivity, labour reducing technologies have been introduced in situations where labour is abundant and cheap, and resource demanding technologies have been introduced where resources are scarce and already fully utilised for the production of sustenance. Traditional economies with a stable ecology have shared with industrially advanced affluent economies the ability to use natural resources to satisfy basic vital needs. The former differ from the latter in two essential ways: first, the same needs are satisfied in industrial societies through longer technological chains requiring higher energy and resource inputs and excluding large numbers without purchasing power; and second, affluence generates new and artificial needs requiring the increased production of industrial goods and services. Traditional economies are not advanced in the matter of non-vital needs satisfaction, but as far as the satisfaction of basic and vital needs is concerned, they are often what Marshall Sahlins has called "the original affluent society." The needs of the Amazonian tribes are more than satisfied by the rich rainforest; their poverty begins with its destruction. The story is the same for the Gonds of Bastar in India or the Penans of Sarawak in Malaysia.

Thus are economies based on indigenous technologies viewed as "backward" and "unproductive." Poverty, as the denial of basic needs, is not necessarily associated with the existence of traditional technologies, and its removal is not necessarily an outcome of the growth of modern ones. On the contrary, the destruction of ecologically sound traditional technologies, often created and used by women, along with the destruction of their material base is generally believed to be responsible for the "feminisation" of poverty in societies which have had to bear the costs of resource destruction.

The contemporary poverty of the Afar nomad is not rooted in the inadequacies of traditional nomadic life, but in the *diversion of the productive pastureland of the Awash Valley*. The erosion of the resource base for survival is increasingly being caused by the demand for resources by the market economy, dominated by global forces. The creation of inequality through economic activity which is ecologically disruptive arises in two ways: first, inequalities in the distribution of privileges make for unequal access to natural resources—these include privileges of both a political and economic nature. Second, resource intensive production processes have access to subsidised raw material on which a substantial number of people, especially from the less privileged economic groups, depend for their survival. The consumption of such industrial raw material is determined purely by market forces, and not by considerations of the social or ecological requirements placed on them. The costs of resource destruction are externalised and unequally divided among various economic groups in society, but are borne largely by women and those who satisfy their basic material needs directly from nature, simply because they have no purchasing power to register their demands on the goods and services provided by the modern production system. Gustavo

Esteva has called development a permanent war waged by its promoters and suffered by its victims.[13]

The paradox and crisis of development arises from the mistaken identification of culturally perceived poverty with real material poverty, and the mistaken identification of the growth of commodity production as better satisfaction of basic needs. In actual fact, there is less water, less fertile soil, less genetic wealth as a result of the development process. Since these natural resources are the basis of nature's economy and women's survival economy, their scarcity is impoverishing women and marginalised peoples in an unprecedented manner. Their new impoverishment lies in the fact that resources which supported their survival were absorbed into the market economy while they themselves were excluded and displaced by it.

The old assumption that with the development process the availability of goods and services will automatically be increased and poverty will be removed, is now under serious challenge from women's ecology movements in the Third World, even while it continues to guide development thinking in centres of patriarchal power. Survival is based on the assumption of the sanctity of life; maldevelopment is based on the assumption of the sacredness of "development." Gustavo Esteva asserts that the sacredness of development has to be refuted because it threatens survival itself. "My people are tired of development," he says, "they just want to live."[14]

The recovery of the feminine principle allows a transcendence and transformation of these patriarchal foundations of maldevelopment. It allows a redefinition of growth and productivity as categories linked to the production, not the destruction, of life. It is thus simultaneously an ecological and a feminist political project which legitimises the way of knowing and being that create wealth by enhancing life and diversity, and which delegitimises the knowledge and practice of a culture of death as the basis for capital accumulation.

Notes

1. Rosa Luxemberg, *The Accumulation of Capital*, London: Routledge and Kegan Paul, 1951.

2. An elaboration of how "development" transfers resources from the poor to the well-endowed is contained in J. Bandyopadhyay and V. Shiva, "Political Economy of Technological Polarisations," in *Economic and Political Weekly*, Vol. XVIII, 1982, pp. 1827–32; and J. Bandyopadhyay and V. Shiva, "Political Economy of Ecology Movements," in *Economic and Political Weekly*, forthcoming.

3. Ester Boserup, *Women's Role in Economic Development*, London: Allen and Unwin, 1970.

4. DAWN, *Development Crisis and Alternative Visions: Third World Women's Perspectives*, Bergen: Christian Michelsen Institute, 1985, p. 21.

5. M. George Foster, *Traditional Societies and Technological Change*, Delhi: Allied Publishers, 1973.

6. Maria Mies, *Patriarchy and Accumulation on a World Scale*, London: Zed Books, 1986.

7. Alice Schlegel (ed.), *Sexual Stratification: A Cross-Cultural Study*, New York: Columbia University Press, 1977.

8. Jonathan Porritt, *Seeing Green*, Oxford: Blackwell, 1984.

9. A. Lovins, cited in S. R. Eyre, *The Real Wealth of Nations*, London: Edward Arnold, 1978.

10. R. Bahro, *From Red to Green*, London: Verso, 1984, p. 211.

11. R. J. Barnet, *The Lean Years*, London: Abacus, 1981, p. 171.

12. U. P. Koehn, "African Approaches to Environmental Stress: A Focus on Ethiopia and Nigeria" in R. N. Barrett (ed.), *International Dimensions of the Environmental Crisis*, Colorado: Westview, 1982, pp. 253–89.

13. Gustavo Esteva, "Regenerating People's Space" in S. N. Mendlowitz and R. B. J. Walker, *Towards a Just World Peace: Perspectives From Social Movements*, London: Butterworths and Committee for a Just World Peace, 1987.

14. G. Esteva, Remarks made at a Conference of the Society for International Development, Rome, 1985.

Rajani Kanth

Postscript: Self-Determination— Birth of a Notion

Looking back now, after almost forty years of "development" theory, ideology, and practice cutting all the way across the political spectrum, it is almost impossible to believe that nearly all of the panaceas advocated by the anointed seers and savants rested on one indelible, if noxious, principle, so obvious as to be unnoticed: *that a set of experts, largely through self-selection, had both the right and the capacity to plan, think, experiment, and hope on behalf of others* upon whom these plans were ultimately to be foisted. All of development theory, Marxist or neoclassical, took this unstated principle as its point of departure, in splendid contempt of what ordinary people—that undistinguished mass of common humanity!—might think, feel, or experience. Both capitalist modernizers and Marxist revolutionaries had prefabricated plans, which required only the seizure of state power or the unwitting acquiescence of common peoples to allow them to be carried out, in experimental fashion and with a sovereign disregard for the rather simple, democratic political precept that it is the people, for better or for worse, who need to exercise the right of choice over their destinies, *even if these choices do not maximize a new dividend as defined by political economists, right or left*, with their own specific political axes to grind. Astonishingly, two hundred years after the great French Revolution and seventy years after the Bolshevik Revolution, neither socialist nor capitalist ideologues would give even nominal credence to this inalienable right of peoples.[1]

It is in the 1990s, today, that the consequences of this Great Default are becoming apparent in the real histories of nations and political systems worldwide, even if the correct political lessons have still not been learned by their leaders. In the case of the self-dissolving socialisms of Eastern Europe, seventy years of paternalism, sometimes benign but often tyrannical, involving major economic and social restructuring and major projects of mass access to basic needs[2]—impressive in their own right, especially in relation to the disgraceful record in the advanced capitalist West in this regard—did little to secure broad legitimacy, let alone any popularity, for these regimes, which were for the best part either endured with sullenness, or evaded, often, by the old stand-bys of silence, cunning, and exile. Even today the Gorbachevian Revolution, obviously to be applauded for the welcome relief (reprieve!) it brings to long-suffering populations, remains a species of the genus of *expert initiatives from above*, originally intended to secure only the greater ultimate glory of the (failed) system. *Once again, people are being seen, by their governing classes, as but means to other ends,*[3] such as growth, development, or progress. It is a major irony, compounding the pre-existing tragedy of the Soviet regime, that *Perestroika* was initially a trickle-down idea and *Glasnost* but a ploy of the ruling elite.

In the capitalist West—the apparent victor in the long-standing East–West encounter—a cynical political system based on voter apathy and a de facto plutocracy masquerades as "democracy" and "freedom" within carefully defined structural bounds of the parametrics of private property and "free" markets, an ideology-cum-institutional set-up now being exported vigorously through the concerted efforts of the multilateral institutions of imperialism, the World Bank, the International Monetary Fund, the Organization for Economic Cooperation and Development, and so forth.[4] The "successes" of the so-called Newly Industrializing Countries (NICs) have already been taken as ready evidence of the hoary old capitalist fantasy of "getting prices right" and "laissez-faire" (in spite of mass evidence, to the contrary, of "getting prices wrong,"[5] as practiced for decades in South Korea and Taiwan, aside from the steady, massive doses of state direction), to say nothing of the rhetoric presenting these nations as the bastions of "freedom" in Asia, despite the easy refutation (also, of the myth that capitalism and democracy are "Siamese twins") in the obvious—indeed, encouraged!—prevalence of dictatorial regimes, in this part of the world, even of the "bloody Taylorist"[6] variety. Nonetheless, despite the rhetoric, resistance to capitalist encroachments on communitarian properties, sentiments, and relations, is as real a trend in the periphery (as it is in the metropolitan centers, with their own growing "Green" initiatives) as is the resistance to Stalinism in Eastern Europe. In a smaller but no less important way, the heroic Chipko villagers of India,[7] much like workers in Poland, bravely resisted "modernization" in favor of self-determination and community values, cocking a snook at the arrogance of power reflected in the self-assurance of Indian government planners and private developers alike, ready to ram "progress" down the throats of people presumed confidently to be powerless, illiterate, and unable to think for themselves.

Although by no means a mass movement, struggles such as that of the Chipko are as much a sign of the times as is the restlessness in eastern Europe, the effulgence of the Greens, and the brave defiance of the defenders of the forest in the Amazon,[8] a sign of the birth of a new consciousness that is *self-directed* and aimed at the preservation of community and self, and *the construction of non-alienating practices*, allowing for both to coexist nonantagonistically. This is a bottom-up, *trickle-up* consciousness that is gathering strength, in an uncoordinated fashion, across north and south, east and west. And, virtually everywhere, it meets the resolve of the planners and their ruling-class partners—securely locked together by the newest catechism of development ideology—to deny them their rights, their rituals, and their practices in the name (always) of a higher rationality, of the calculus of efficiency and the maximand of growth.

Indeed, it is in this fetishism of productivity and the worship of economic growth (indeed, the standard economist, Marxist or neoclassical, is the guardian high priest at the temple of capital accumulation) that conventional Marxists join their class enemies, the neoclassicals, in a passionate embrace of *economism*, the idea that increases in social productivity are necessary *at any cost*—social, demographic, ecological, etc.—to anyone.[9] And it is this fetish that united the otherwise divided house of the developmentalists, the majority group among state planners, virtually everywhere. Villages could be overrun, cultures destroyed, entire histories submerged and flooded, and peoples relocated and uprooted, with complete impunity, in both socialist and capitalist variants of this rabid crusade. The idea that, in a human society, such choices involve recourse to values, rather than inexorable historical necessities, never once disturbed the tranquillity of these economic *determinists*, of both right and left, who were ready to act out the inevitable historical agenda on behalf (if not at the behest!) of their hapless wards. *That people, be they peasants, workers, the homeless, or women, have the right to make their own decisions—even if these be judged incorrect decisions by some outside agency—has never been acknowledged.*[10] But they do—and must—have that right, even if it only amounts to a *right to be wrong*.

The central issue of all development theory has therefore always been—once again, so obvious as to be unmentioned—*political power and its exercise*. The development crusaders have battened on this power (a power denied to the helpless objects of policy), however illegitimately attained. Indeed, economists have never questioned the legitimacy of power in any existential context, simply taking it as a highly instrumental given—managing to inflict unbelievable human suffering in the process, making "mistakes" that rarely return to visit the remote architects of policy.[11] There is a political moral here, one that will be drawn (indeed, *is* being drawn) by many more in the future: that the *subalternity*[12] of the masses and the minority rule of the masters of the polity—the twin bases of despotism—are unlikely to be a tolerable or tolerated condition for much longer. For self-determination is an idea that is flouting traditional notions of representation and democracy; and it is a movement that will continue to trouble and challenge the smug elitism of both Marxists and the mainstream as they go about trying to change the world—even, as they have in the past, *against its will*.

Notes

1. In the case of capitalist ideology, past or present, with its insistence on the essential safety of elite rule (Mosca, Pareto in the past; Kornhauser, Pye, and Verba in the

present) based on mass apathy, the question is not even posed; of course, in the case of Marxian political thinking, one might be misled into hoping for something better, but the very title of an early Lenin pamphlet, "Better Fewer, But Better," puts the matter to rest quite effectively.

2. The discovery of the "basic needs" approach to the development matters, announced to the world in the mid-1970s by the International Labour Organisation and the catechism of the United Nations for a short while thereafter, before the great Reagan reversal, illustrates the lateness of bourgeois perceptions and their inherent political cannibalism. The idea was central to the Bolshevik Revolution—indeed, to virtually all visions of socialism—and revived again in China by Mao; that is, it was a socialist idea long before the development establishment co-opted it, briefly, to secure legitimacy for their international depredations. In similar vein, the United Nations Development Programme, in the 1990s, has recently discovered "human development" as a selling vehicle (under the tutelage of Professor Mahbub-ul-Haq, only lately a member of a murderous military regime in Pakistan); at this rate, somewhere in the twenty-first century, the World Bank will discover the existence of "people," and announce it in full-color glossies. After all, as a recent International Monetary Fund journal banner announced, it is time the poor were made "more productive" (*Finance and Development*, September 1990).

3. For a perspective on this idea, see Maxine Molyneux, "The 'Woman Question' in the age of Perestroika," *New Left Review* no. 183 (September-October 1990): 23–49; also T. Friedgut and L. Siegelbaum, "Perestroika from Below," *New Left Review* no. 181 (May-June 1990): 5–32.

4. For a dip into the bottomless pit of capitalist machinations, see S. Branford and B. Kucinski, *The Debt Squads* (London: Zed Books, 1988). On the other hand, the speeches of Reaganite World Bank presidents since A. W. Clausen are models of clarity with respect to the export of capitalism.

5. For some detail on this issue, see Alice Amsden, "Third World Industrialization: 'Global Fordism' or New Model?" *New Left Review* no. 182 (July-August 1990): 5–31.

6. A term used by Alain Lipietz, *Mirages and Miracles: The Crisis of Global Fordism* (London: Verso, 1987).

7. See, for a full account, J. Bandhopadhyay and V. Shiva, "Chipko: Politics of Ecology," *Seminar* no. 330 (1987): 33–39.

8. The martyred heroism of Chico Mendes and his intrepid band is now part of folklore. For the story in his own words, see Chico Mendes, *Fight for the Forest* (New York: Monthly Review Press, 1989); for a detailed account, see Susanna Hecht and Alexander Cockburn, *The Fate of the Forest* (London: Verso, 1989).

9. Whether in the construction of the Aswan Dam, which destroyed Nubian settlements and buried priceless treasures, or in the toxic poisoning of Lake Baikal (or, for that matter, of Love Canal) and the cover-up at Chernobyl, or in the many depredations on tribal and village lands and rights in India, the record—capitalist or socialist—is a sorry one. Let no one apologize for these *Himalayan blunders* that will stand as a bloody testament to the worship of growth.

10. A lone but fearless contemporary voice (still a voice in the wilderness, for all practical purposes) speaking to this has been that of the tireless Paul Feyerabend—mediated through invective and satire—to call attention to the covert tyranny of science and reason; see his *Science in a Free Society* (London: Verso, 1979); and *Farewell to Reason* (London: Verso, 1987). One must also acknowledge, in this regard, the gentler musings of Gandhi and the wisdom therein.

11. "Errors" made by elite planners rarely come back to haunt the original schemers: The designers of the Ford Pinto or the planners of Gosplan, who misallocated food supplies, could not have been the immediate sufferers of their gross negligence. For an attempt to construct a different vision of a cooperative society of producers, one with real accountability, see the imaginative paper by Ernest Mandel, "In Defence of Socialist Planning" (*New Left Review* no. 159 September-October 1986: 5–37), which remains interesting despite its utopianism, or perhaps because of it.

12. Perhaps the pithiest definition of subalternity as a social condition comes from the pen of Rudolph Bahro, erstwhile political prisoner in East Germany and now an organizer of the Greens in Germany. See the paper penned in his earlier phase of radical Marxism, titled "The Alternative in Eastern Europe," *New Left Review* no. 177 (September-October 1989): 3–37.

A Guide to Further Reading

Development has proved a lucrative business for scholars, publishers, policy analysts, governments, and funding agencies, and it is no wonder that a titanic assemblage of the most diverse literature awaits the hapless student who strays in this direction. Fortunately, however, the bulk of the tracts, treatises, and tomes in this genre are best forgotten, having yielded royalties and revenues but little else of enduring value. For the serious undergraduate, I therefore offer but a few suggestions for further reading by way of commentary, analysis, and discussion of the critical papers presented in this book (for the graduate student I offer no direction: in that area, learning is principally by doing).

For the mainstream student, I recommend Diana Hunt, *Economic Theories of Development* (Savage, MD: Barnes & Noble, 1989), which offers a schematic discussion of the various "paradigms" in development theory. For a right-wing skew to matters, P. T. Bauer's *Dissent on Development* (Cambridge, MA: Harvard University Press, 1976) remains the magisterial statement of reaction. For the Marxist scholar, Ronald Chilcote and Dale Johnson, *Theories of Development: Mode of Production or Dependency?* (Newbury Park, CA: Sage Publications, 1983), situates the issues squarely; Michael Redclift and David Goodman, *From Peasant to Proletarian* (Oxford: Basil Blackwell, 1981), builds on the problematic; additionally, a useful, but not sympathetic, account of Marxist ideas is available in A. Brewer, *Marxist Theories of Imperialism* (London: Routledge & Kegan Paul, 1980). For the radical student not up to the stresses of Marxist histrionics, I recommend M. Blomstrom and B. Hettne, *Development Theory in Transition* (London: Zed Books, 1984), and Ankie Hoogvelt, *The Third World in Global Development* (London: Macmillan, 1982). For the feminist and ecologist, I can do no better than offer Vandana Shiva and Maria Mies, *Ecofeminism* (London: Zed Books, 1993), which poses matters clearly and forcefully.

Index

Accumulation, 6–8, 35, 40–41, 44, 58–60, 62–63, 67, 72, 74, 80, 83–84, 86–90, 92, 95–96, 109–15, 117–120, 127–135, 138–140, 142, 145, 147, 161–164, 167–175, 177*n.*, 182–83, 187, 194, 209*n.17*, 212–13, 215, 217–19, 243, 249, 252, 253*n.6*, 257

Adams, Brooks, 133

Advanced countries, 18, 21, 28–32, 36, 41–43, 45*n.1*, 53–54, 56, 95, 111, 115–19, 126, 144, 158, 164, 199, 201, 207, 249

Afghanistan, 215–16

Africa, 4, 8, 13*n.16*, 24, 28–29, 35–39, 45, 60, 67, 95, 130, 137, 141–42, 146*n.28*, 185–87, 188*n.18*, 191, 201, 204, 207, 213, 216, 249, 253*n.12*

  East, 38

  North, 186

  South, 216, 226*n.9*

  West, 29, 37–39

Agriculture, 43, 51–52, 66–67, 71–72, 84–85, 96, 99–103, 108, 120, 134, 136, 139, 158–59, 169, 177, 179, 181–87, 188*nn.14–15*, 196, 199, 208*n.5*, 222, 231, 245, 250

  agricultural output, 127, 139, 208*n.5*, 225

  agricultural produce, 128, 163

  agricultural revolution, 85

  cocoa, 37, 92

  coffee, 153, 155, 158

  cotton, 134

  crops, 33, 36–38, 40, 91–92, 99, 131, 185, 222, 244, 250

  foodgrains, 185–86

  groundnuts, 37, 45

  millets, 250

Agriculture *(continued)*

  palm oil, 37

  peanuts, 90, 92

  peasant, 38, 66, 82

  rice, 37, 222, 231

  sugar, 91–92, 157–59, 181

  wheat, 90–91, 158

  yams, 37

  see also Farming

Aid

  foreign, 50, 57, 187, 200

  grants-in-aid, 23, 57

Aird, J., 228*nn.27, 32*, 229

Alailima, P., 227*n.18*, 229

Alamgir, M., 228*n.23*, 229

Algeria, 185

America, 3–4, 8–9, 29–30, 35, 42, 49, 53–54, 60, 82, 104–6, 130, 137, 141–42, 145*n.10*, 148*n.51*, 149, 151–55, 157–59, 165, 171, 179–80, 182–83, 186–87, 191, 199, 202, 204, 207–9, 213–14, 249

  see also Latin America; North America; South America; United States of America

Amin, Samir, ix, 9, 12*n.13*, 13*nn.14, 15*, 161–64

Amsden, Alice, 258*n.5*

Anstey, Vera, 145*nn.16–17*

Aptheker, Herbert, 148*n.47*

Argentina, 94, 102, 154–57, 216, 219

Arrighi, G., 188*nn.19–20*, 209*n.12*

Arrow, K. J., 227*n.22*, 229

Asia, 4, 8, 28–29, 37–38, 59, 86–87, 95, 127, 130, 134, 137, 141–44, 161, 180–81, 183, 188*n.23*, 191, 204, 207, 213, 227*n.13*, 229, 231, 256

  South, 229, 231

Wages *(continued)*
70–74, 78, 83–96, 139, 163, 169–70,
172, 178–80, 184–85, 201, 208*n.5*,
221–22, 239
level of, 70, 163
real, 62, 67–68, 74, 78, 83–85, 87, 90,
92, 95–96, 201, 239
subsistence, 59, 62, 87, 90, 92, 94, 96
see also Earnings
Warren, Bill 12*nn.11, 12*, 204, 209*n.17*
Water, 21, 62, 66, 83, 245–46, 248, 250,
252
irrigation, 21, 76, 79–80, 84, 99, 182
Weber, Max, 125
Welfare, 34–35, 42, 57, 68, 101, 105–6,
122, 200, 208*n.10*, 230–31, 236,
238–39, 247
economic, 34, 236, 238

Welfare *(continued)*
economics, 34, 42, 236
social, 34, 105
Williams, Eric, 145*n.9*
Wilson, T., 46*n.4*
Women, 62–63, 230, 243–53, 257
see also Feminism
Woolf, Leonard, 146*n.28*
World Bank, 9–11, 206, 233*n.*, 256,
258*nn.2, 4*
see also International Bank for
Reconstruction and Development

Yamada, M., 147*n.39*
Yugoslavia, 215–18

Zhu Zhengzhi, 224, 228*n.28*, 232
Zimmerman, E. W., 148*n.48*

About the Editor

Professor Rajani Kannepalli Kanth was educated in India at the Delhi School of Economics, and in the United States at Columbia University and the New School for Social Research, securing graduate degrees in both Economics and Social Anthropology. His teaching career, spanning two decades, began at the Jawaharlal Nehru University in New Delhi, 1971-74, interrupted by a two-year stint at the United Nations, in New York, only to be contlnued at the State University of New York (1981-85) and then on to the University of Utah, in Salt Lake City, where he is currentlY based. Author of *Polltical Economy and Laissez-Faire* (1986), and *Capitalism and Social Theory* (1992) and principal editor of *Explorations in Political Economy* (1991), (his forthcoming books, projected for 1993/94, include *Economics and Epistemology: A Realist Critique*, and *Science and Society:Essays in Critical Political Economy*), he has held Visiting Fellowships at Oxford University, England, and the University of Bielefeld, Germany. His teaching and research interests include political economy, philosophy, and social theory.